RANMA 1/2

VOLUME TWO

STORY & ART BY
RUMIKO TAKAHASHI

B **XTREE**

First published in Great Britain in 1994 by Boxtree Limited

© Rumiko Takahashi/Shogakukan, Inc. 1993
RANMA 1/2 is a trademark of Viz Communications, Inc.
All rights reserved. No unauthorized reproduction allowed.
The stories, characters, and incidents mentioned in this
publication are entirely fictional.

1 2 3 4 5 6 7 8 9 10

Translation/Gerard Jones & Matt Thorn
Touch-Up & Lettering/Wayne Truman
Editors/Satoru Fujii & Trish Ledoux

Boxtree Limited
Broadwall House
21 Broadwall
London SE1 9PL

A CIP catalogue entry for this book is available
from the British Library

ISBN 0 7522 0861 6

Printed in Finland

PART EIGHT

Because There's a Girl He Likes

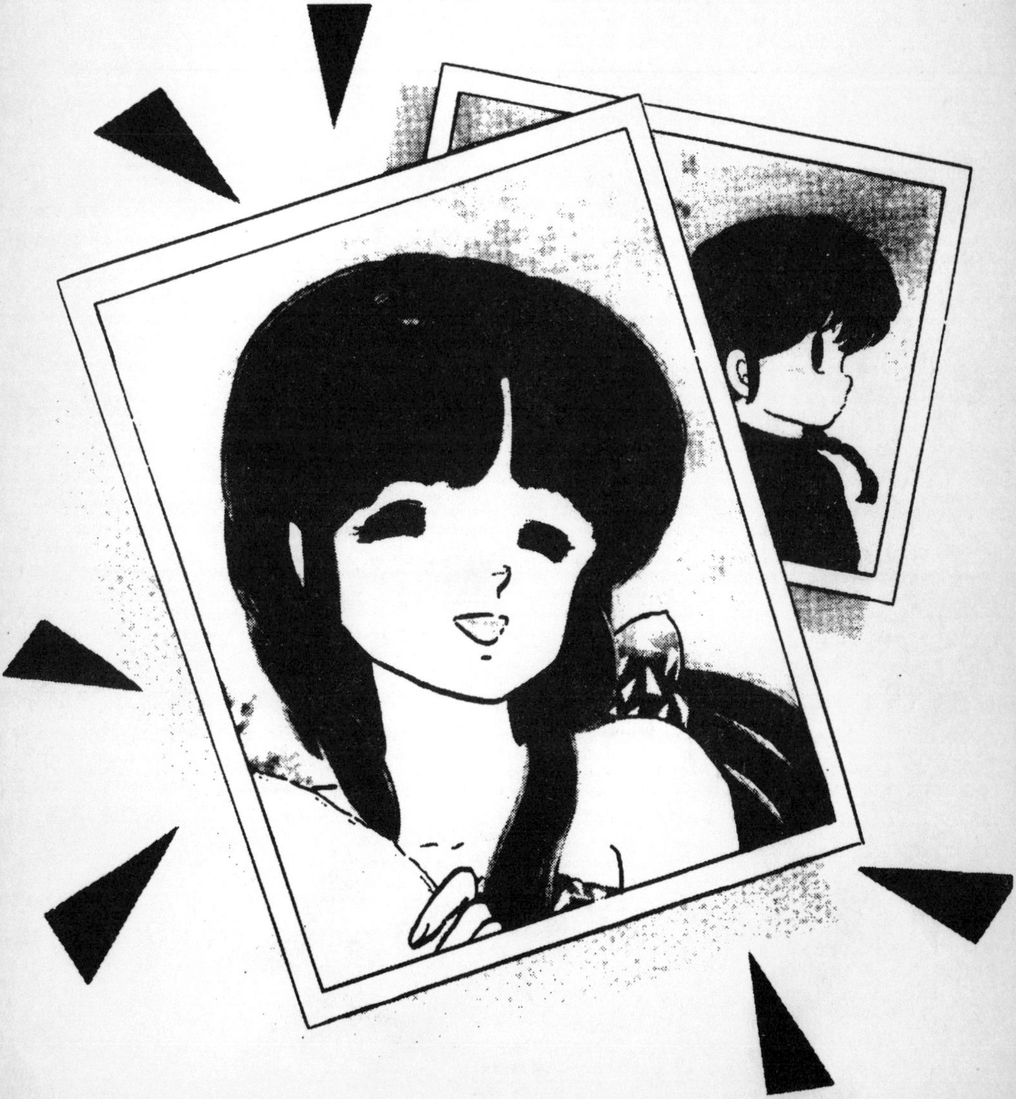

Parts 1-7 are found in Ranma ½ Volume One: also from Boxtree

SNEAK PREVIEW: VOLUME TWO

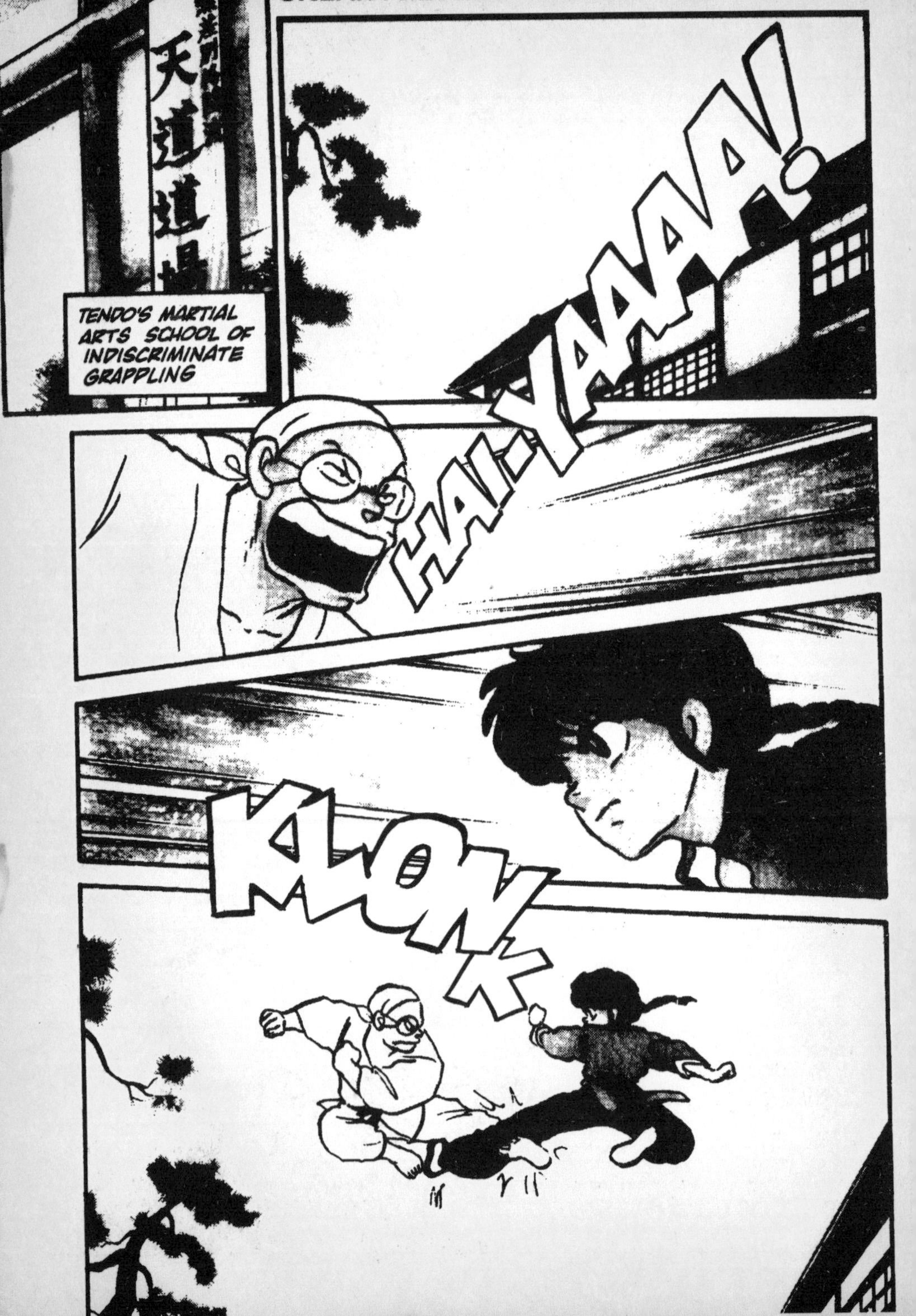

天道道場
TENDO'S MARTIAL ARTS SCHOOL OF INDISCRIMINATE GRAPPLING
HAI-YAAAAA!
KLONK

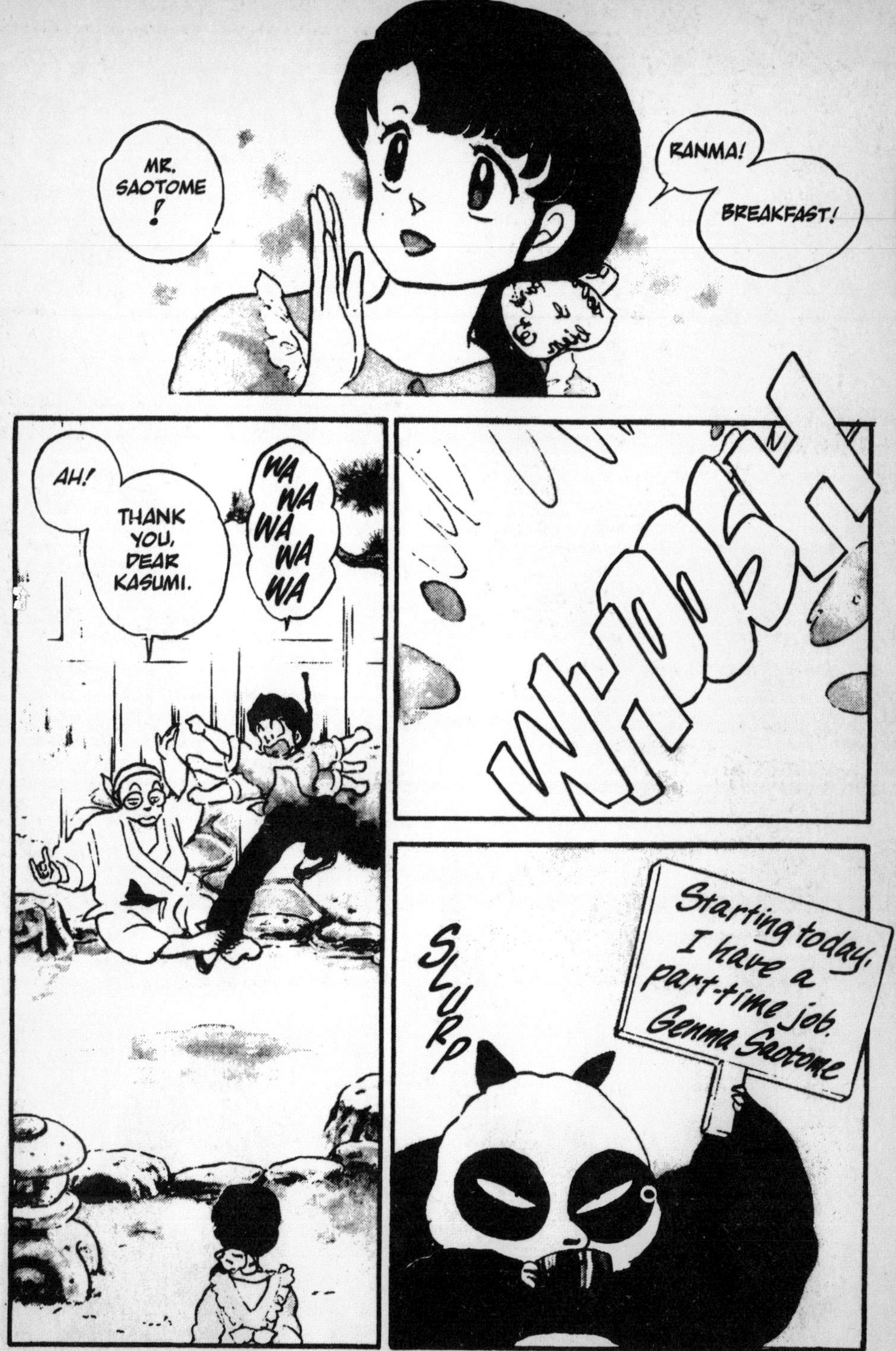
RANMA! BREAKFAST!
MR. SAOTOME!
WHOOSH
AH! THANK YOU, DEAR KASUMI.
WA WA WA WA WA WA
...
SLURP
Starting today, I have a part-time job. Genma Saotome

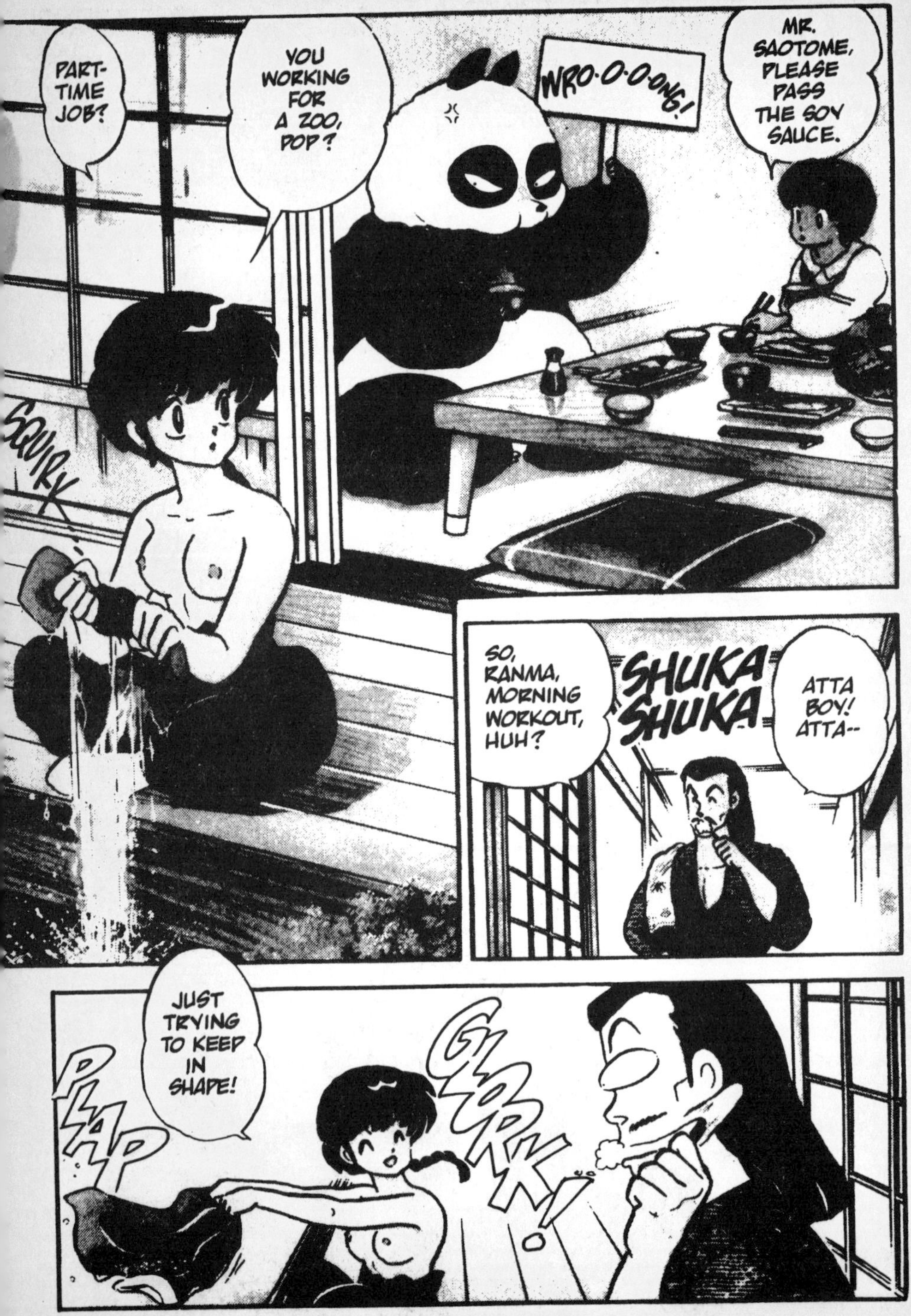

PART-TIME JOB?
YOU WORKING FOR A ZOO, POP?
WRO·O·O·ONG!
MR. SAOTOME, PLEASE PASS THE SOY SAUCE.
SQUIRK
SO, RANMA, MORNING WORKOUT, HUH?
SHUKA SHUKA
ATTA BOY! ATTA--
JUST TRYING TO KEEP IN SHAPE!
PLAP
GLORK!

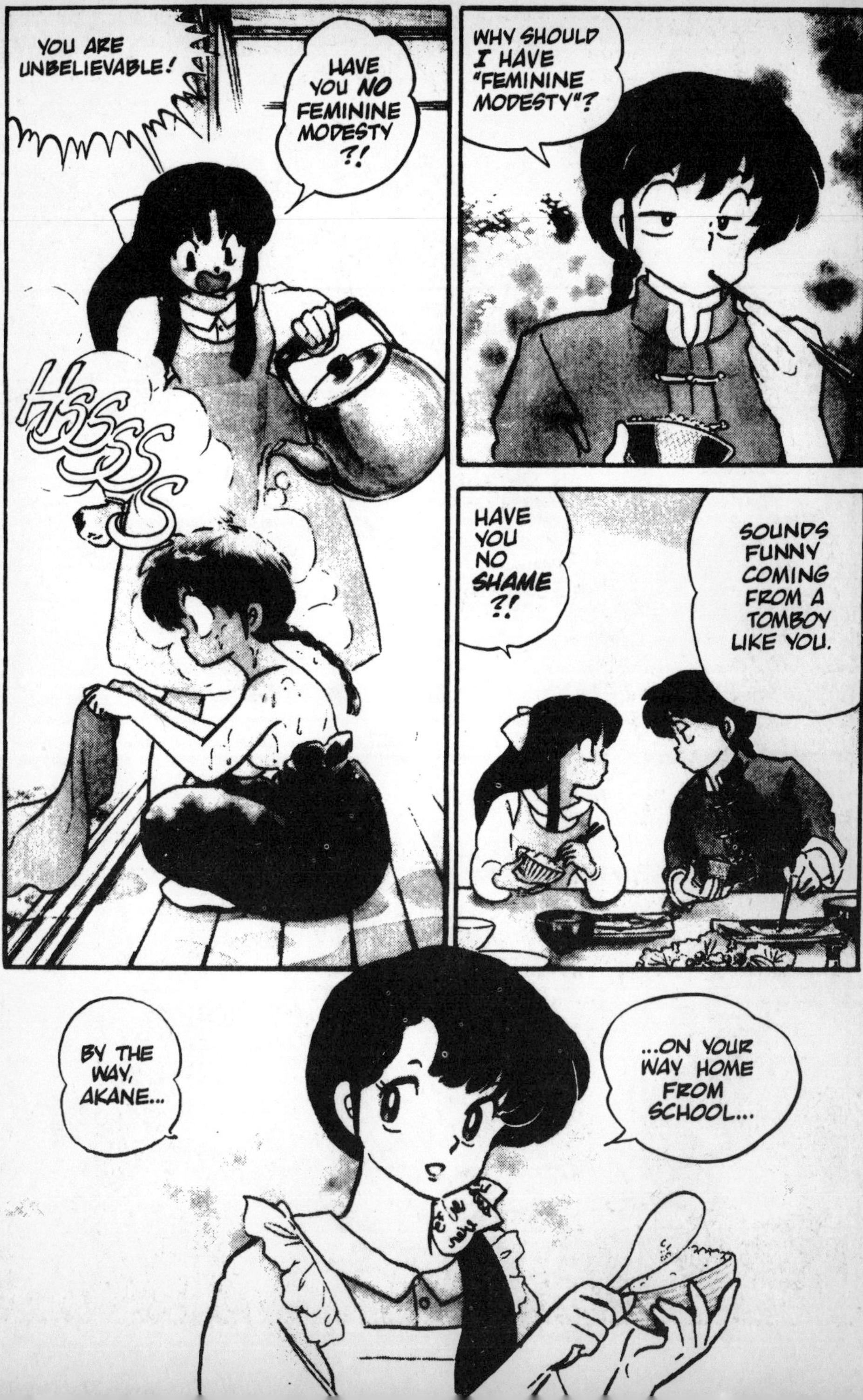

YOU ARE UNBELIEVABLE!
HAVE YOU NO FEMININE MODESTY ?!
HSSSSS
WHY SHOULD I HAVE "FEMININE MODESTY"?
HAVE YOU NO SHAME ?!
SOUNDS FUNNY COMING FROM A TOMBOY LIKE YOU.
BY THE WAY, AKANE...
...ON YOUR WAY HOME FROM SCHOOL...

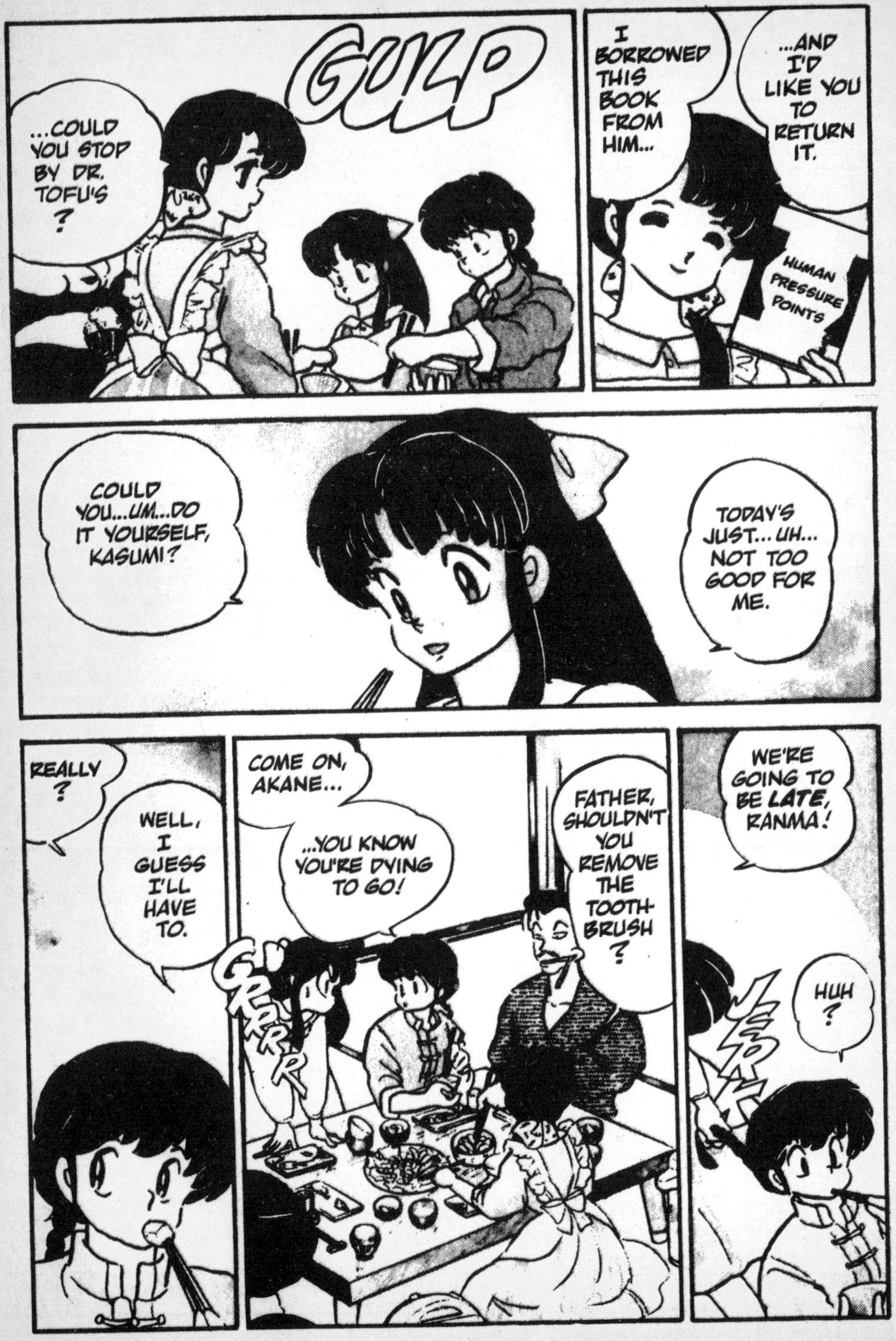
GULP
...COULD YOU STOP BY DR. TOFU'S?
I BORROWED THIS BOOK FROM HIM...
...AND I'D LIKE YOU TO RETURN IT.
HUMAN PRESSURE POINTS
COULD YOU...UM...DO IT YOURSELF, KASUMI?
TODAY'S JUST...UH... NOT TOO GOOD FOR ME.
REALLY?
WELL, I GUESS I'LL HAVE TO.
COME ON, AKANE...
...YOU KNOW YOU'RE DYING TO GO!
GRRRR
FATHER, SHOULDN'T YOU REMOVE THE TOOTH-BRUSH?
WE'RE GOING TO BE LATE, RANMA!
HUH?

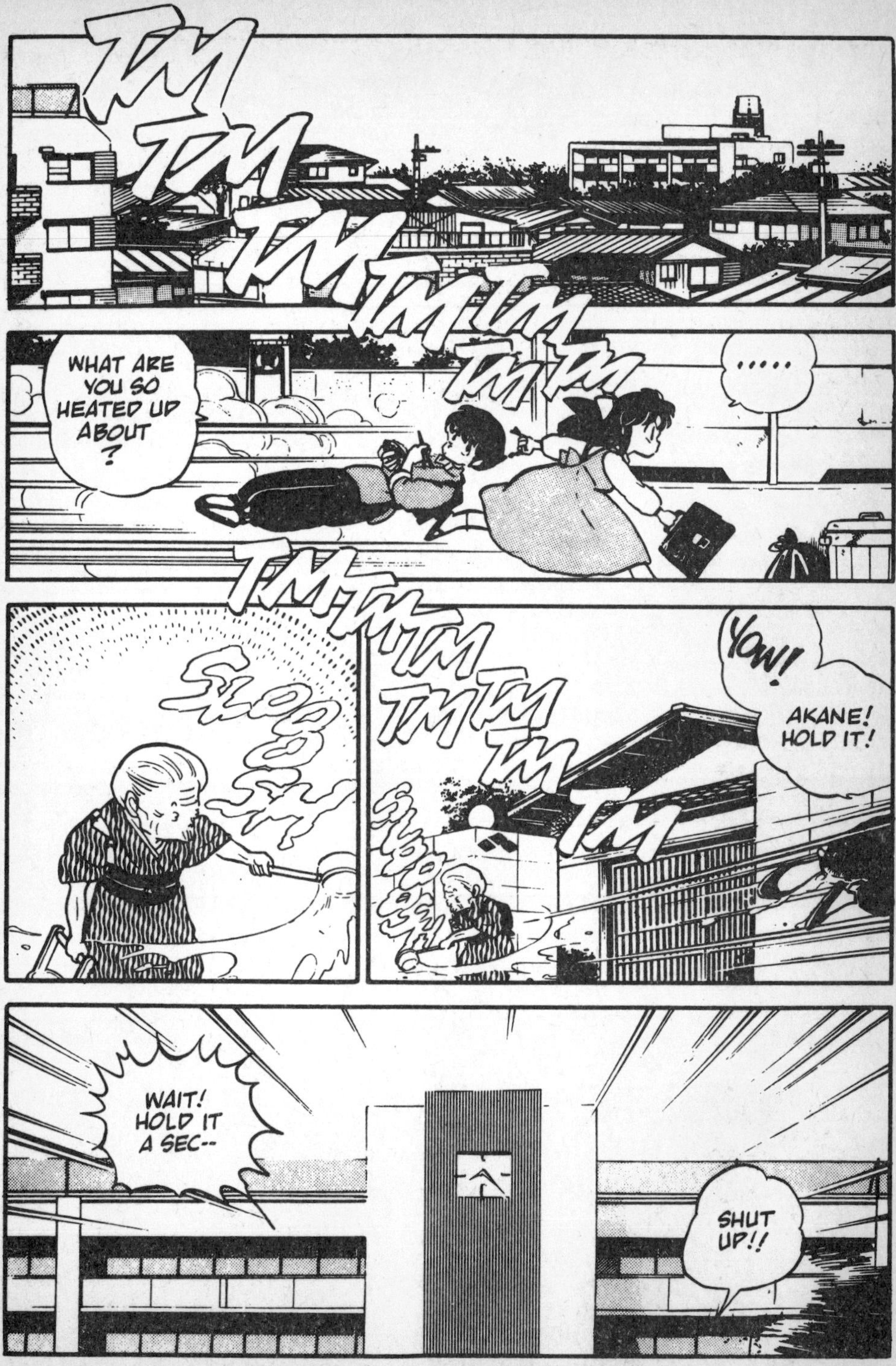

TM TM TM TMTMTM TM TM
WHAT ARE YOU SO HEATED UP ABOUT?
.....
TMTMTMTM TMTM TM TM
SLOOOSH
YOW!
AKANE! HOLD IT!
WAIT! HOLD IT A SEC--
SHUT UP!!

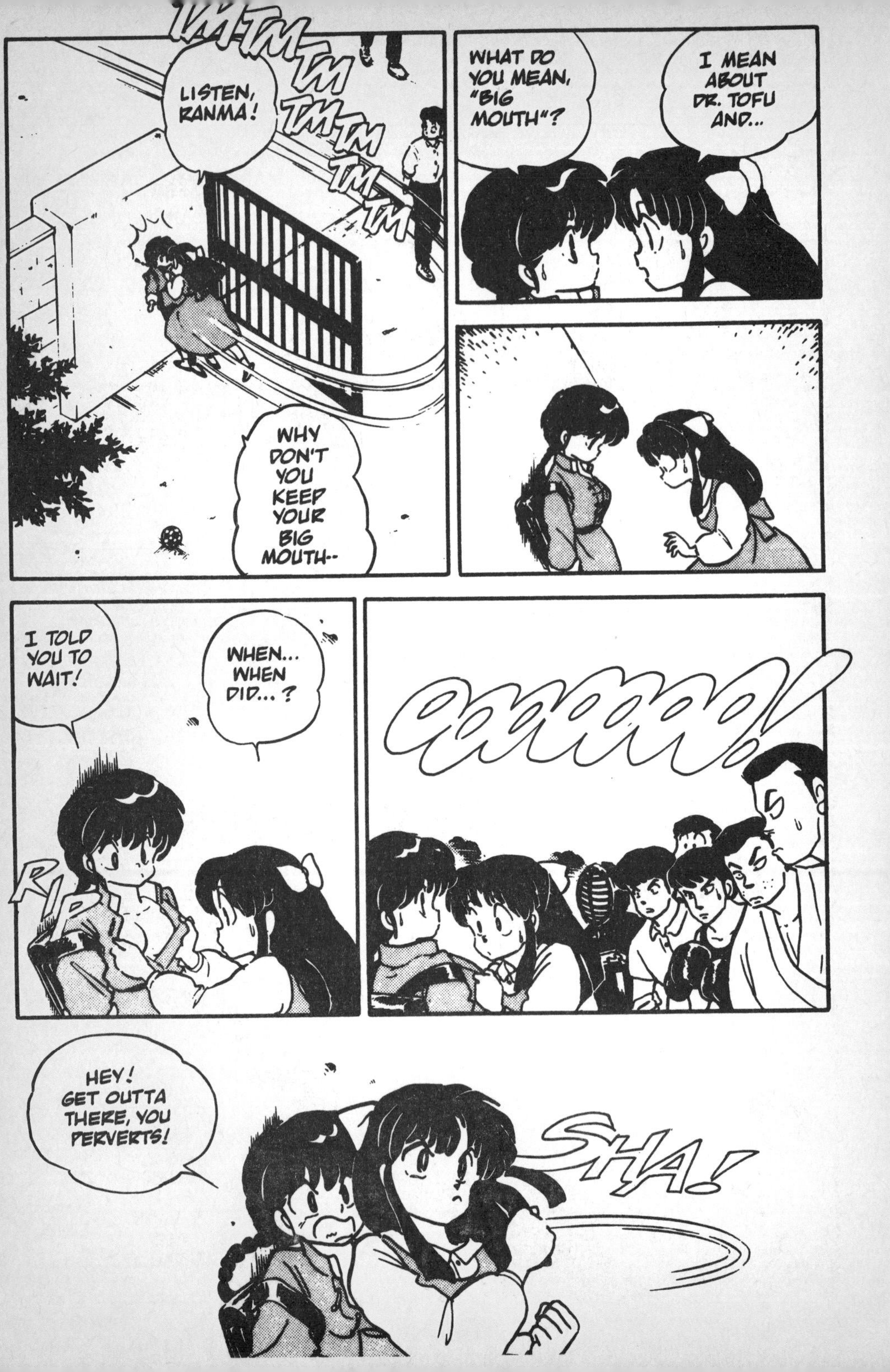
TMTMTMTMTMTMTMTMTM
LISTEN, RANMA!
WHY DON'T YOU KEEP YOUR BIG MOUTH--
WHAT DO YOU MEAN, "BIG MOUTH"?
I MEAN ABOUT DR. TOFU AND...
I TOLD YOU TO WAIT!
WHEN... WHEN DID...?
RIP
OOOOOO!
HEY! GET OUTTA THERE, YOU PERVERTS!
SHA!

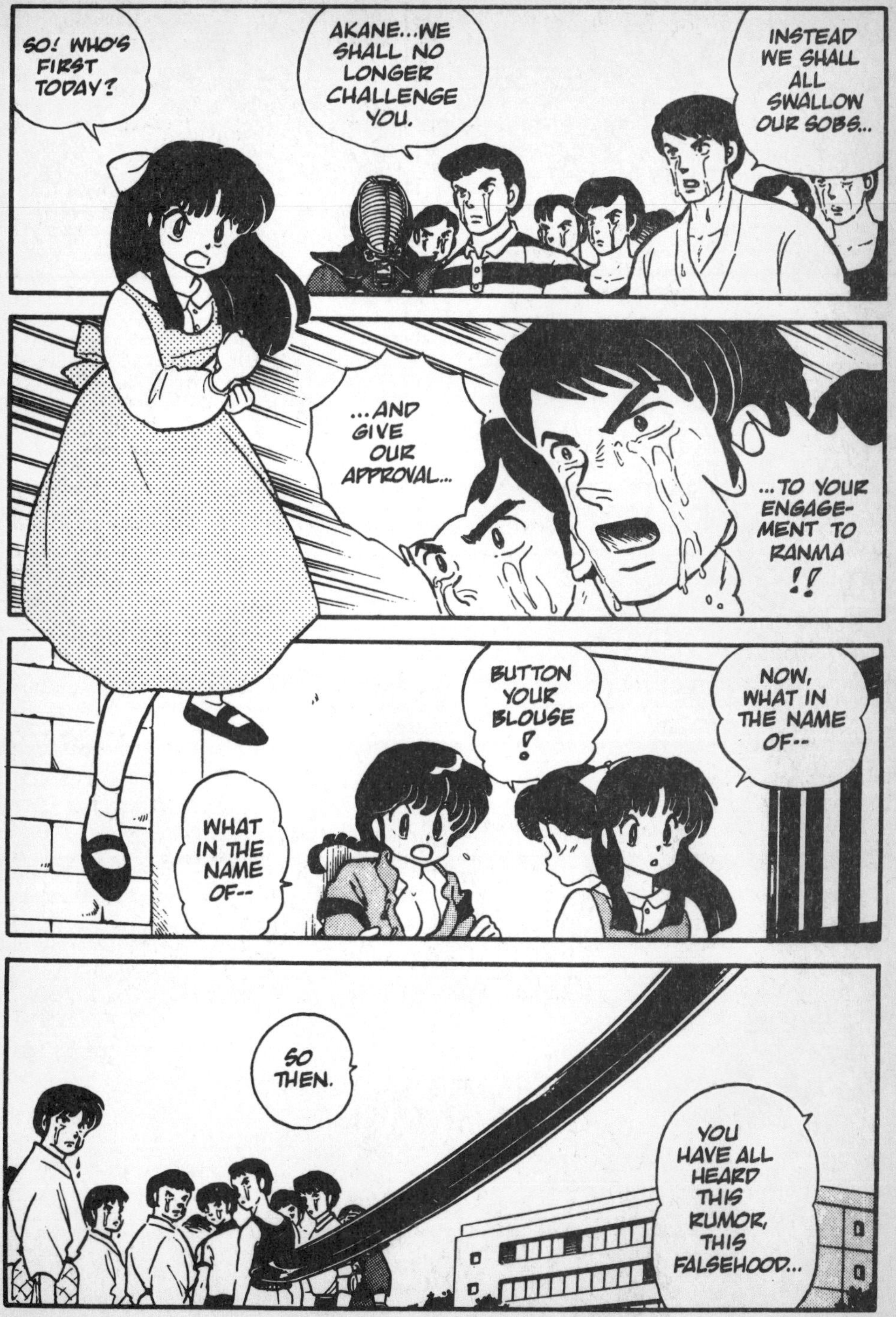
SO! WHO'S FIRST TODAY?
AKANE...WE SHALL NO LONGER CHALLENGE YOU.
INSTEAD WE SHALL ALL SWALLOW OUR SOBS...
...AND GIVE OUR APPROVAL...
...TO YOUR ENGAGEMENT TO RANMA!!
BUTTON YOUR BLOUSE!
NOW, WHAT IN THE NAME OF--
WHAT IN THE NAME OF--
SO THEN.
YOU HAVE ALL HEARD THIS RUMOR, THIS FALSEHOOD...

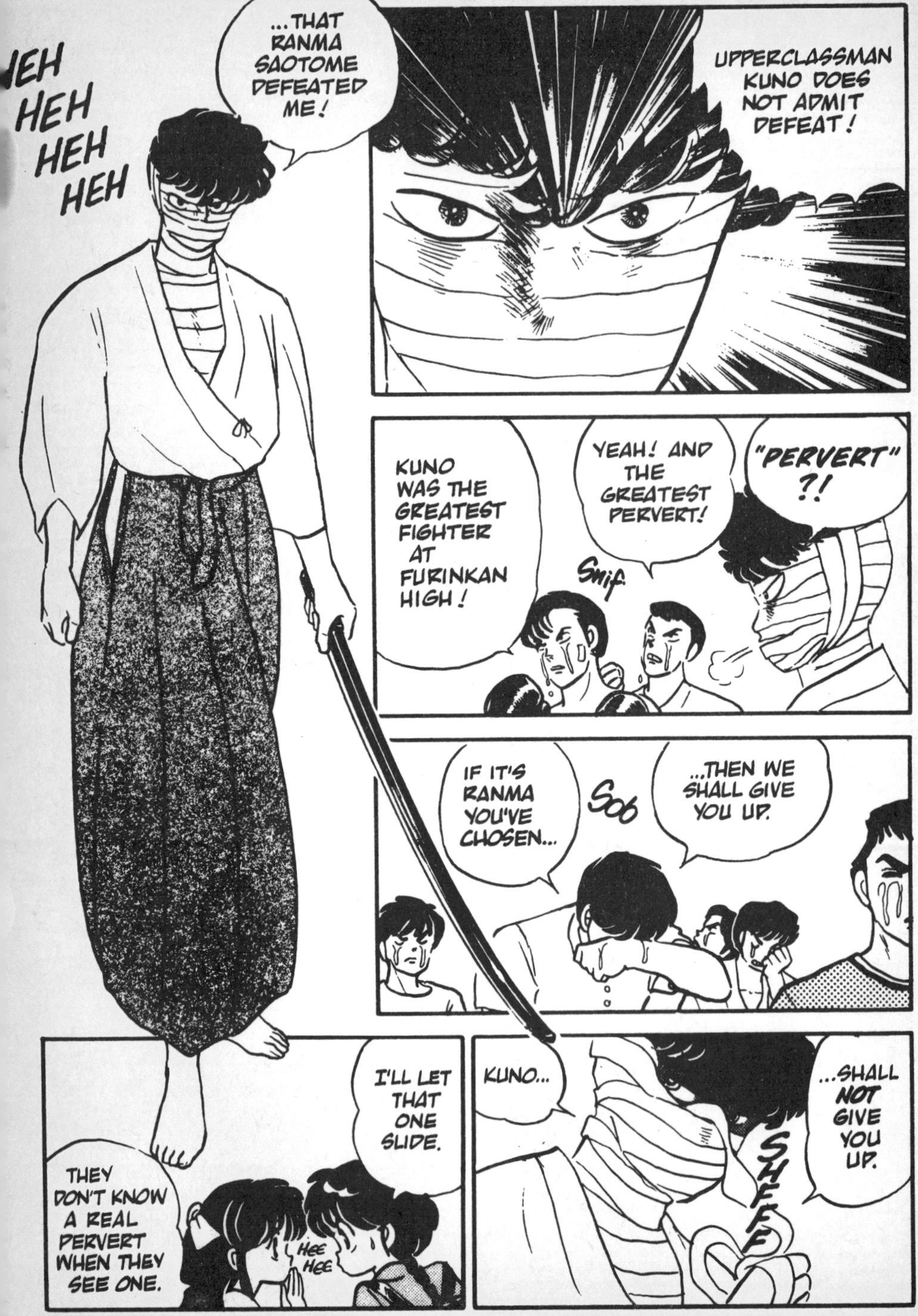
HEH HEH HEH HEH
...THAT RANMA SAOTOME DEFEATED ME!
UPPERCLASSMAN KUNO DOES NOT ADMIT DEFEAT!
KUNO WAS THE GREATEST FIGHTER AT FURINKAN HIGH!
YEAH! AND THE GREATEST PERVERT!
Snif
"PERVERT" ?!
IF IT'S RANMA YOU'VE CHOSEN...
Sob
...THEN WE SHALL GIVE YOU UP.
THEY DON'T KNOW A REAL PERVERT WHEN THEY SEE ONE.
HEE HEE
I'LL LET THAT ONE SLIDE.
KUNO...
...SHALL NOT GIVE YOU UP.
SHFFF

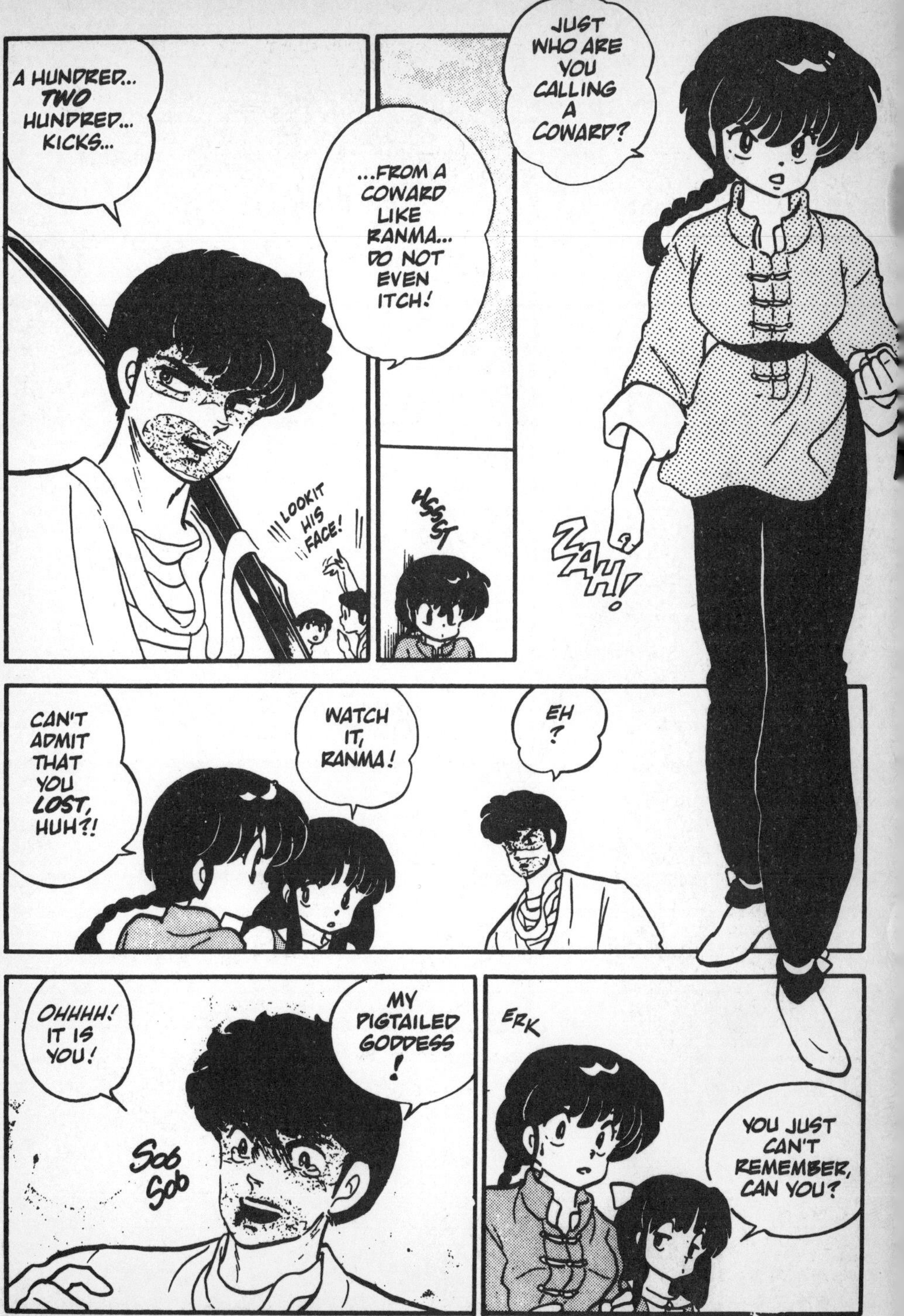
JUST WHO ARE YOU CALLING A COWARD?
ZAAH!
...FROM A COWARD LIKE RANMA... DO NOT EVEN ITCH!
HSSST
A HUNDRED... TWO HUNDRED... KICKS...
LOOKIT HIS FACE!
EH?
WATCH IT, RANMA!
CAN'T ADMIT THAT YOU LOST, HUH?!
ERK
YOU JUST CAN'T REMEMBER, CAN YOU?
MY PIGTAILED GODDESS!
OHHHH! IT IS YOU!
Sob Sob

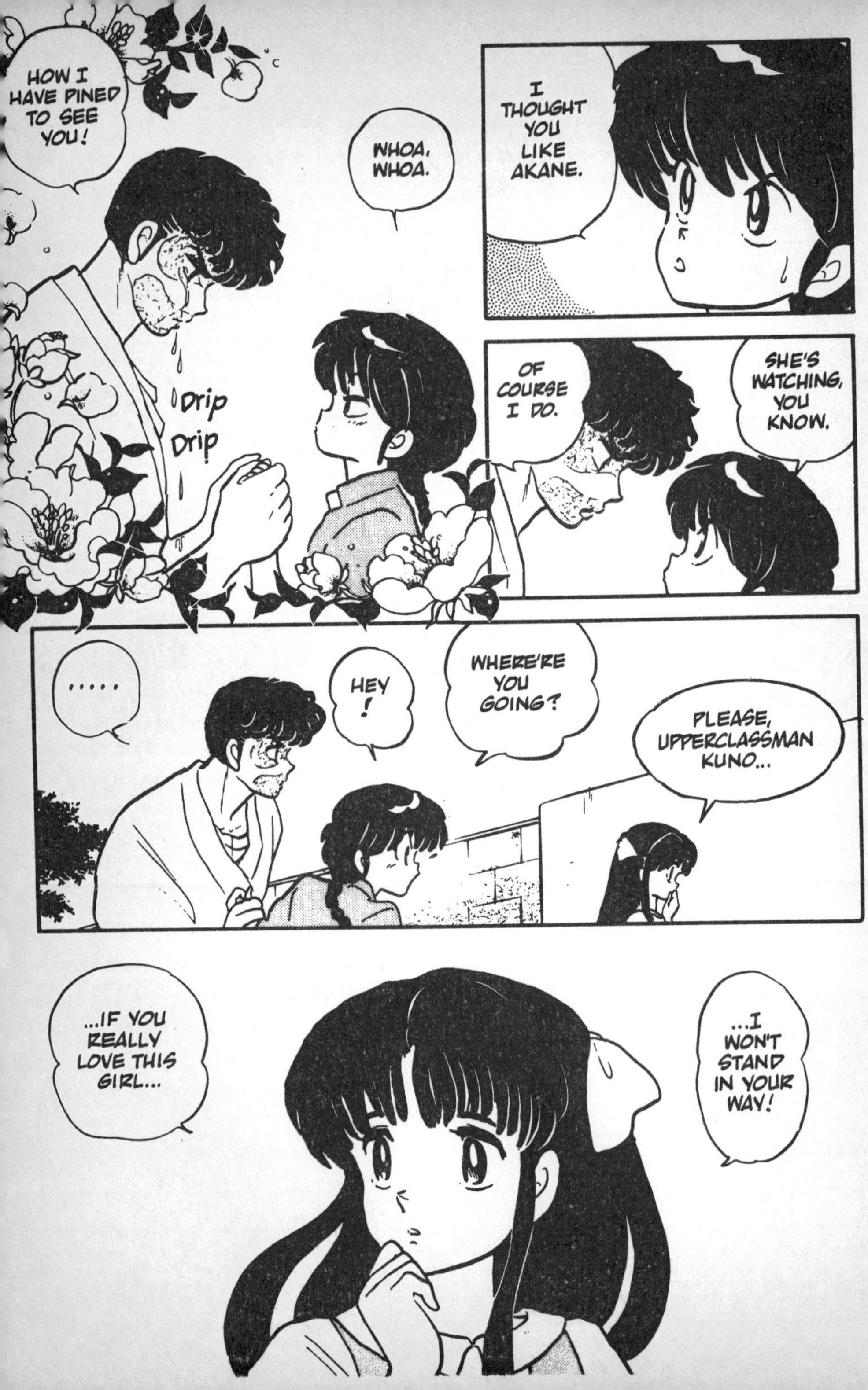

HOW I HAVE PINED TO SEE YOU!
Drip Drip
WHOA, WHOA.
I THOUGHT YOU LIKE AKANE.
OF COURSE I DO.
SHE'S WATCHING, YOU KNOW.
.....
HEY!
WHERE'RE YOU GOING?
PLEASE, UPPERCLASSMAN KUNO...
...IF YOU REALLY LOVE THIS GIRL...
...I WON'T STAND IN YOUR WAY!

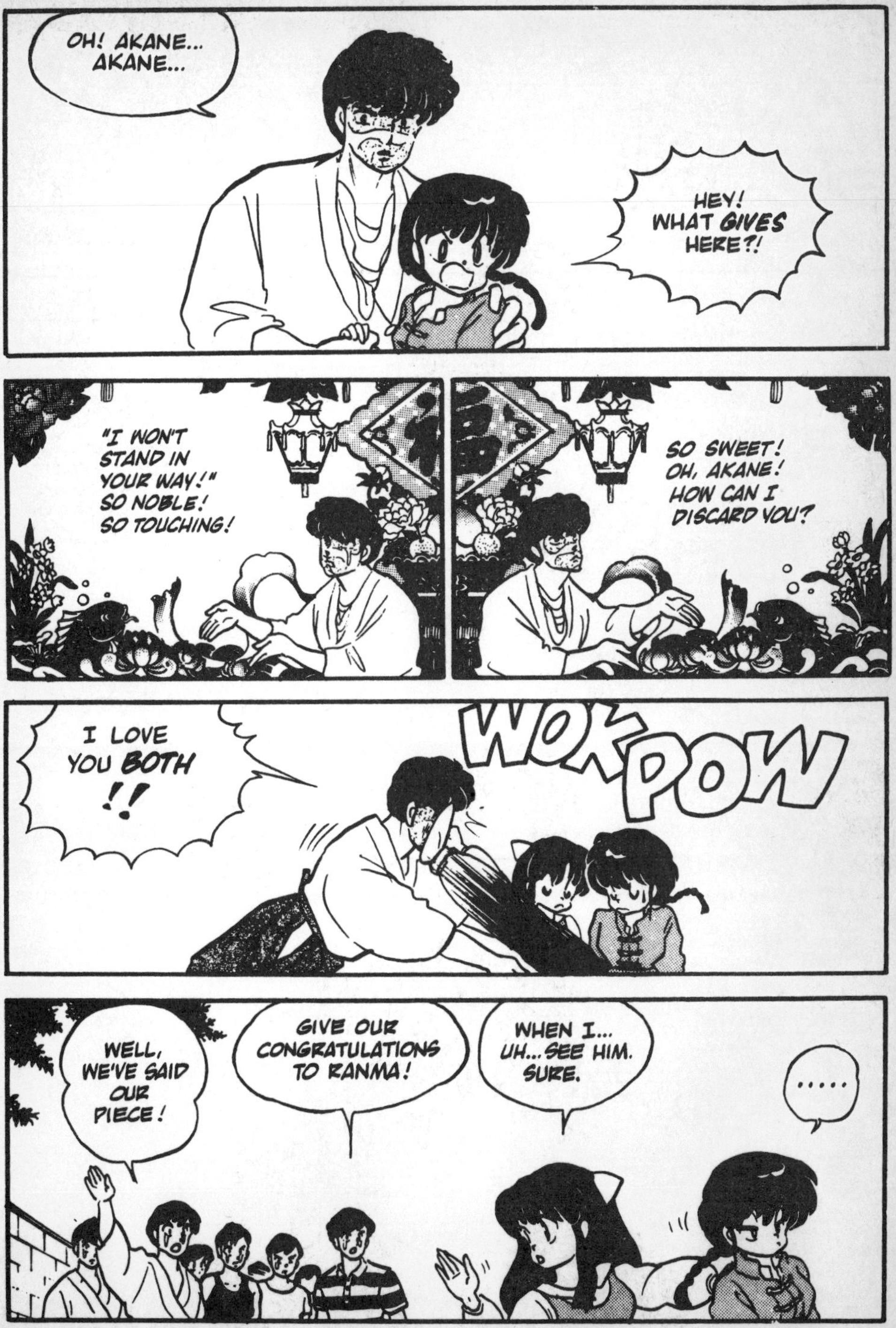
OH! AKANE... AKANE...
HEY! WHAT GIVES HERE?!
"I WON'T STAND IN YOUR WAY!" SO NOBLE! SO TOUCHING!
SO SWEET! OH, AKANE! HOW CAN I DISCARD YOU?
I LOVE YOU BOTH !!
WOK
POW
WELL, WE'VE SAID OUR PIECE!
GIVE OUR CONGRATULATIONS TO RANMA!
WHEN I... UH... SEE HIM. SURE.
.....

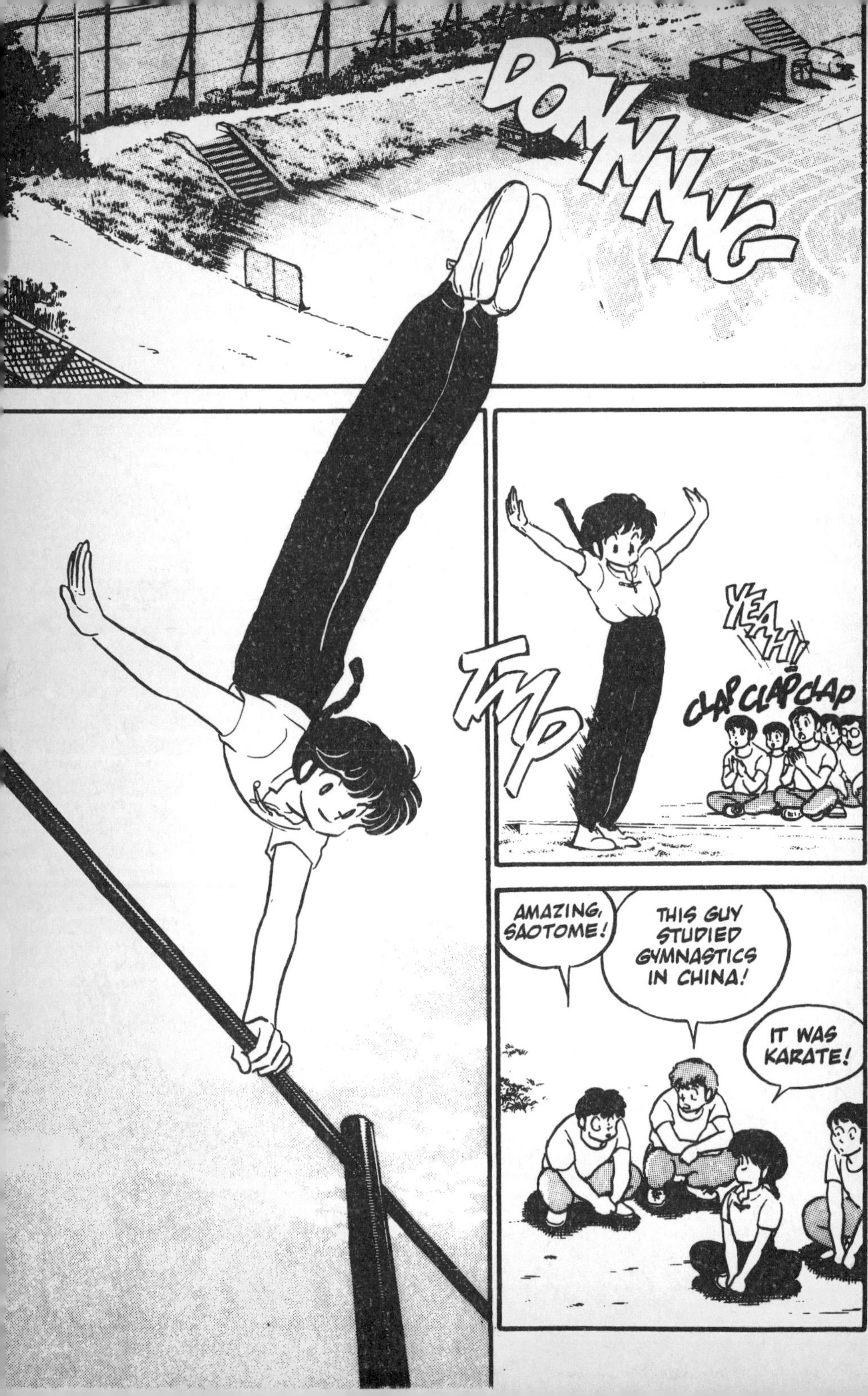

DOINNNG
TMP
YEAAH!
CLAP CLAP CLAP
AMAZING, SAOTOME!
THIS GUY STUDIED GYMNASTICS IN CHINA!
IT WAS KARATE!

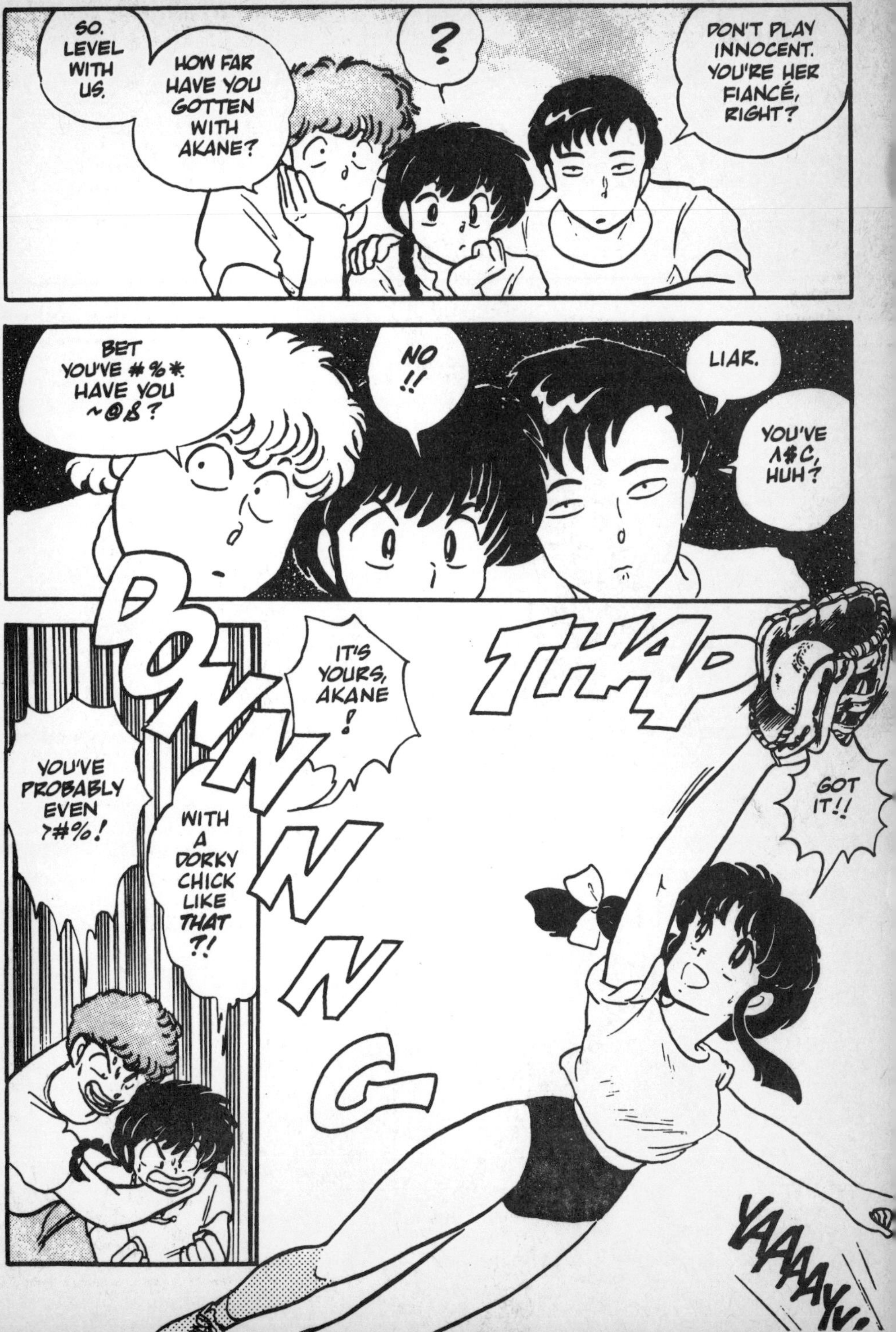
SO. LEVEL WITH US.
HOW FAR HAVE YOU GOTTEN WITH AKANE?
?
DON'T PLAY INNOCENT. YOU'RE HER FIANCÉ, RIGHT?
BET YOU'VE #%* HAVE YOU ~@&?
NO!!
LIAR.
YOU'VE ∧$C, HUH?
DOWNNNNG
YOU'VE PROBABLY EVEN 7#%!
WITH A DORKY CHICK LIKE THAT?!
IT'S YOURS, AKANE!
THAP
GOT IT!!
YAAAAY

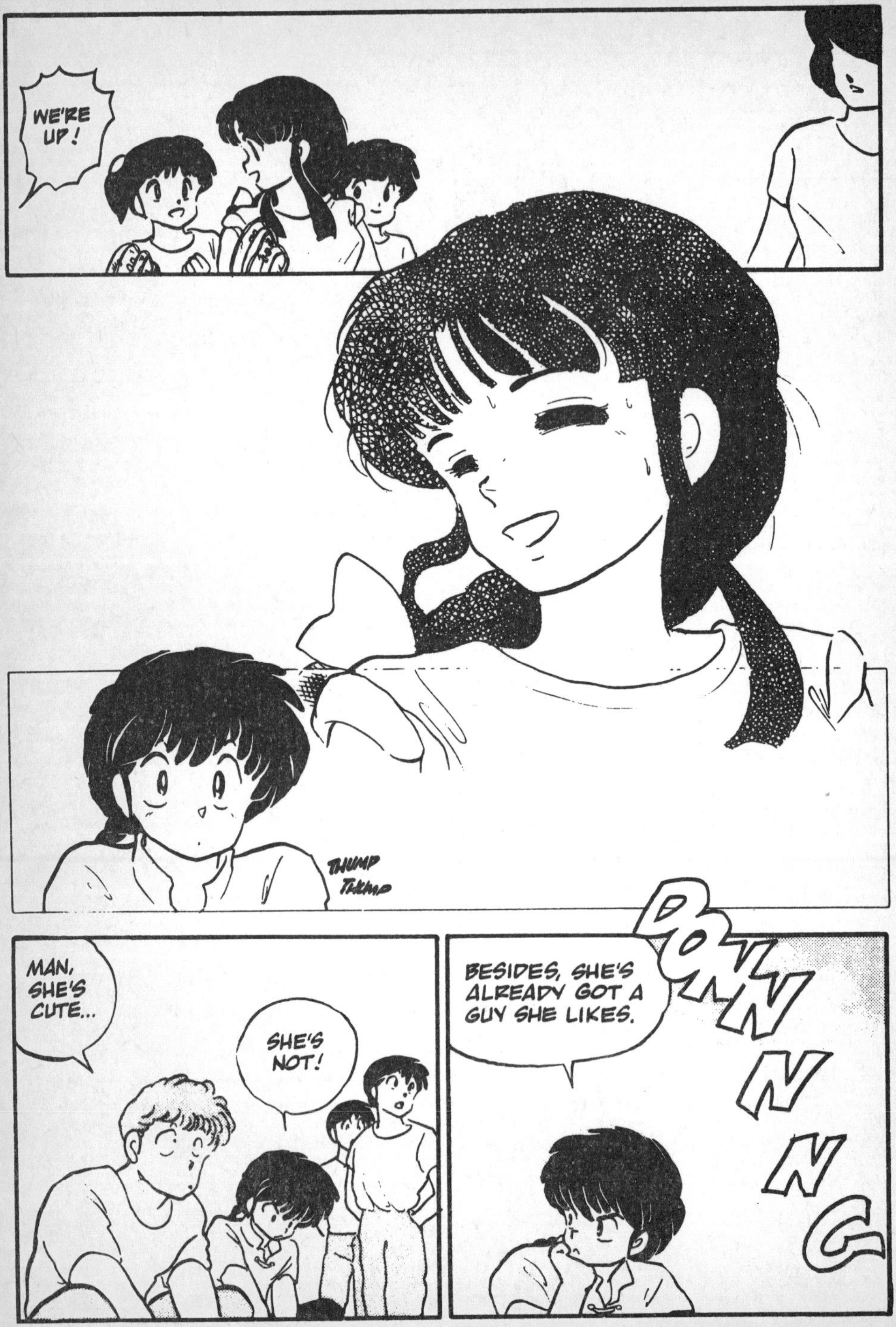

WE'RE UP!
THUMP THUMP
MAN, SHE'S CUTE...
SHE'S NOT!
DONNNNG
BESIDES, SHE'S ALREADY GOT A GUY SHE LIKES.

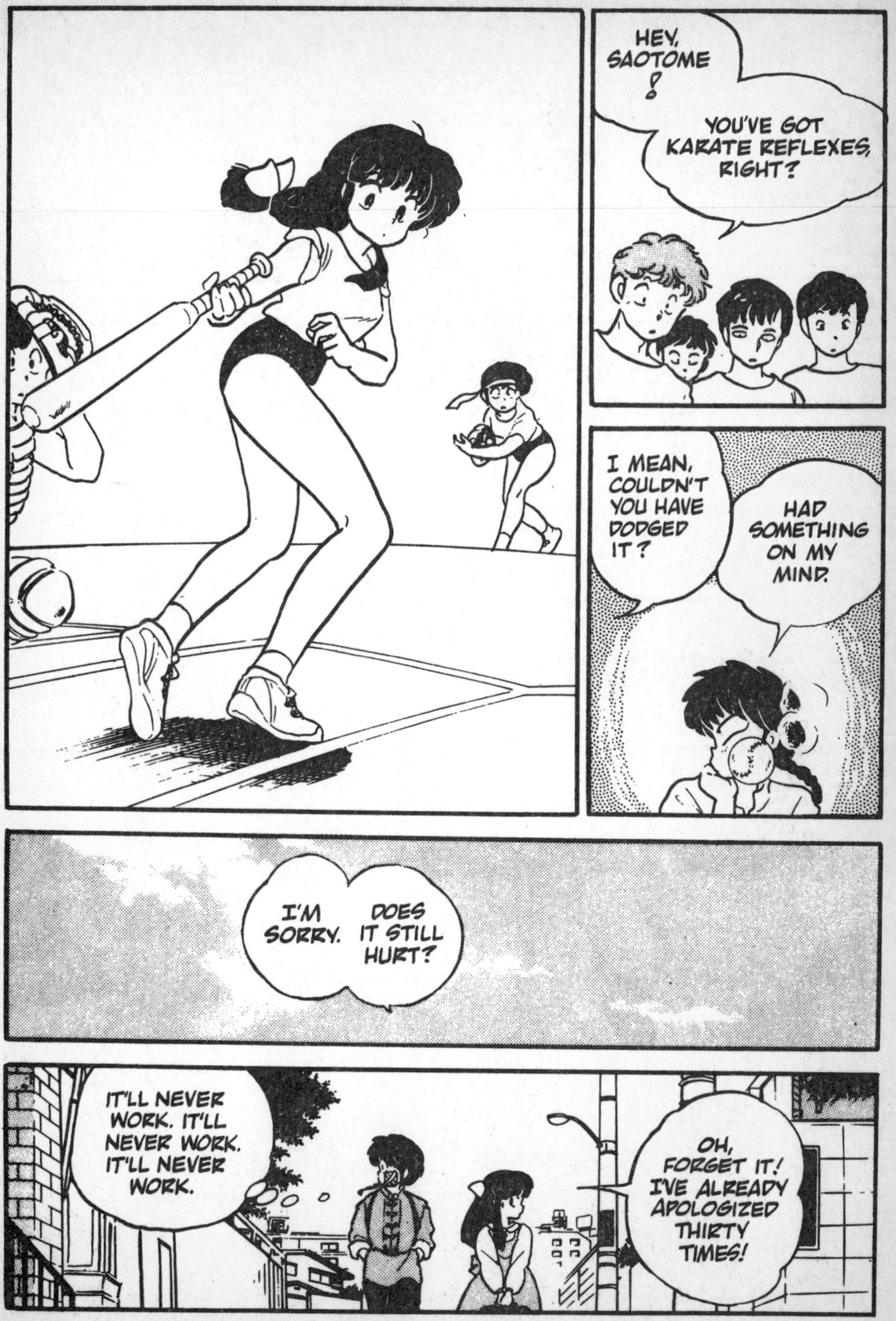
HEY, SAOTOME!
YOU'VE GOT KARATE REFLEXES, RIGHT?
I MEAN, COULDN'T YOU HAVE DODGED IT?
HAD SOMETHING ON MY MIND.
I'M SORRY.
DOES IT STILL HURT?
IT'LL NEVER WORK. IT'LL NEVER WORK. IT'LL NEVER WORK.
OH, FORGET IT! I'VE ALREADY APOLOGIZED THIRTY TIMES!

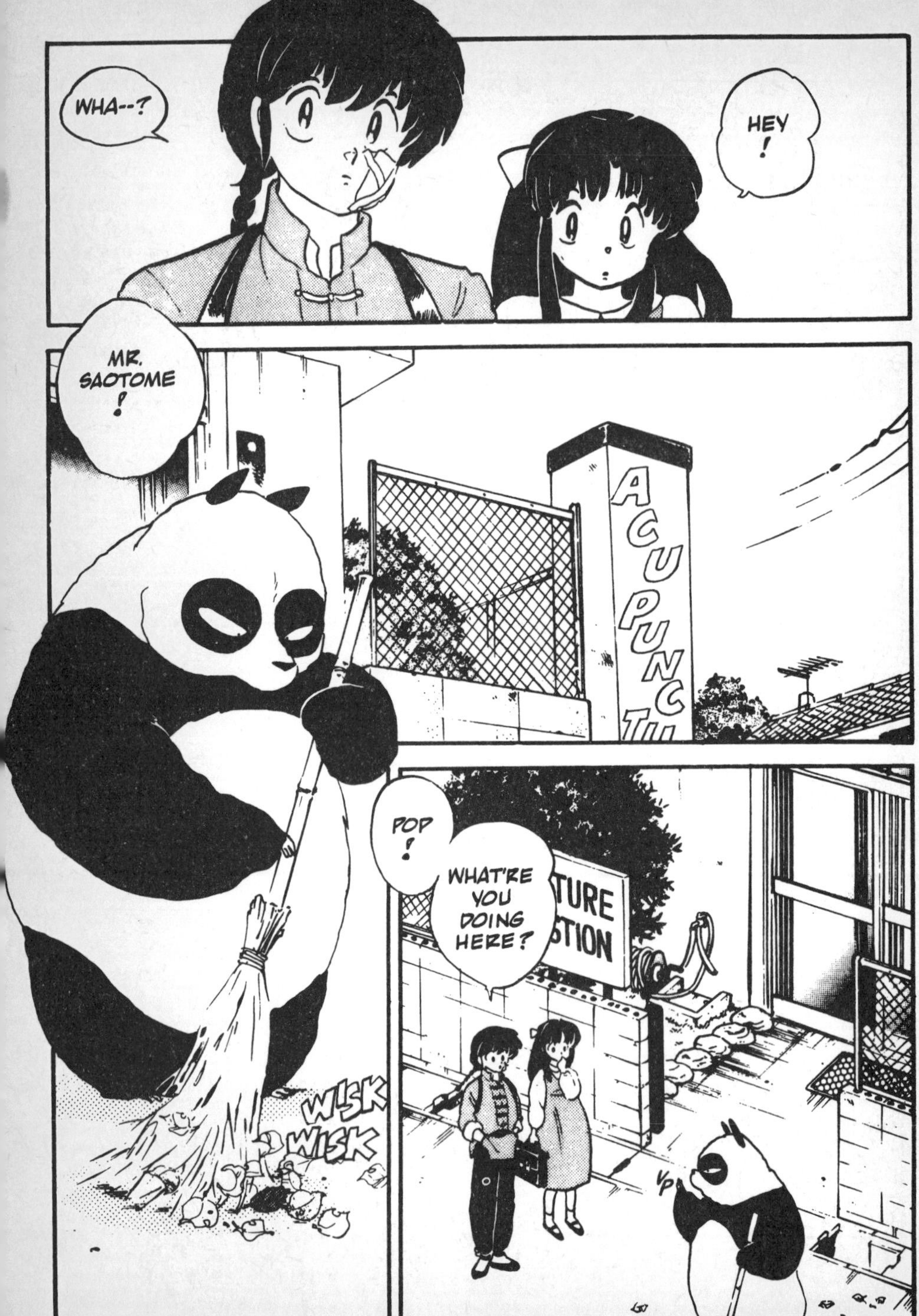
WHA--?
HEY!
MR. SAOTOME!
ACUPUNC
WISK WISK
POP!
WHAT'RE YOU DOING HERE?
TURE
STION

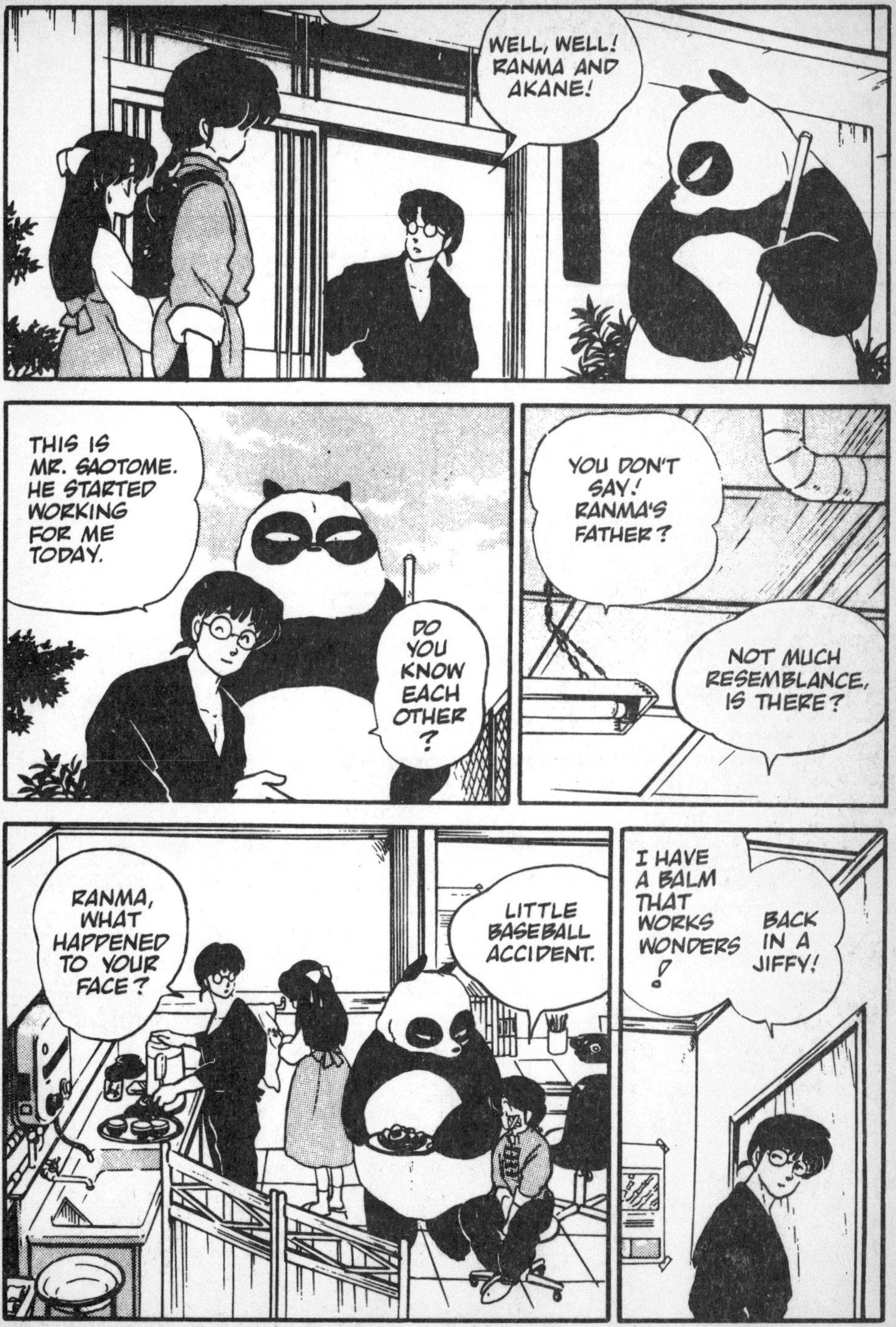
WELL, WELL! RANMA AND AKANE!
THIS IS MR. SAOTOME. HE STARTED WORKING FOR ME TODAY.
DO YOU KNOW EACH OTHER?
YOU DON'T SAY! RANMA'S FATHER?
NOT MUCH RESEMBLANCE, IS THERE?
RANMA, WHAT HAPPENED TO YOUR FACE?
LITTLE BASEBALL ACCIDENT.
I HAVE A BALM THAT WORKS WONDERS!
BACK IN A JIFFY!

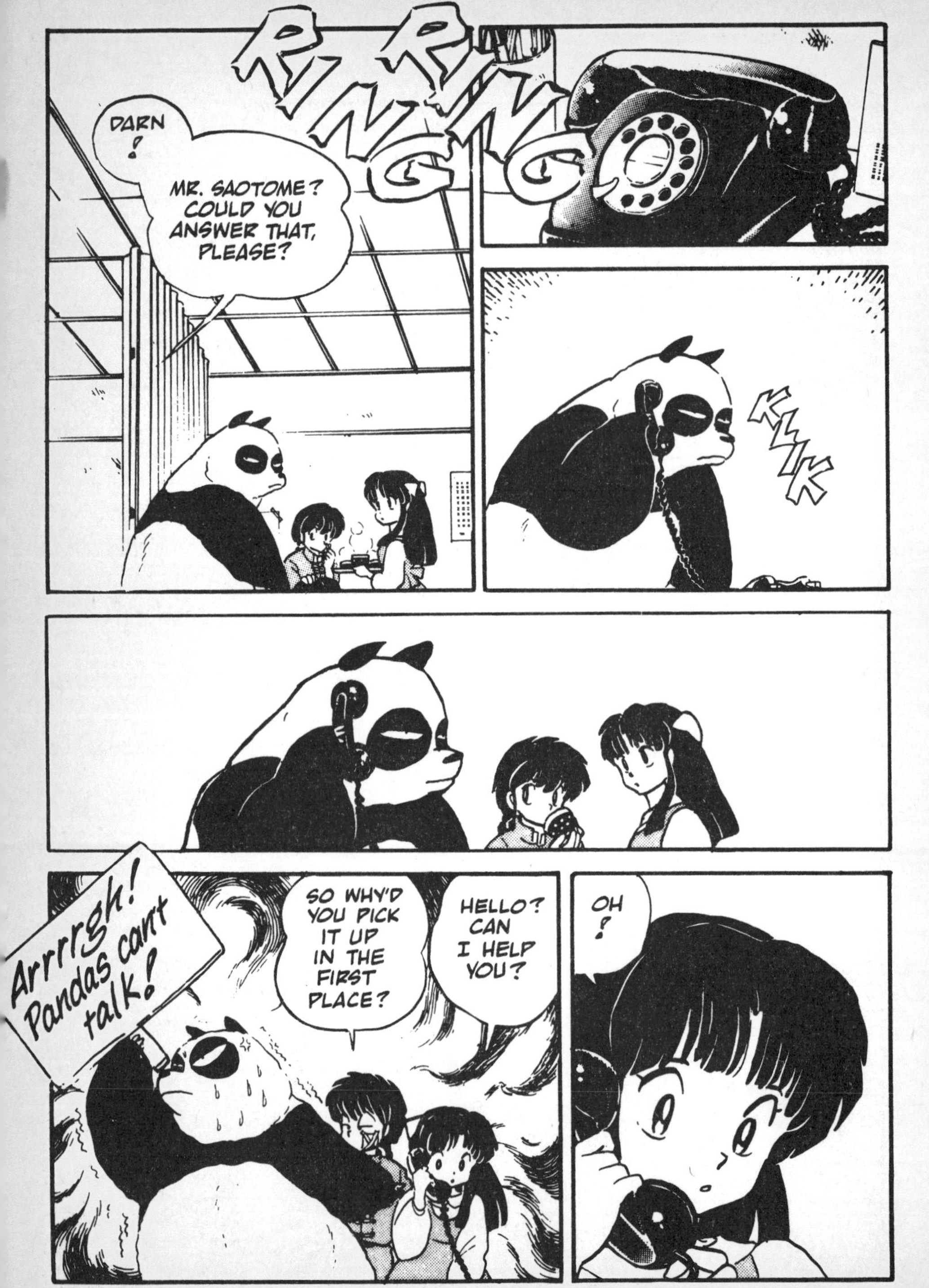
RINNNGGG
DARN!
MR. SAOTOME? COULD YOU ANSWER THAT, PLEASE?
KLIK
HELLO? CAN I HELP YOU?
SO WHY'D YOU PICK IT UP IN THE FIRST PLACE?
Arrrrgh! Pandas can't talk!
OH!

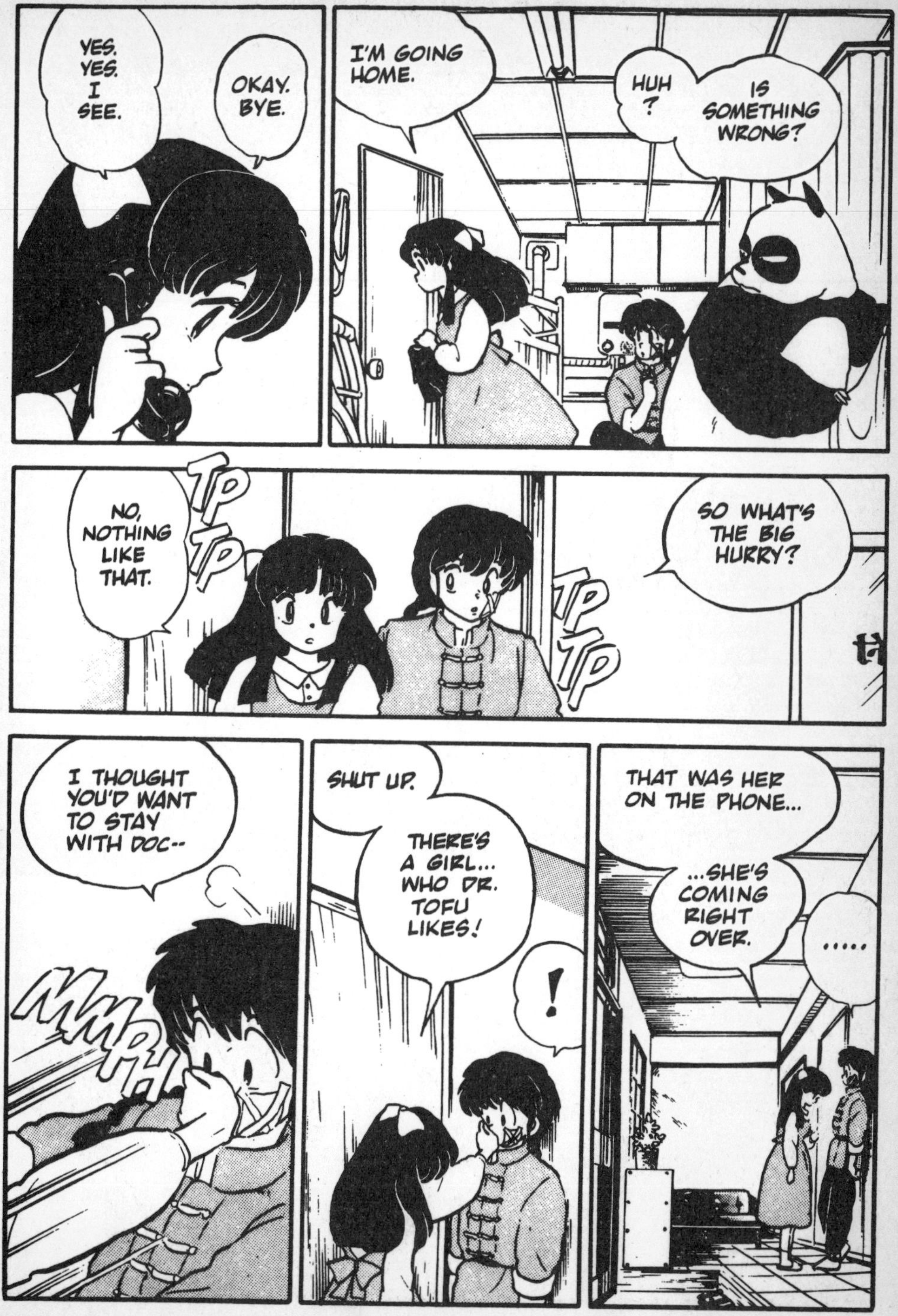
YES. YES. I SEE.
OKAY. BYE.
I'M GOING HOME.
HUH?
IS SOMETHING WRONG?
NO, NOTHING LIKE THAT.
TP TP
TP TP
SO WHAT'S THE BIG HURRY?
I THOUGHT YOU'D WANT TO STAY WITH DOC--
MMPH
SHUT UP.
THERE'S A GIRL... WHO DR. TOFU LIKES!
!
THAT WAS HER ON THE PHONE...
...SHE'S COMING RIGHT OVER.
.....

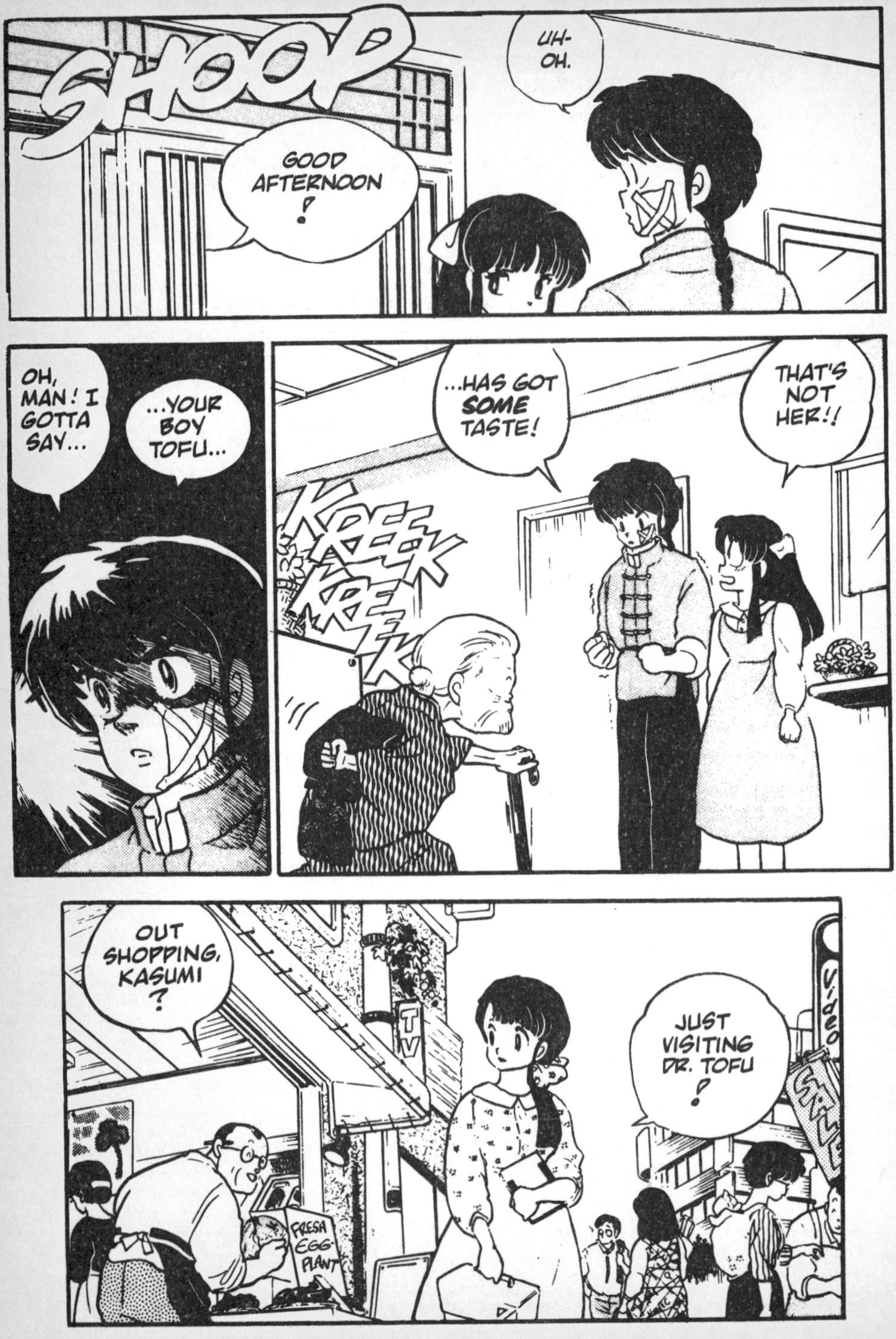
SHOOP
GOOD AFTERNOON!
UH-OH.
OH, MAN! I GOTTA SAY...
...YOUR BOY TOFU...
...HAS GOT SOME TASTE!
KREEK KREEK
THAT'S NOT HER!!
OUT SHOPPING, KASUMI?
JUST VISITING DR. TOFU!
TV
Video
FRESH EGG-PLANT

PART NINE

You're Cute When You Smile

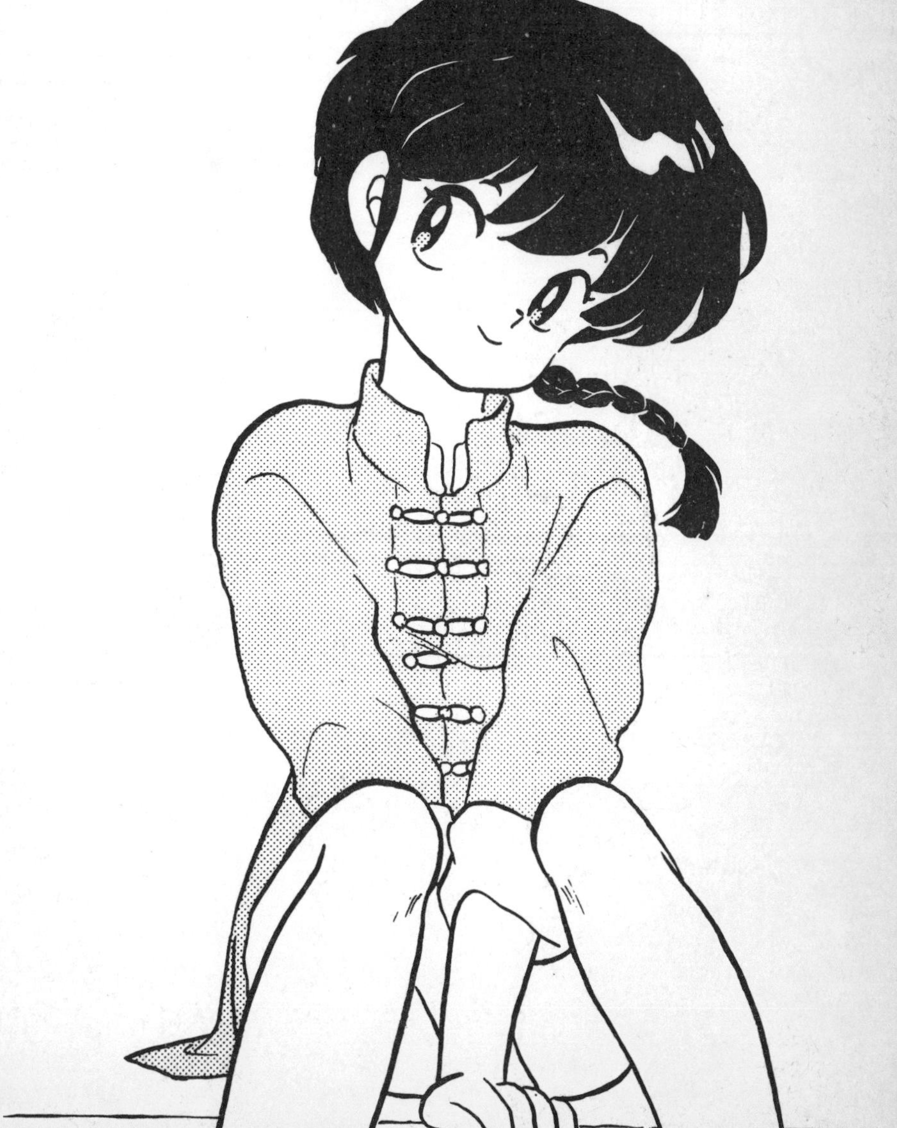

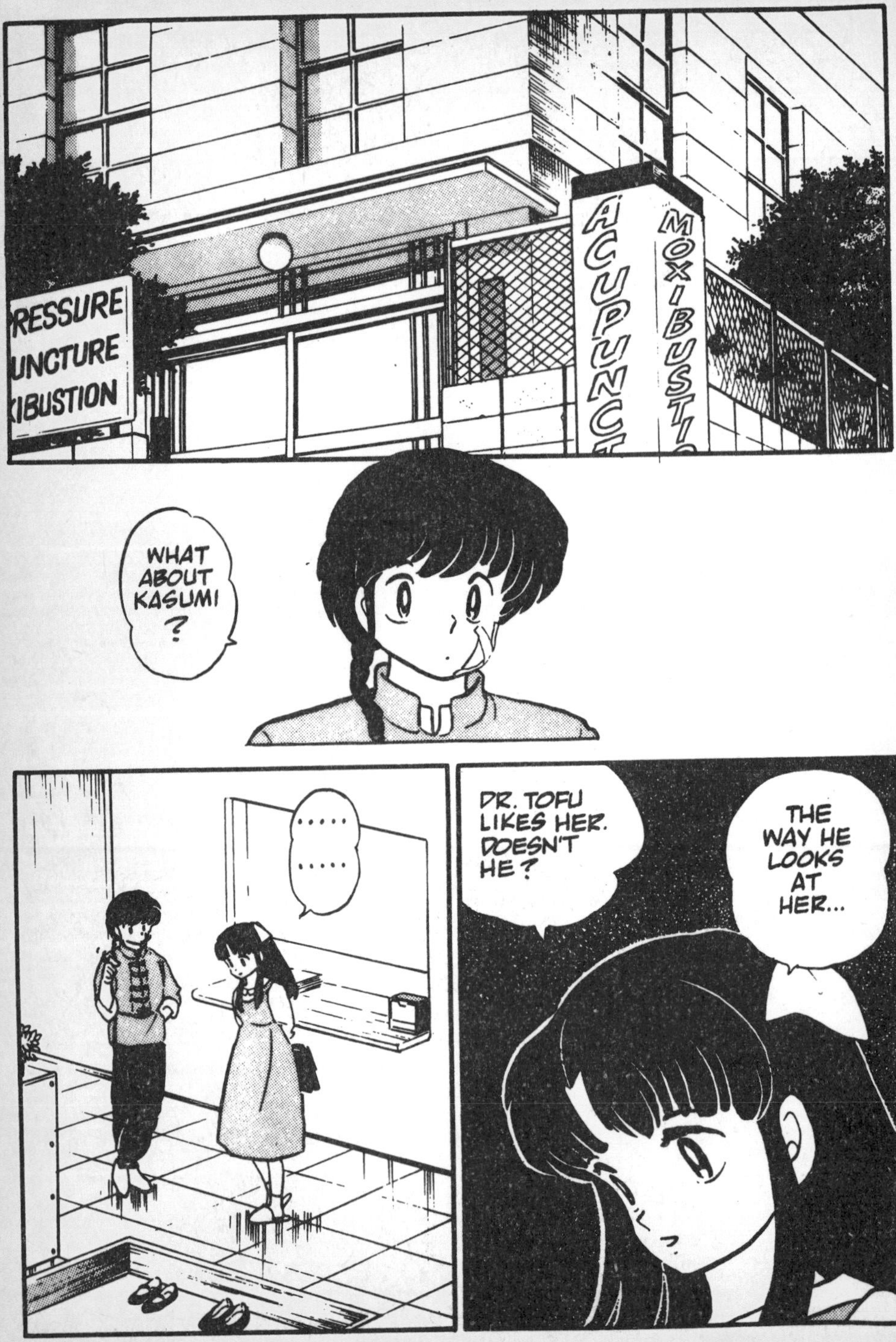
PRESSURE
UNCTURE
XIBUSTION
ACUPUNCT
MOXIBUSTIO
WHAT ABOUT KASUMI ?
.....
.....
DR. TOFU LIKES HER. DOESN'T HE ?
THE WAY HE LOOKS AT HER...

WHAT ARE YOU TWO DOING?
HUH ?
UH... NOTHING !
RIGHT ?
POP
I'M RANMA'S POP! (GET IT?)
THANK YOU FOR THAT INTERRUPTION.

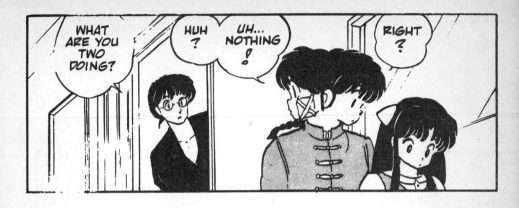

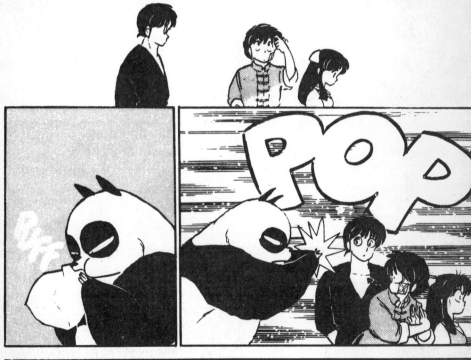

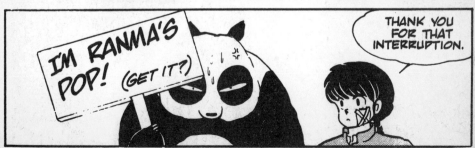

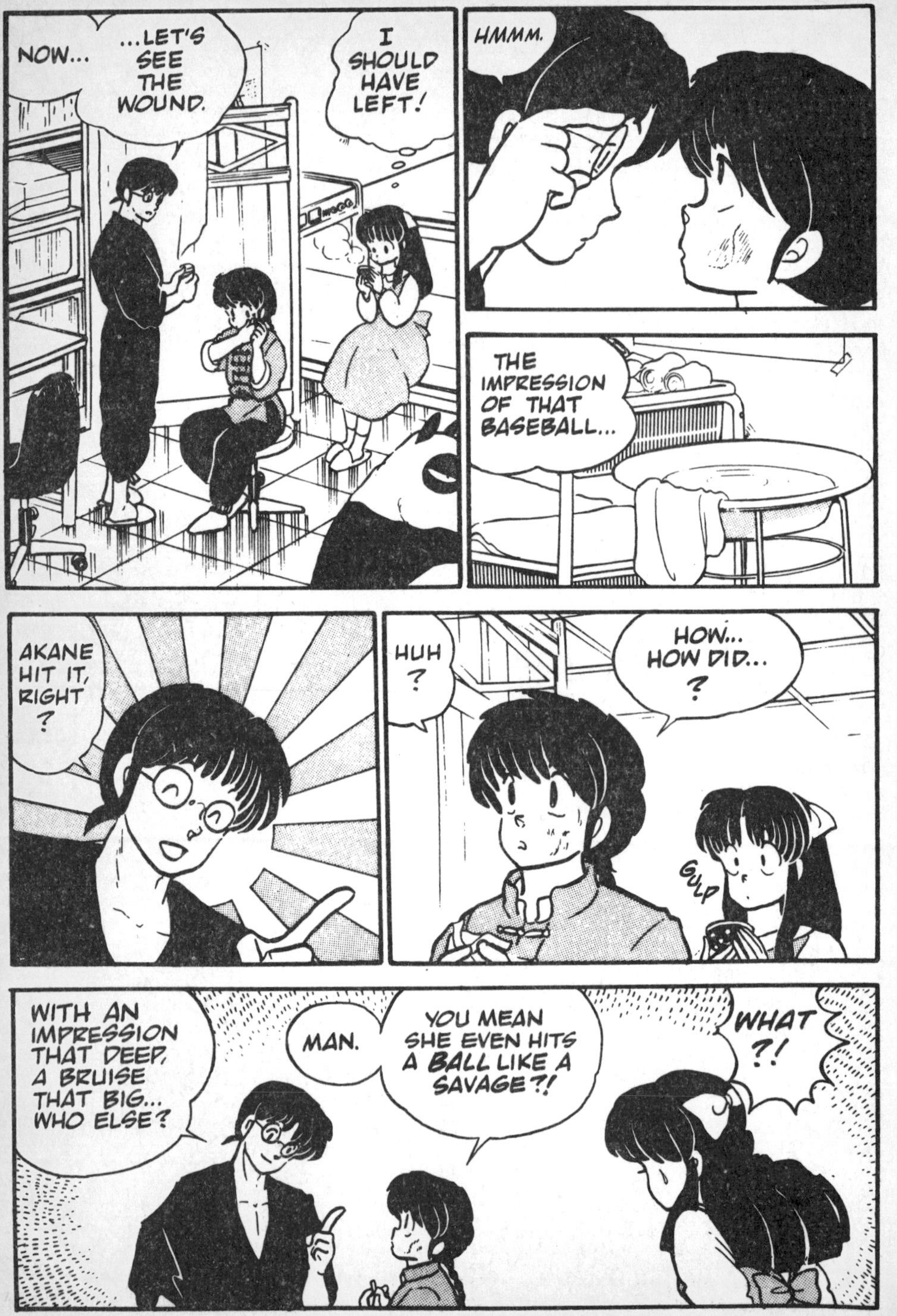
NOW...
...LET'S SEE THE WOUND.
I SHOULD HAVE LEFT!
HMMM.
THE IMPRESSION OF THAT BASEBALL...
AKANE HIT IT, RIGHT ?
HUH ?
HOW... HOW DID... ?
GULP
WITH AN IMPRESSION THAT DEEP, A BRUISE THAT BIG... WHO ELSE?
MAN.
YOU MEAN SHE EVEN HITS A BALL LIKE A SAVAGE?!
WHAT ?!

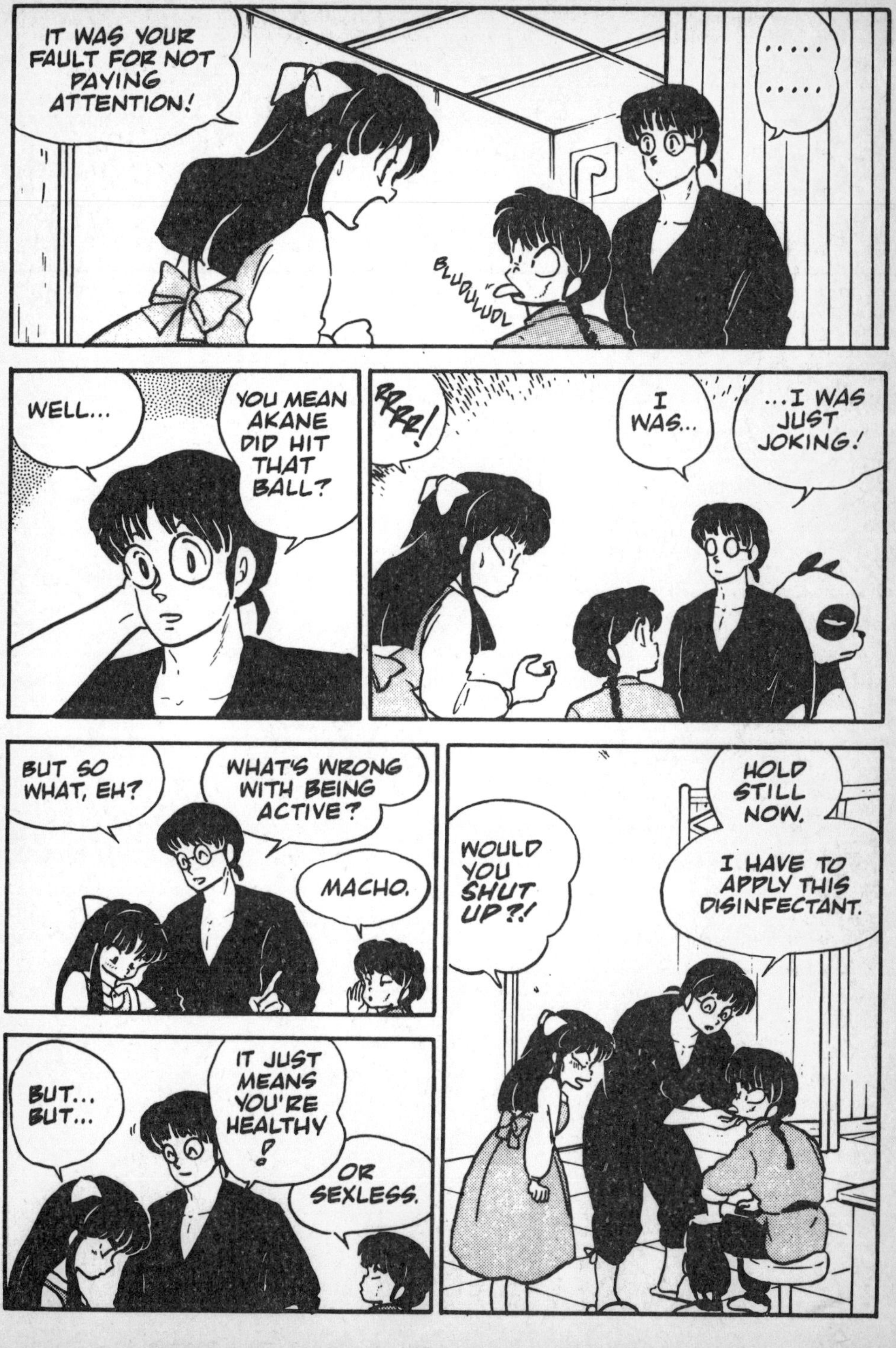
IT WAS YOUR FAULT FOR NOT PAYING ATTENTION!
....
BLUDULUDL
WELL...
YOU MEAN AKANE DID HIT THAT BALL?
RRRR!
I WAS...
...I WAS JUST JOKING!
BUT SO WHAT, EH?
WHAT'S WRONG WITH BEING ACTIVE?
MACHO.
BUT... BUT...
IT JUST MEANS YOU'RE HEALTHY!
OR SEXLESS.
HOLD STILL NOW.
I HAVE TO APPLY THIS DISINFECTANT.
WOULD YOU SHUT UP?!

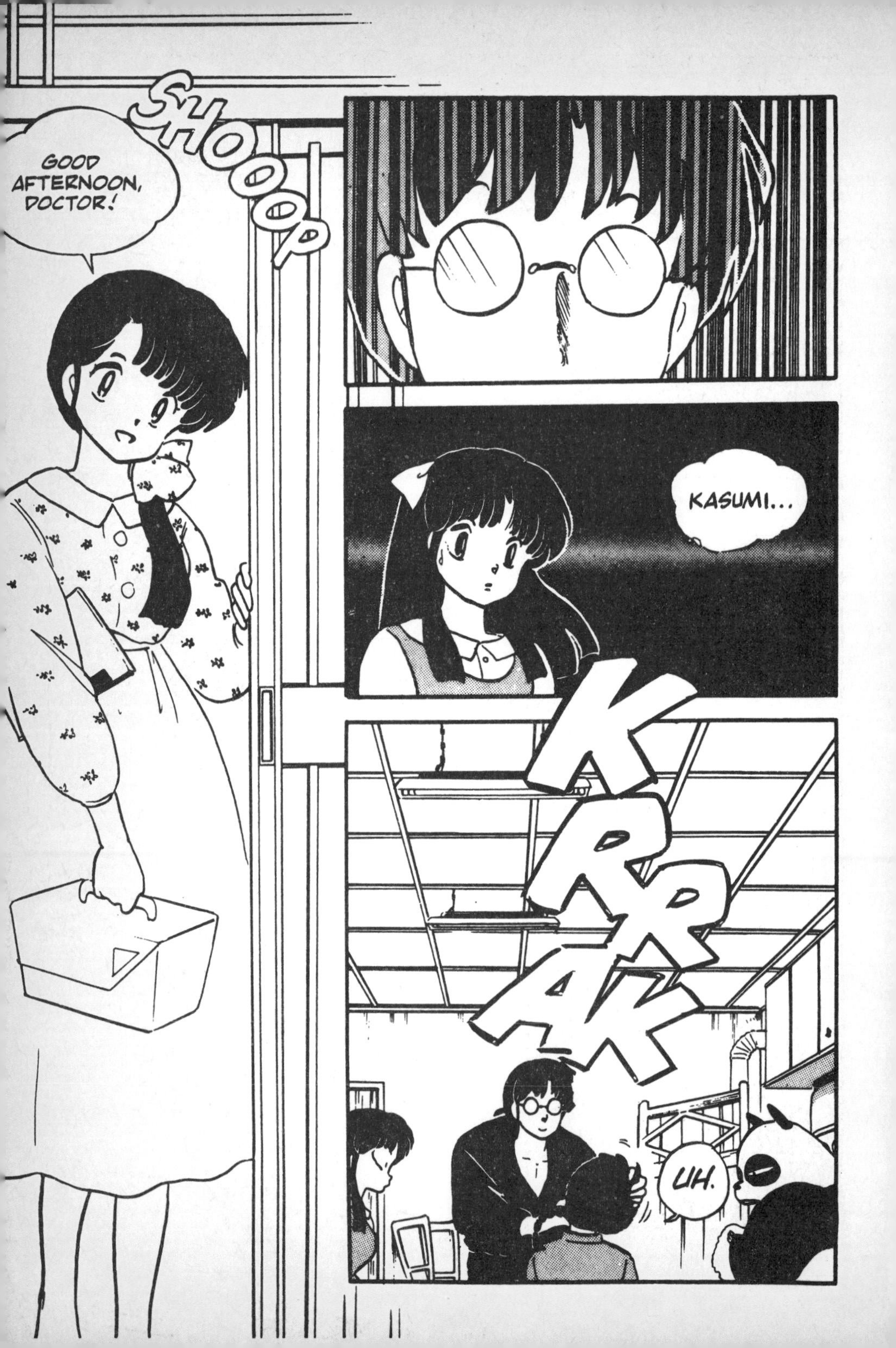
SHOOOP
GOOD AFTERNOON, DOCTOR!
KASUMI...
KRRAK
UH.

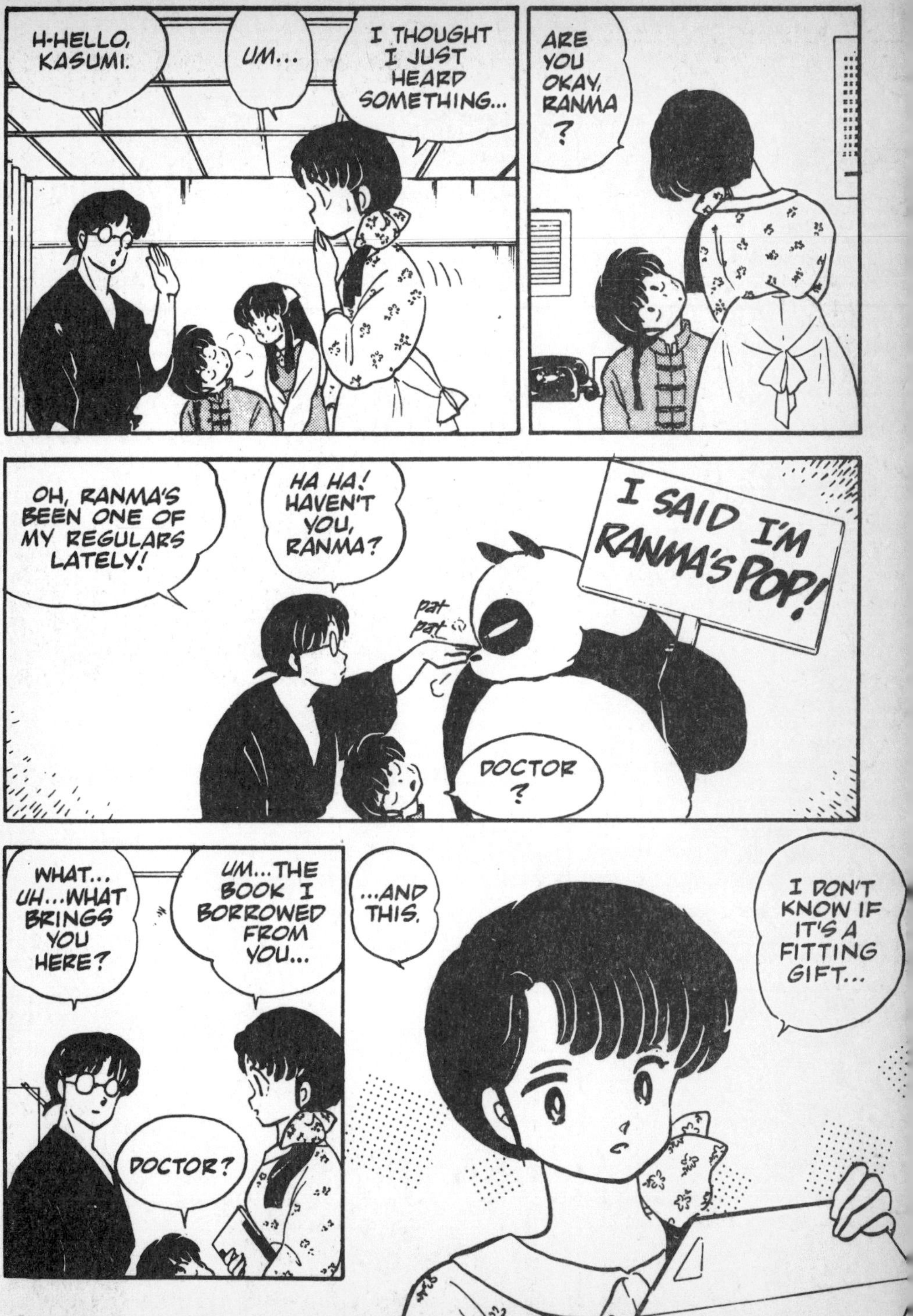
H-HELLO, KASUMI.
UM...
I THOUGHT I JUST HEARD SOMETHING...
ARE YOU OKAY, RANMA ?
OH, RANMA'S BEEN ONE OF MY REGULARS LATELY!
HA HA! HAVEN'T YOU, RANMA?
pat pat
I SAID I'M RANMA'S POP!
DOCTOR ?
WHAT... UH...WHAT BRINGS YOU HERE?
UM...THE BOOK I BORROWED FROM YOU...
...AND THIS.
I DON'T KNOW IF IT'S A FITTING GIFT...
DOCTOR?

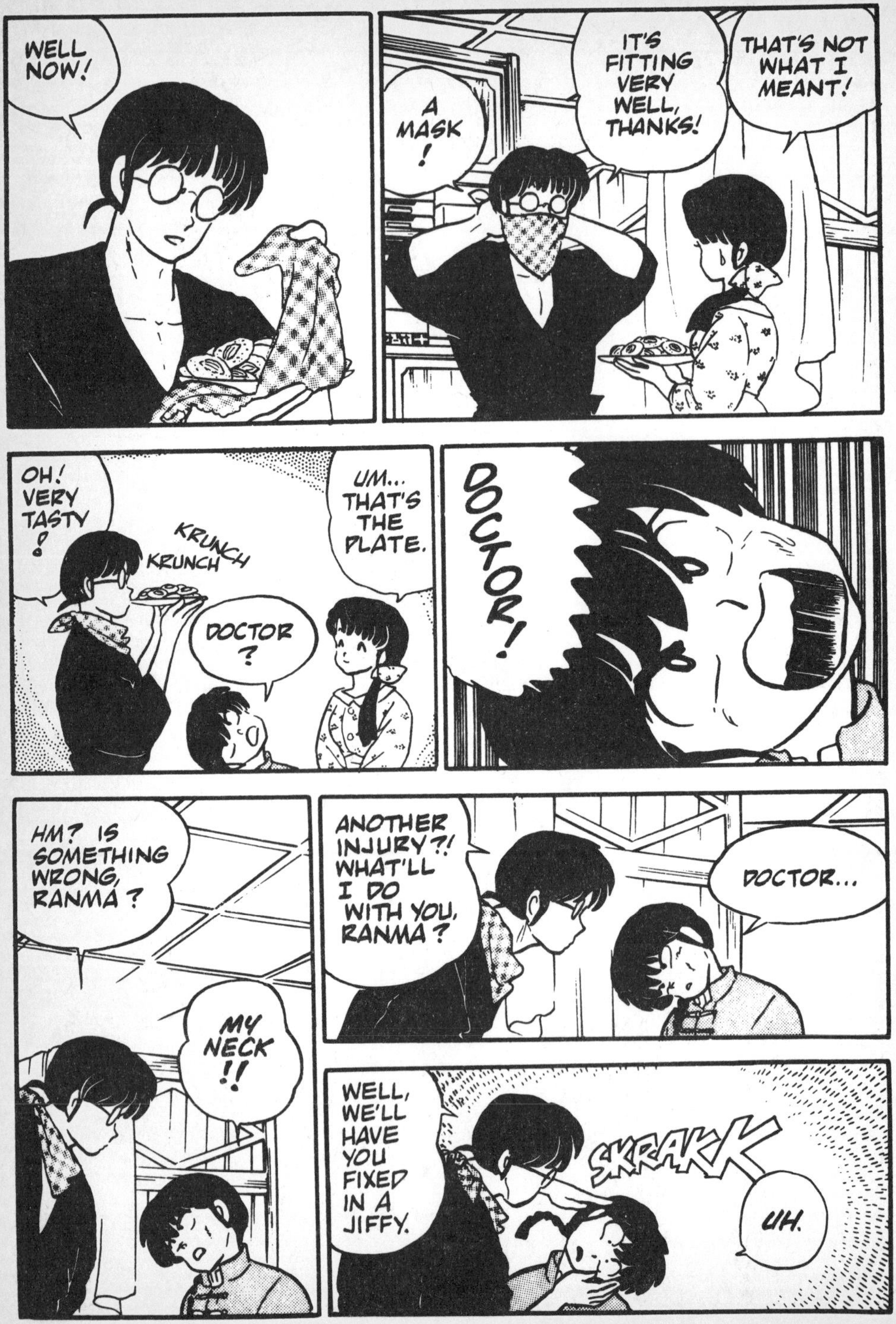
WELL NOW!
A MASK!
IT'S FITTING VERY WELL, THANKS!
THAT'S NOT WHAT I MEANT!
OH! VERY TASTY!
KRUNCH
KRUNCH
UM... THAT'S THE PLATE.
DOCTOR?
DOCTOR!
HM? IS SOMETHING WRONG, RANMA?
MY NECK!!
ANOTHER INJURY?! WHAT'LL I DO WITH YOU, RANMA?
DOCTOR...
WELL, WE'LL HAVE YOU FIXED IN A JIFFY.
SKRAKK
UH.

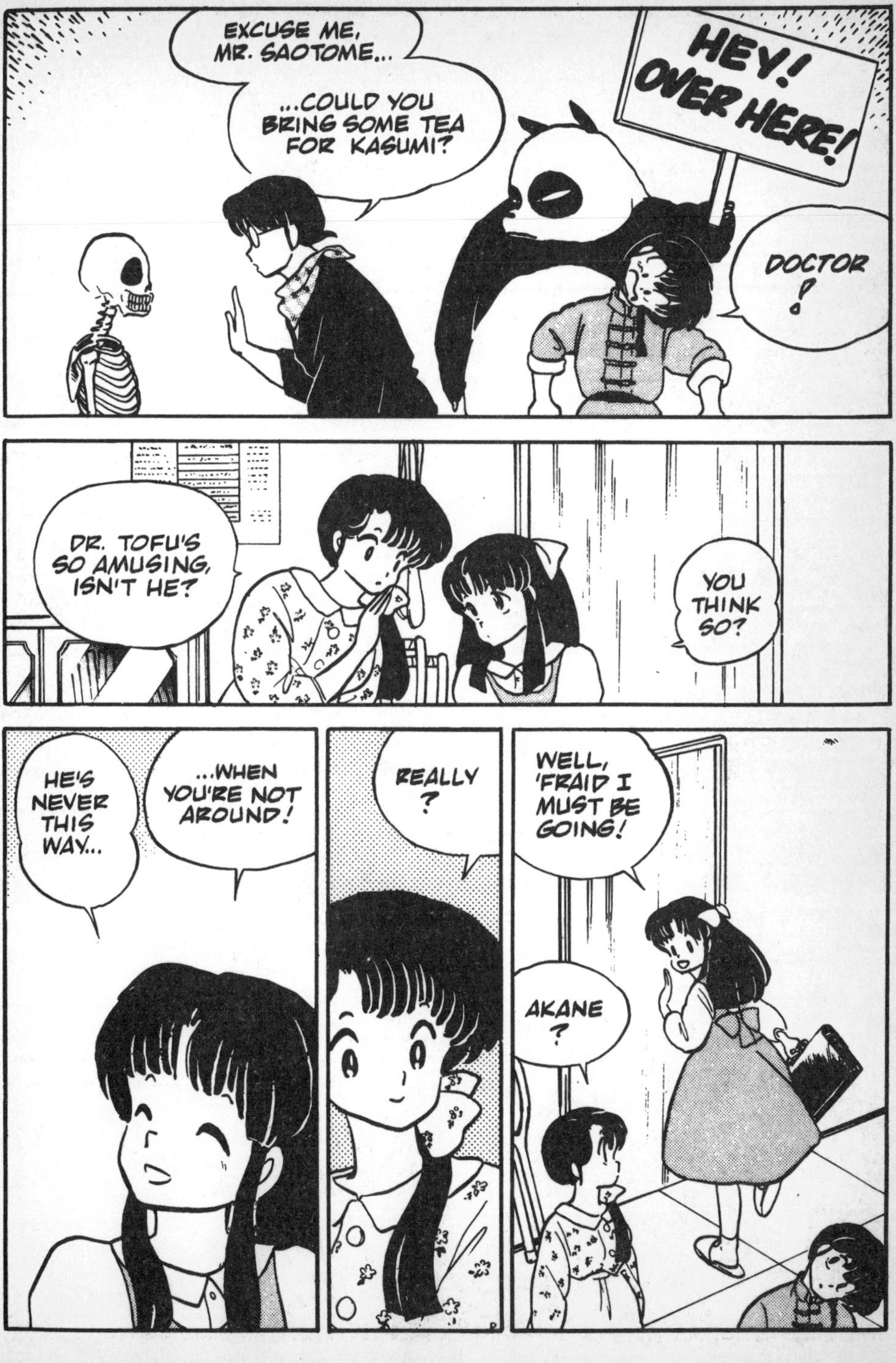
EXCUSE ME, MR. SAOTOME...
...COULD YOU BRING SOME TEA FOR KASUMI?
HEY! OVER HERE!
DOCTOR!
DR. TOFU'S SO AMUSING, ISN'T HE?
YOU THINK SO?
HE'S NEVER THIS WAY...
...WHEN YOU'RE NOT AROUND!
REALLY?
WELL, 'FRAID I MUST BE GOING!
AKANE?

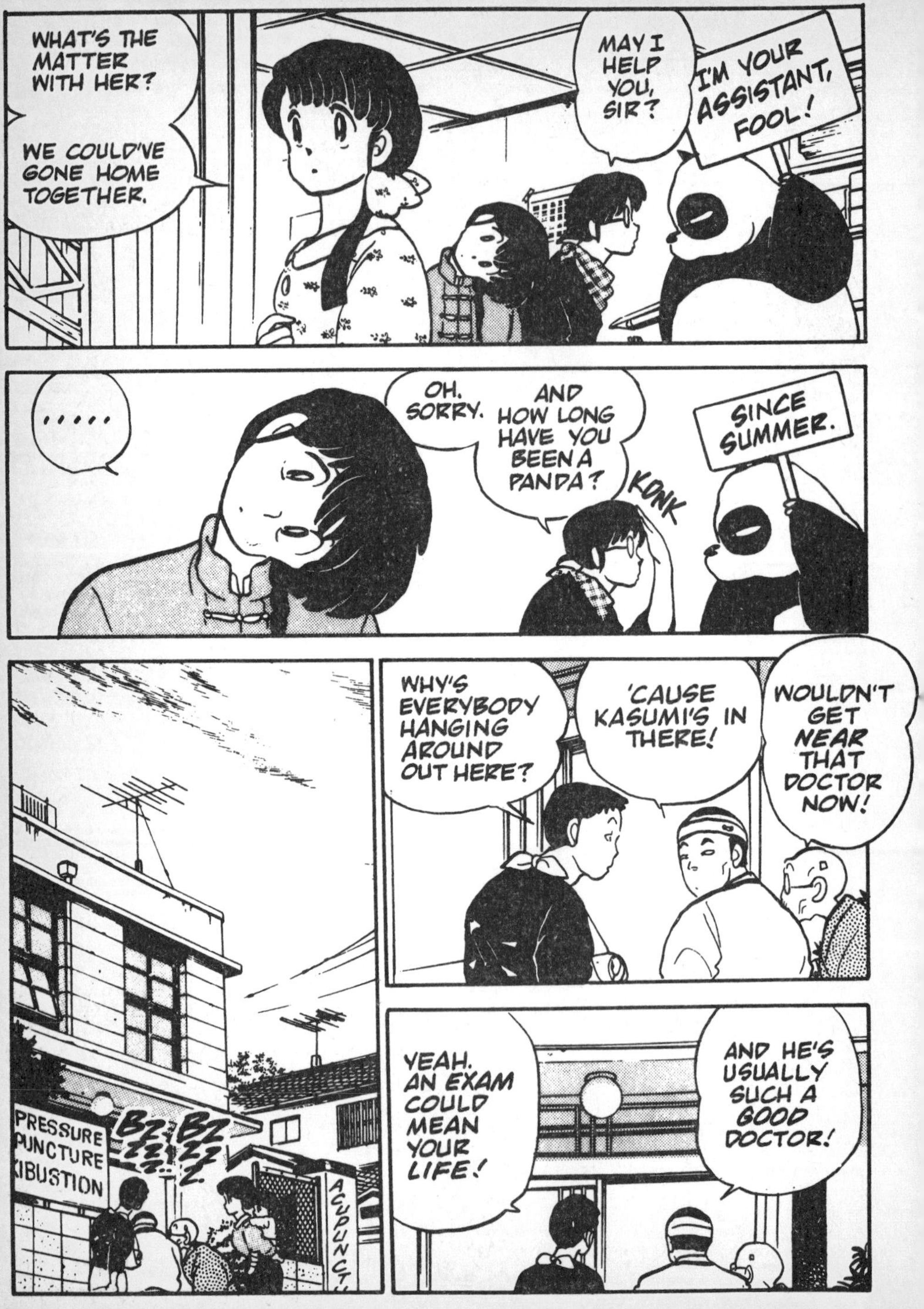
WHAT'S THE MATTER WITH HER?
WE COULD'VE GONE HOME TOGETHER.
MAY I HELP YOU, SIR?
I'M YOUR ASSISTANT, FOOL!
.....
OH. SORRY.
AND HOW LONG HAVE YOU BEEN A PANDA?
KONK
SINCE SUMMER.
PRESSURE
PUNCTURE
XIBUSTION
WHY'S EVERYBODY HANGING AROUND OUT HERE?
'CAUSE KASUMI'S IN THERE!
WOULDN'T GET NEAR THAT DOCTOR NOW!
YEAH. AN EXAM COULD MEAN YOUR LIFE!
AND HE'S USUALLY SUCH A GOOD DOCTOR!

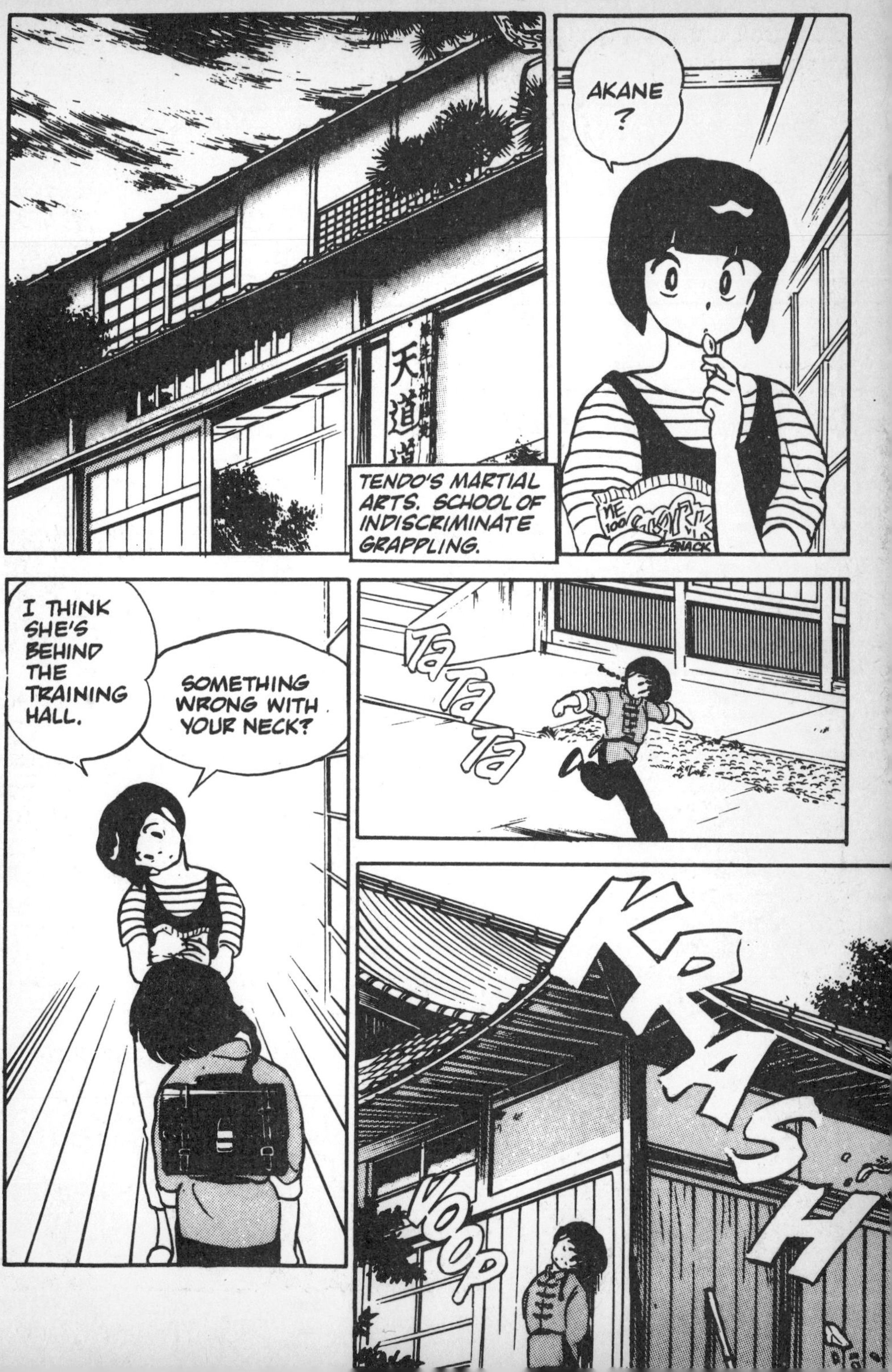
TENDO'S MARTIAL ARTS. SCHOOL OF INDISCRIMINATE GRAPPLING.
天道道
AKANE ?
SNACK
I THINK SHE'S BEHIND THE TRAINING HALL.
SOMETHING WRONG WITH YOUR NECK?
Ta Ta Ta
KRASH
VOOP

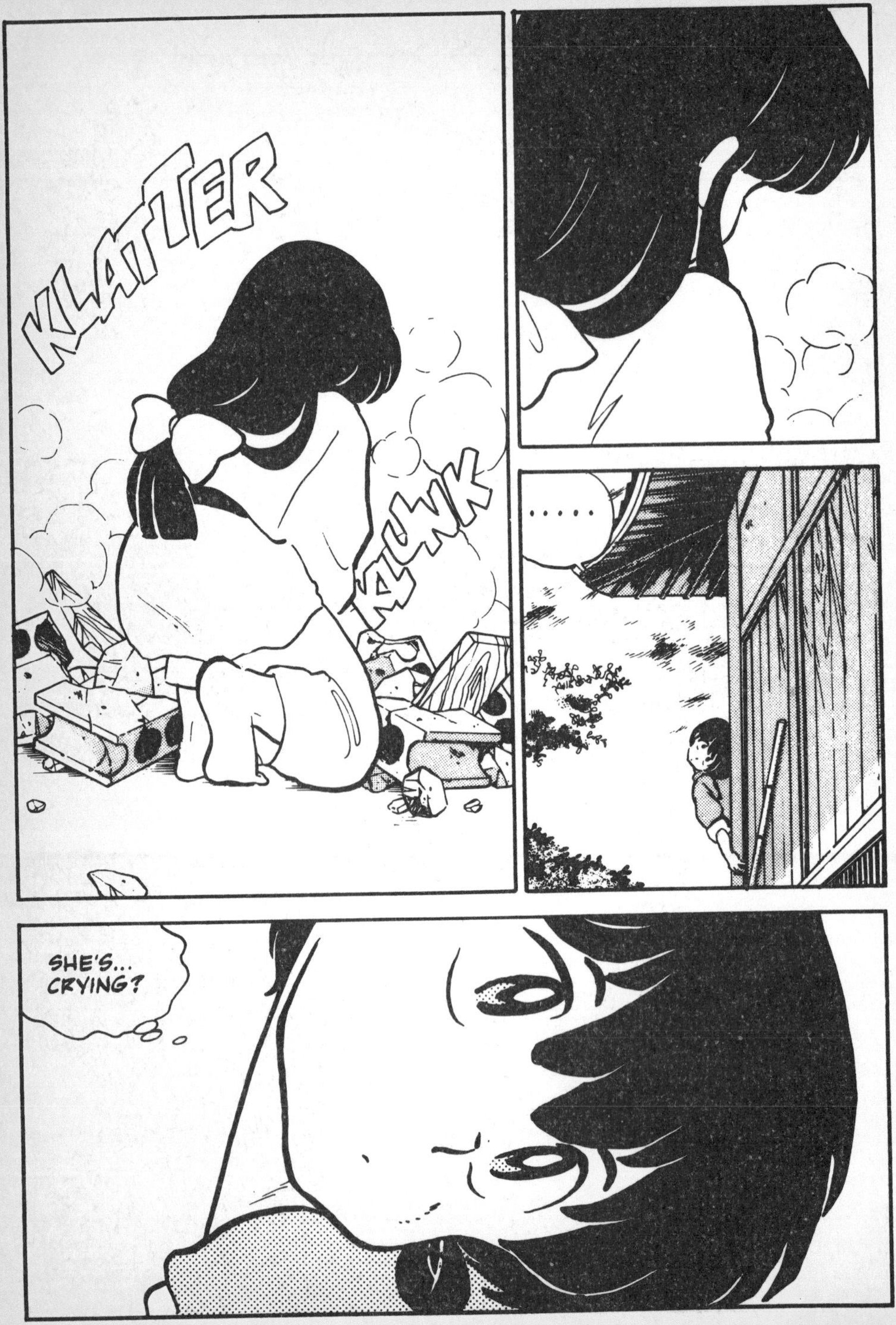
KLATTER
KLUNK
......
SHE'S... CRYING?

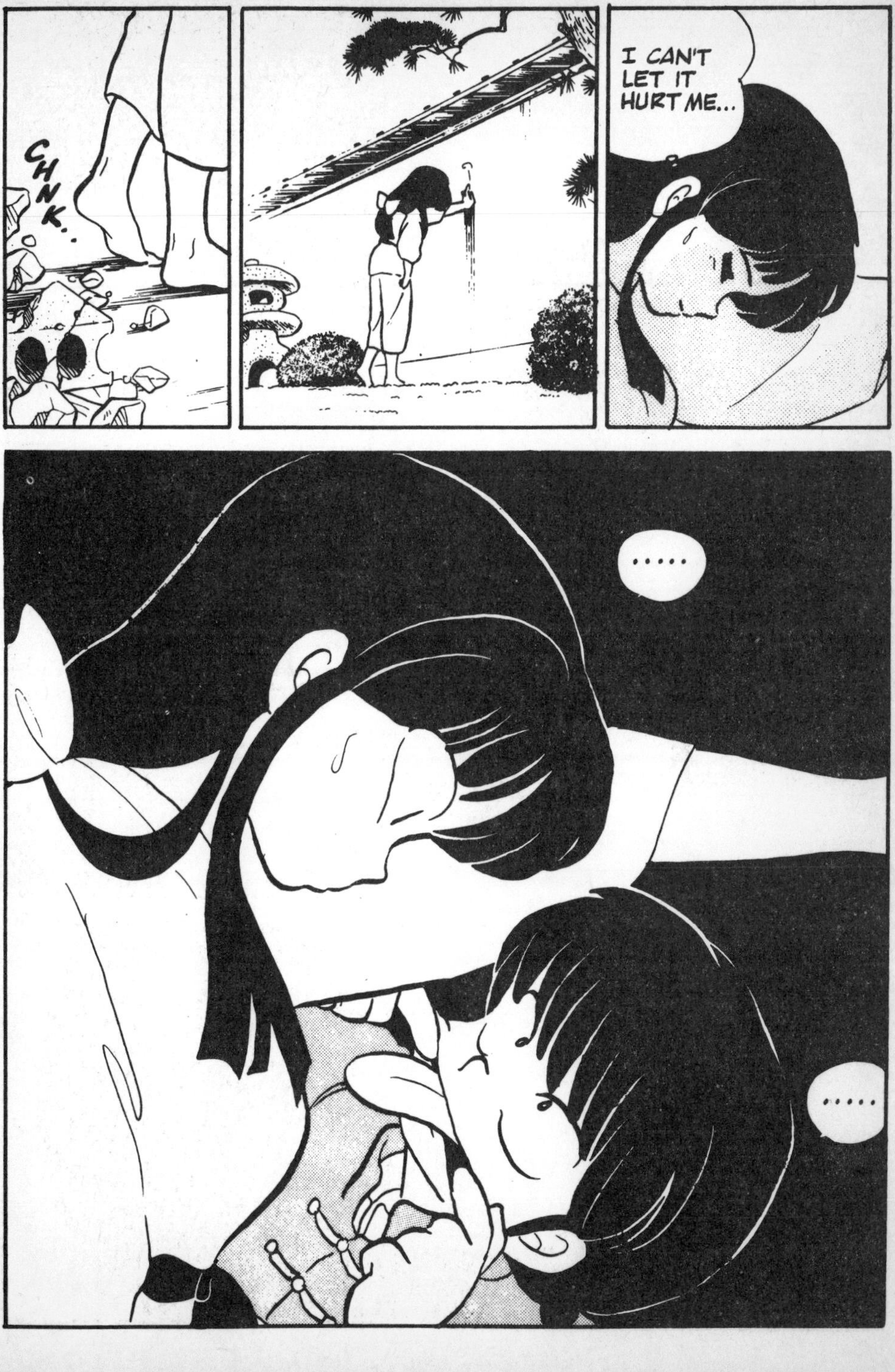
CHNK...
I CAN'T LET IT HURT ME...
......
......

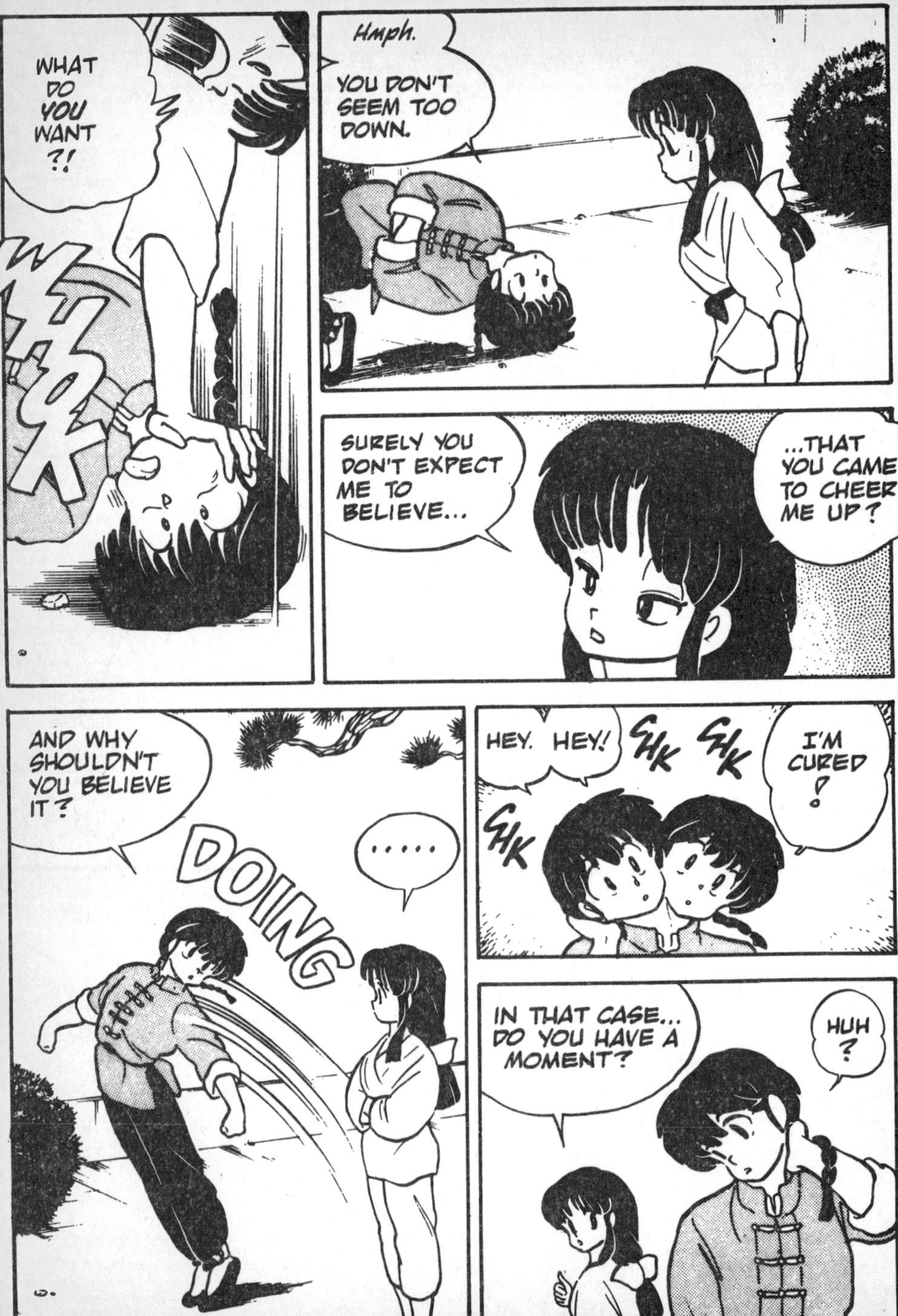
WHAT DO YOU WANT ?!
WHOK
Hmph.
YOU DON'T SEEM TOO DOWN.
SURELY YOU DON'T EXPECT ME TO BELIEVE...
...THAT YOU CAME TO CHEER ME UP?
AND WHY SHOULDN'T YOU BELIEVE IT?
DOING
.....
HEY. HEY!
CHK
CHK
CHK
I'M CURED!
IN THAT CASE... DO YOU HAVE A MOMENT?
HUH?

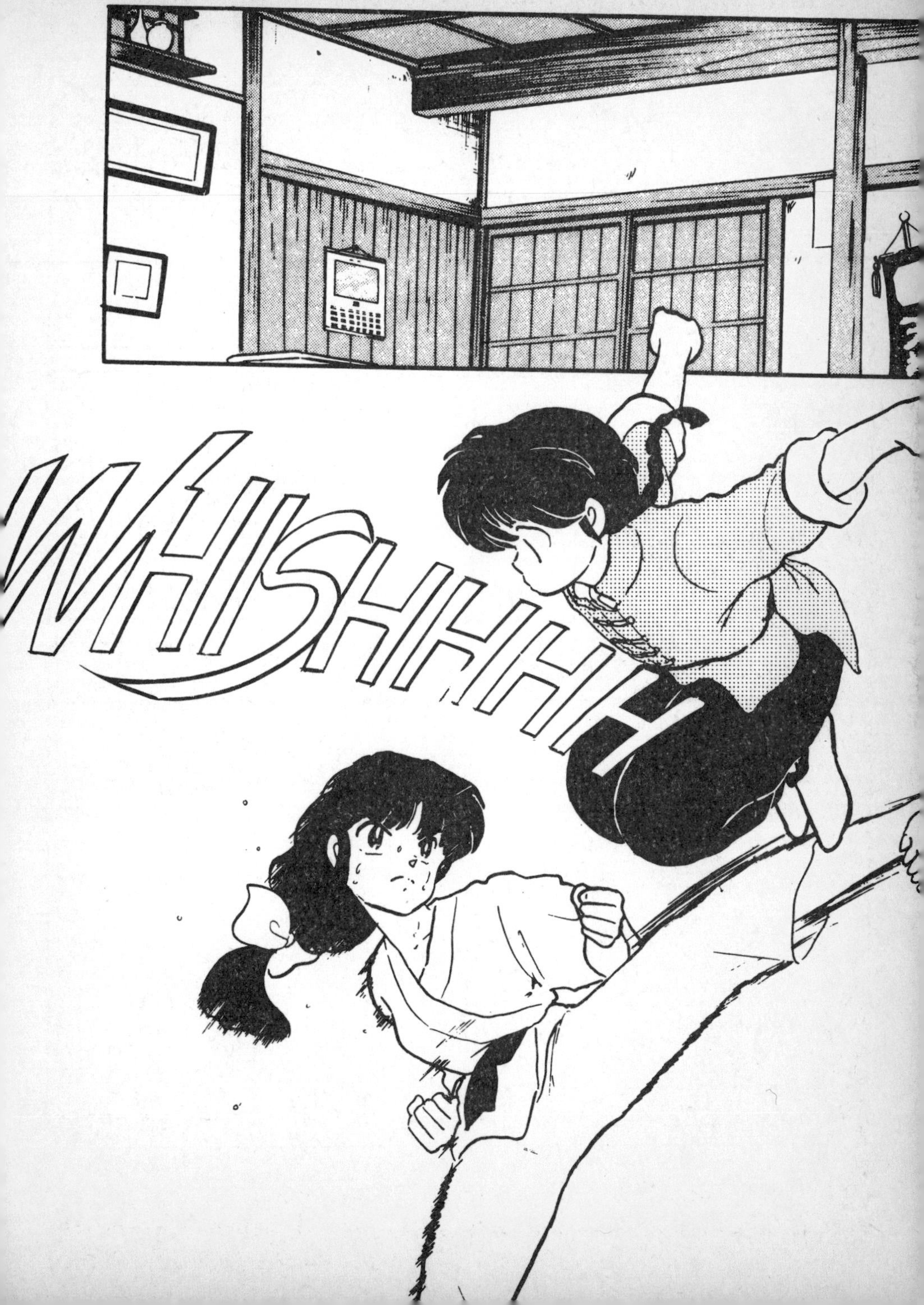
WHISHHHH

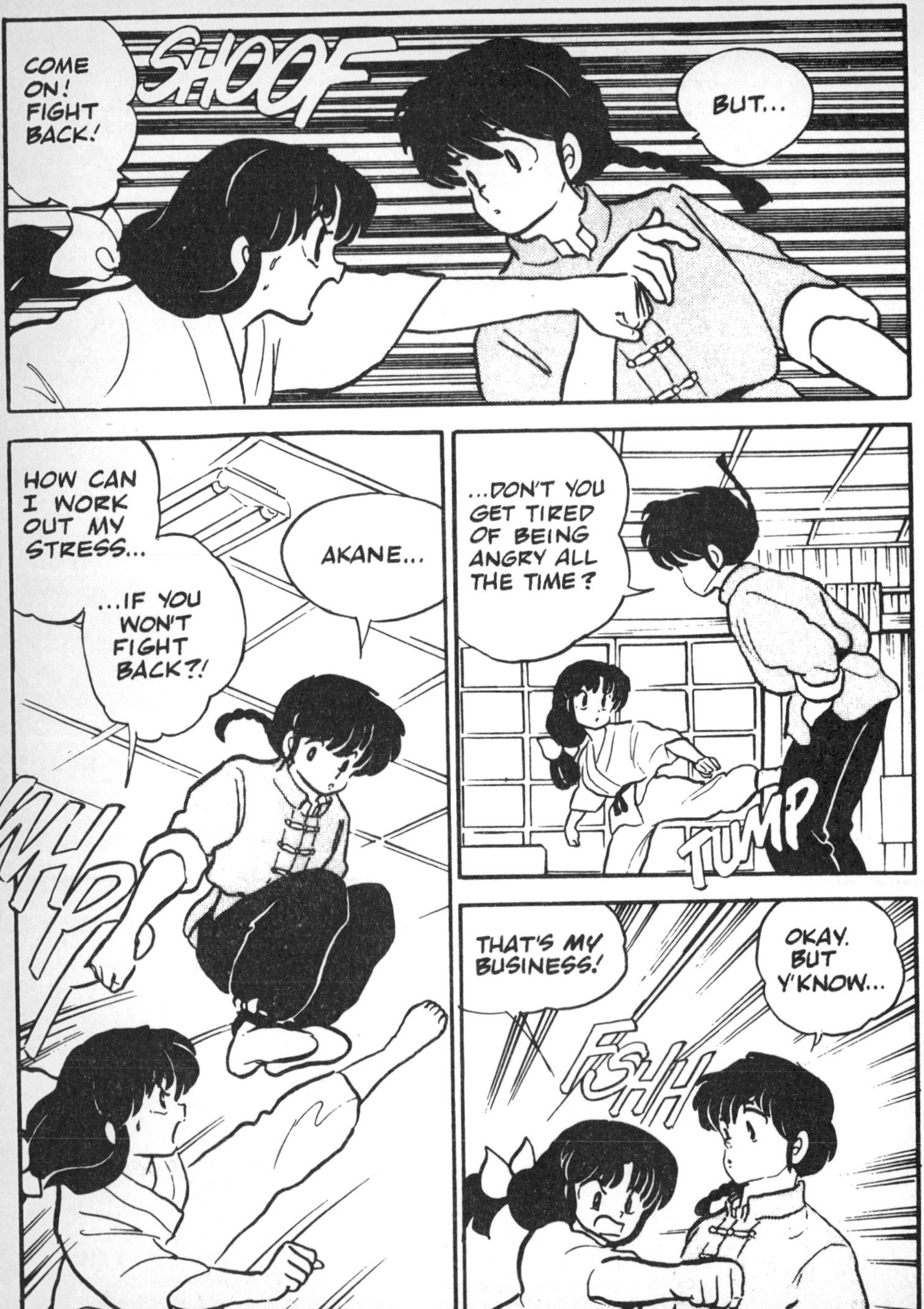
COME ON! FIGHT BACK!
SHOOF
BUT...
HOW CAN I WORK OUT MY STRESS...
...IF YOU WON'T FIGHT BACK?!
AKANE...
WHIP
...DON'T YOU GET TIRED OF BEING ANGRY ALL THE TIME?
TUMP
THAT'S MY BUSINESS!
OKAY. BUT Y'KNOW...
FSHH

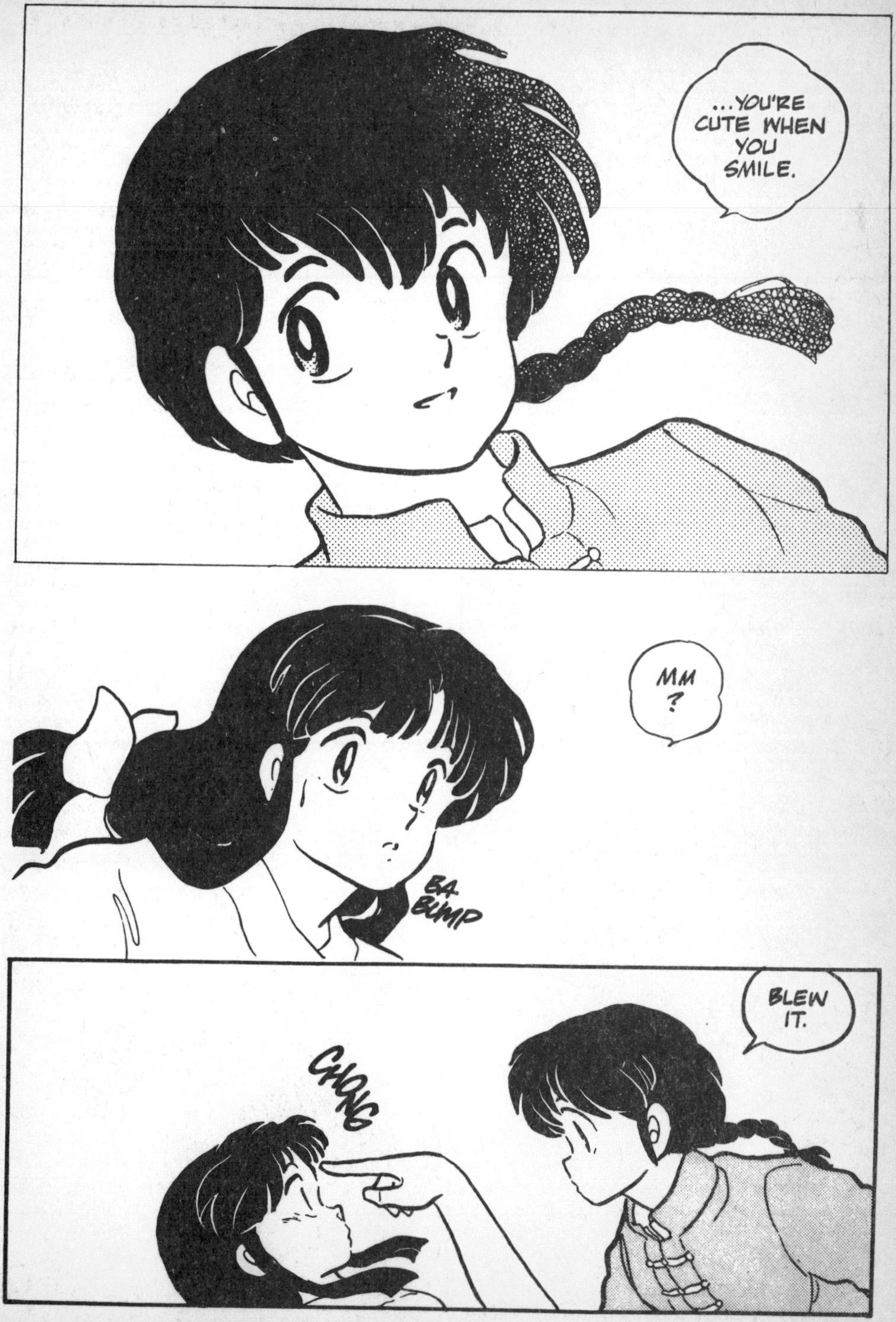
...YOU'RE CUTE WHEN YOU SMILE.
MM ?
BA BUMP
BLEW IT.
CHONG

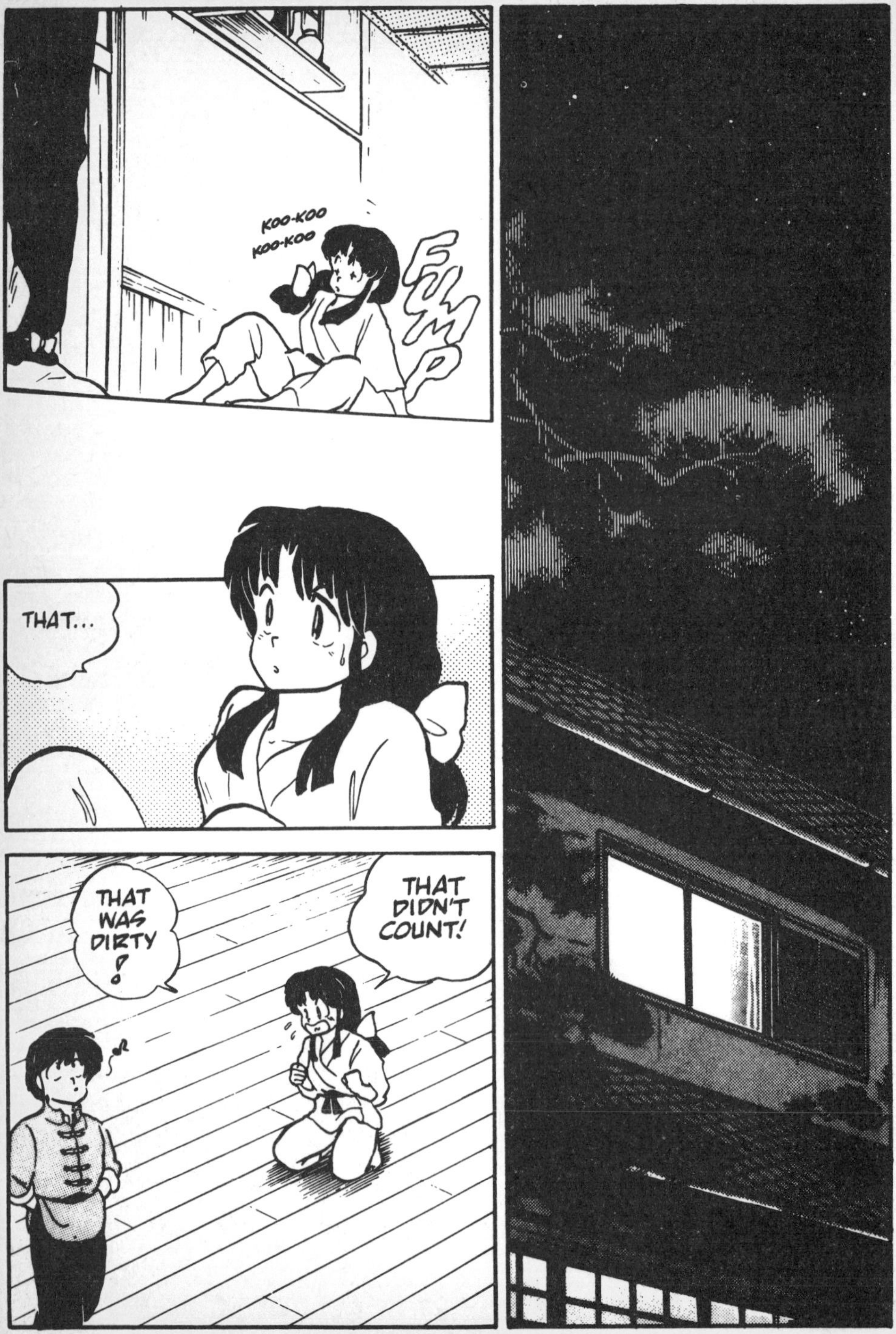
KOO-KOO
KOO-KOO
FUMP
THAT...
THAT WAS DIRTY!?
THAT DIDN'T COUNT!

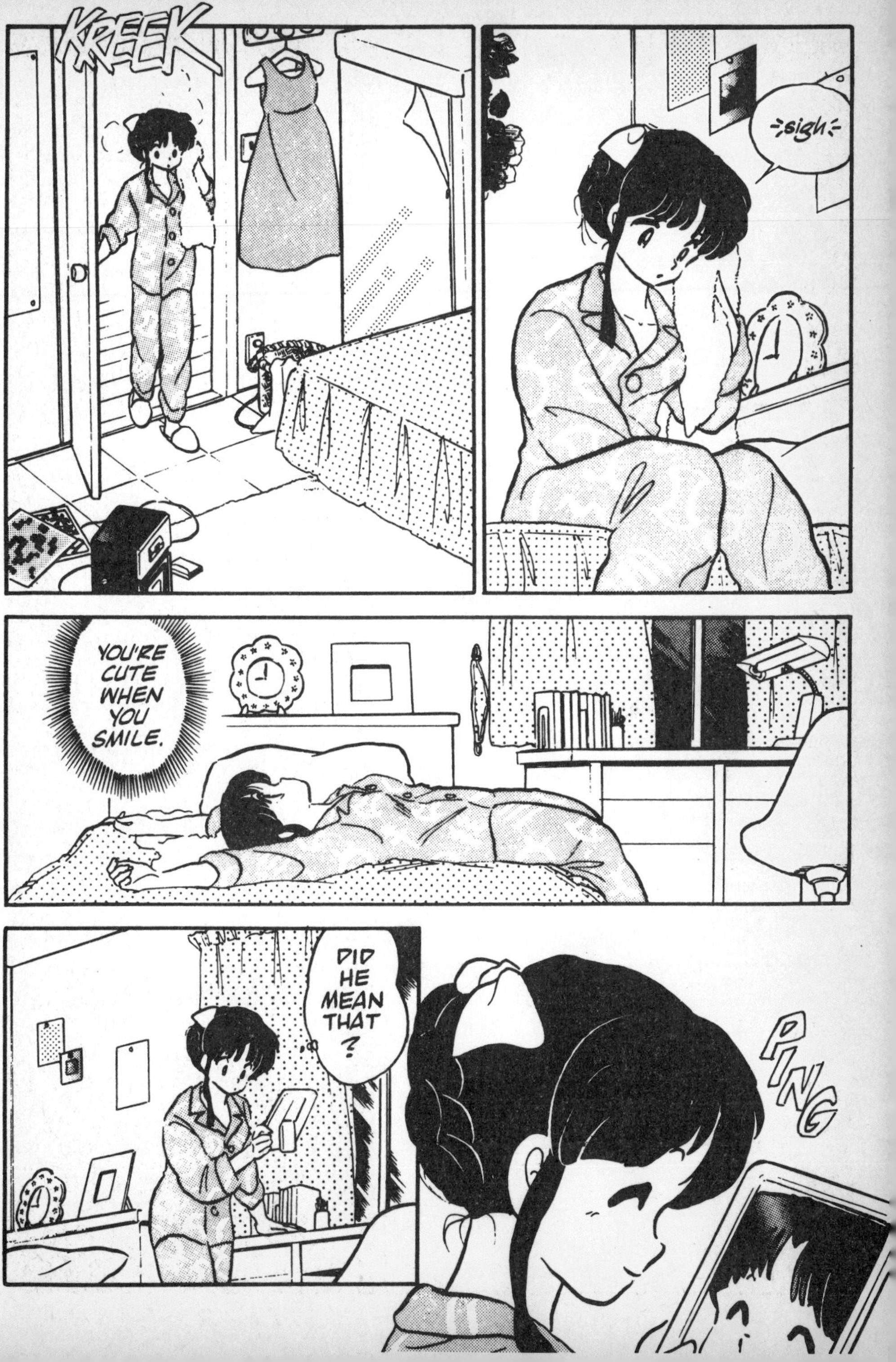
KREEK
sigh
YOU'RE CUTE WHEN YOU SMILE.
DID HE MEAN THAT ?
PING

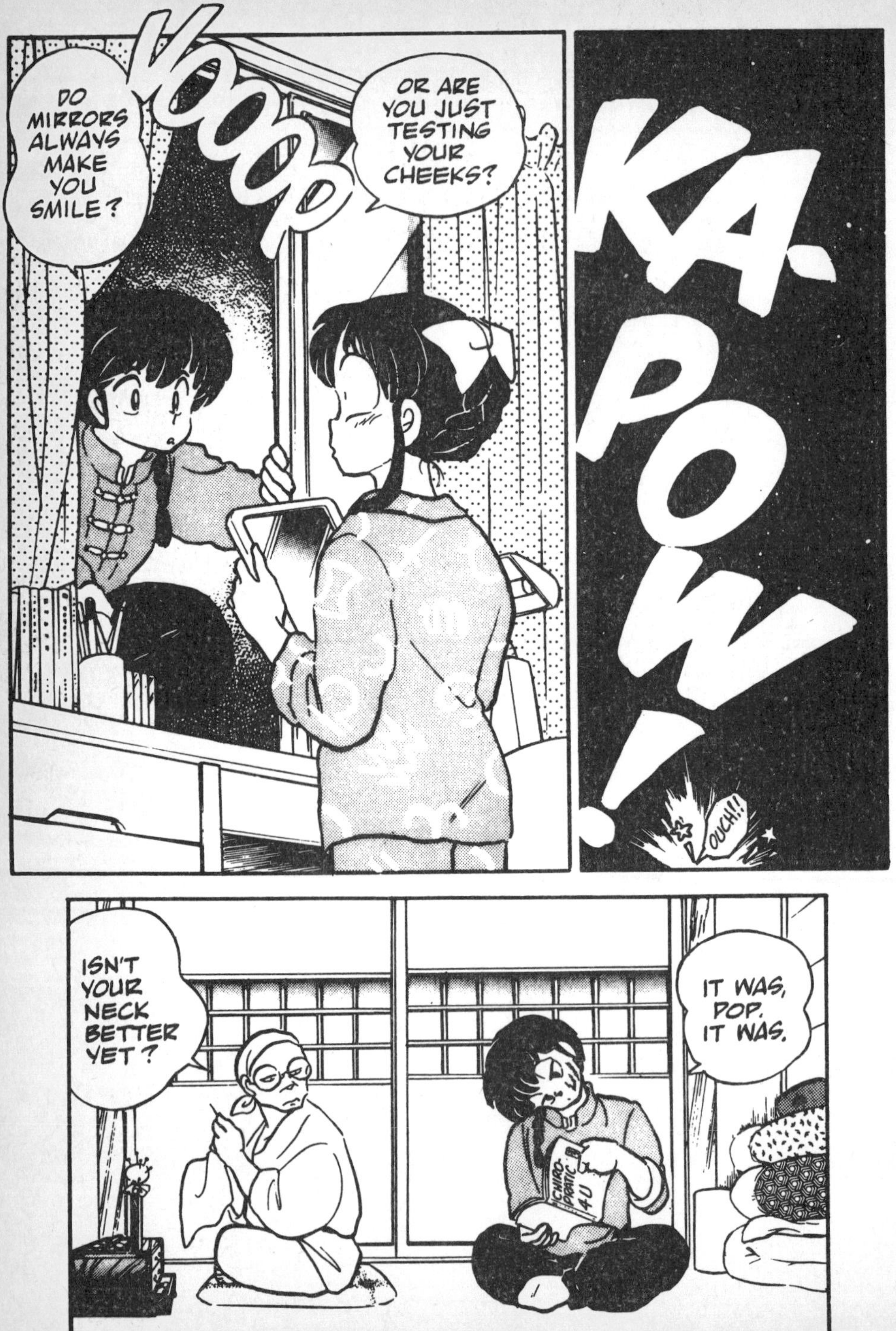
DO MIRRORS ALWAYS MAKE YOU SMILE?
VOOOP
OR ARE YOU JUST TESTING YOUR CHEEKS?
KA-POW!
OUCH!!
ISN'T YOUR NECK BETTER YET?
IT WAS, POP. IT WAS.

PART TEN
The Hunter

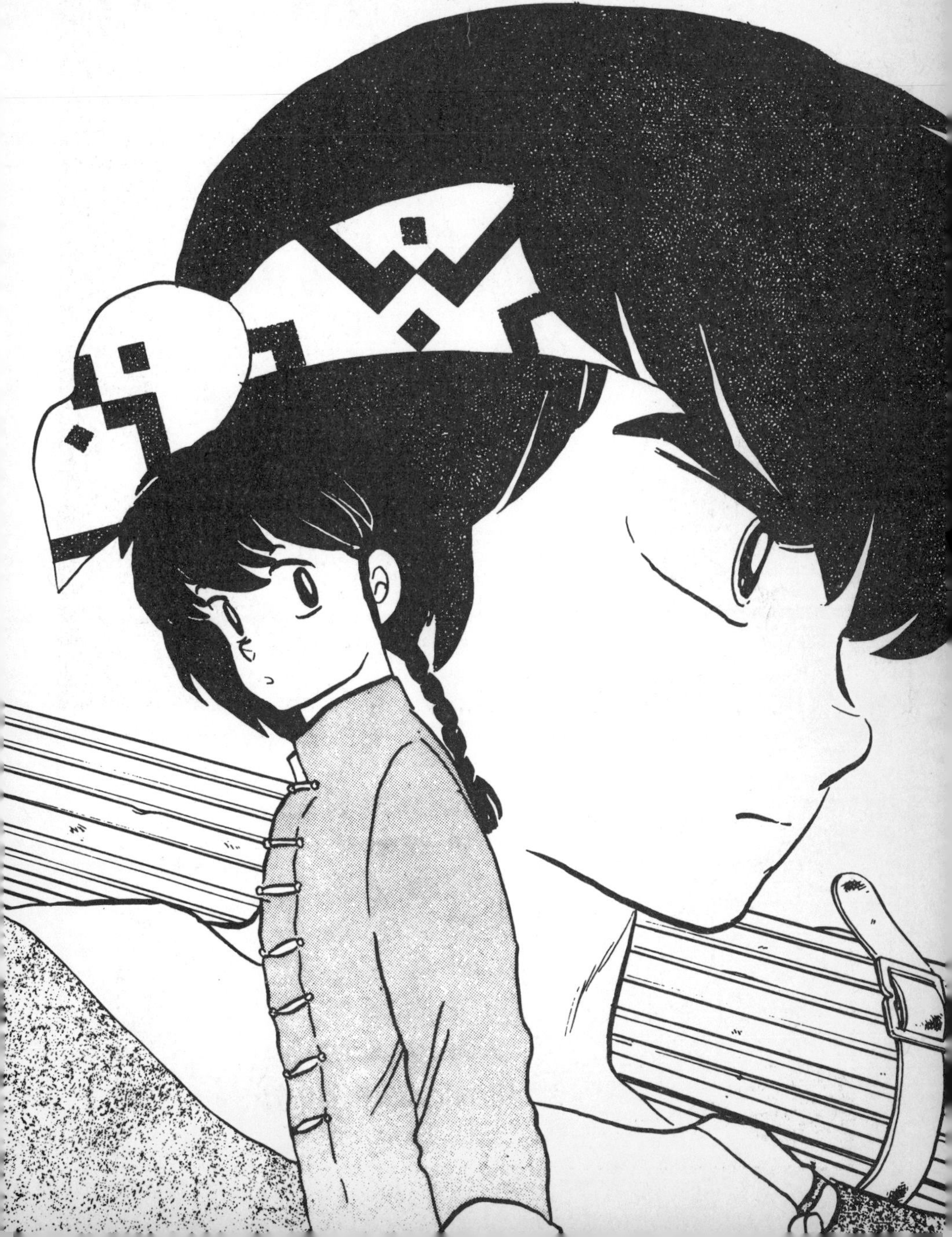

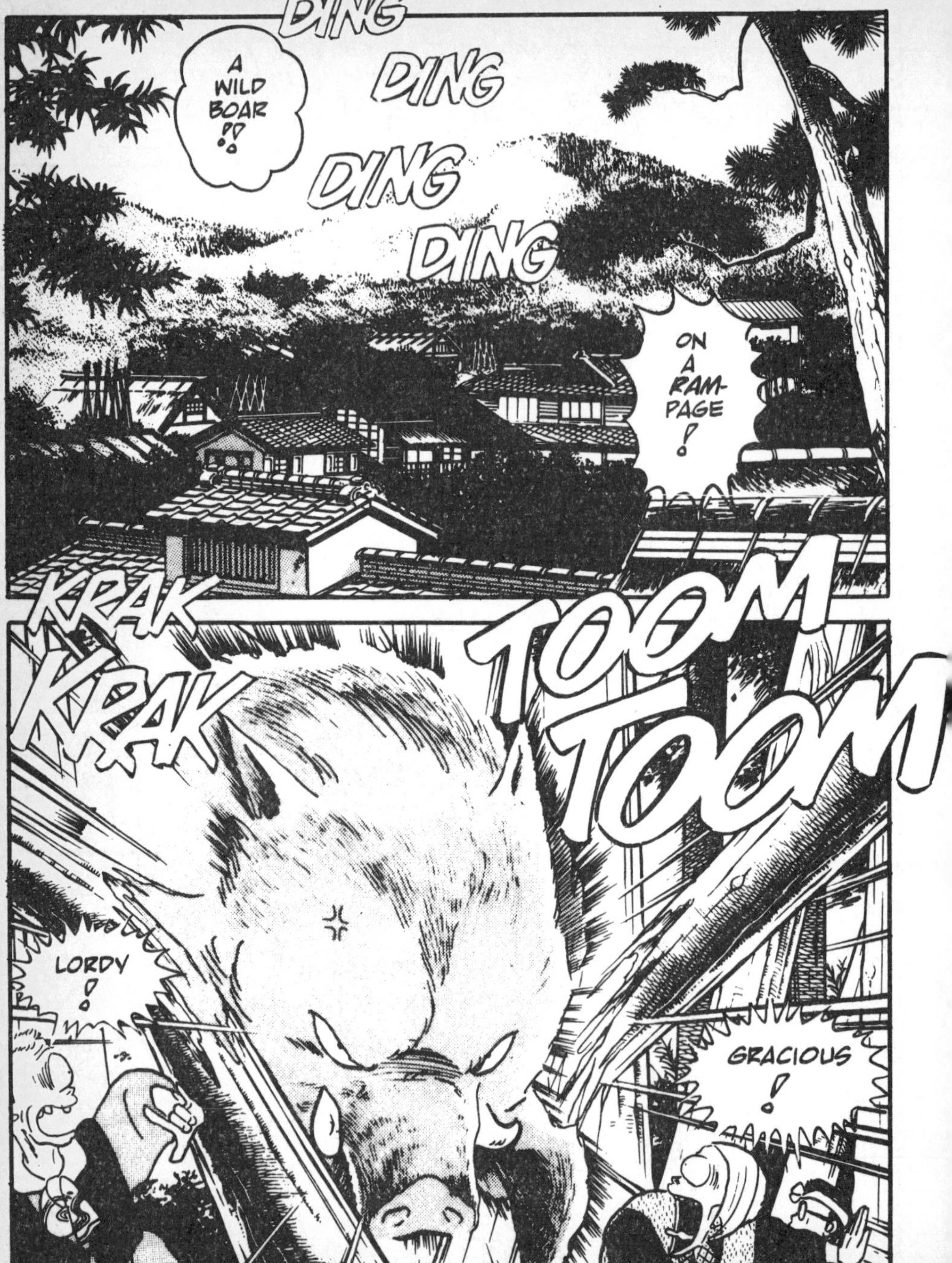
DING
A WILD BOAR!?
DING
DING
DING
ON A RAM-PAGE!
KRAK
KRAK
TOOM
TOOM
LORDY!
GRACIOUS!

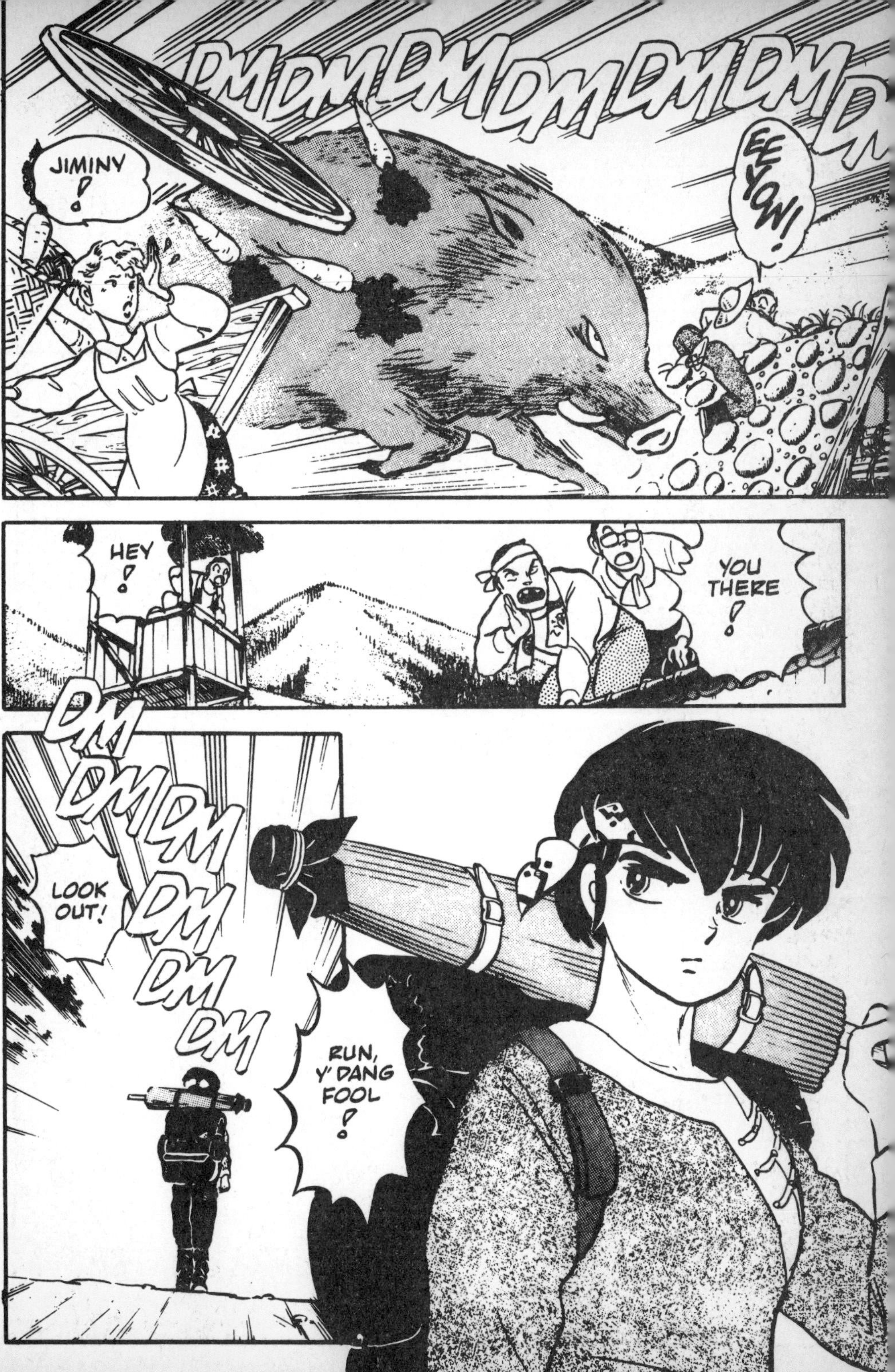
DMDMDMDMDMDMDMDMD
JIMINY!
EEYOW!
HEY!
YOU THERE!
DMDMDMDMDMDMDM
LOOK OUT!
RUN, Y' DANG FOOL!

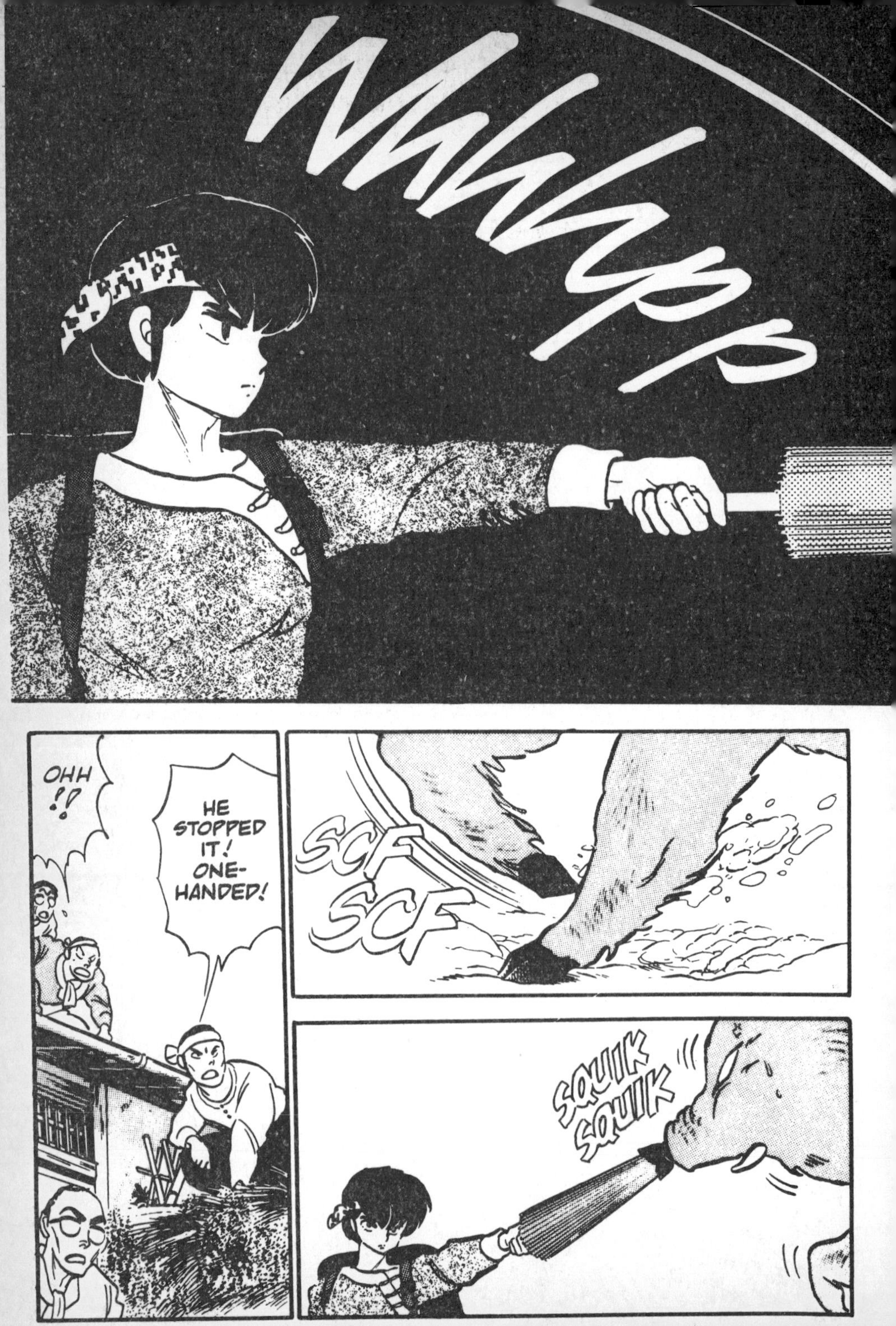
WHHUPP
OHH !!
HE STOPPED IT! ONE-HANDED!
SCF SCF
SQUIK SQUIK

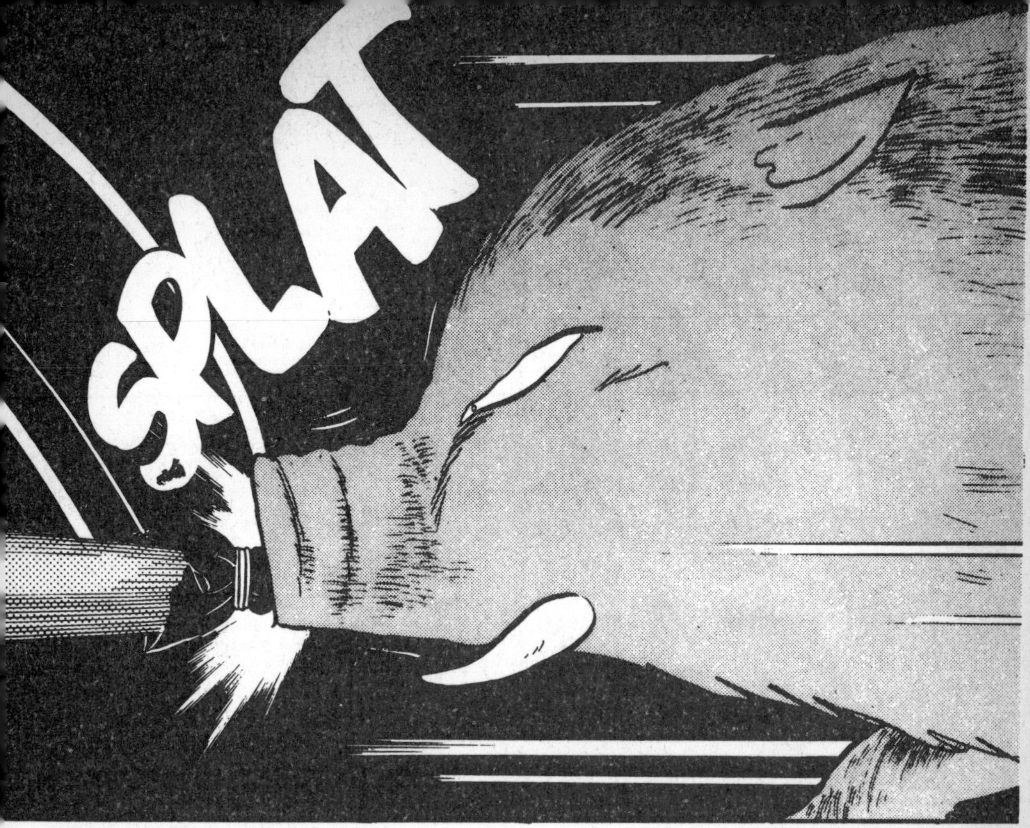
SPLAT
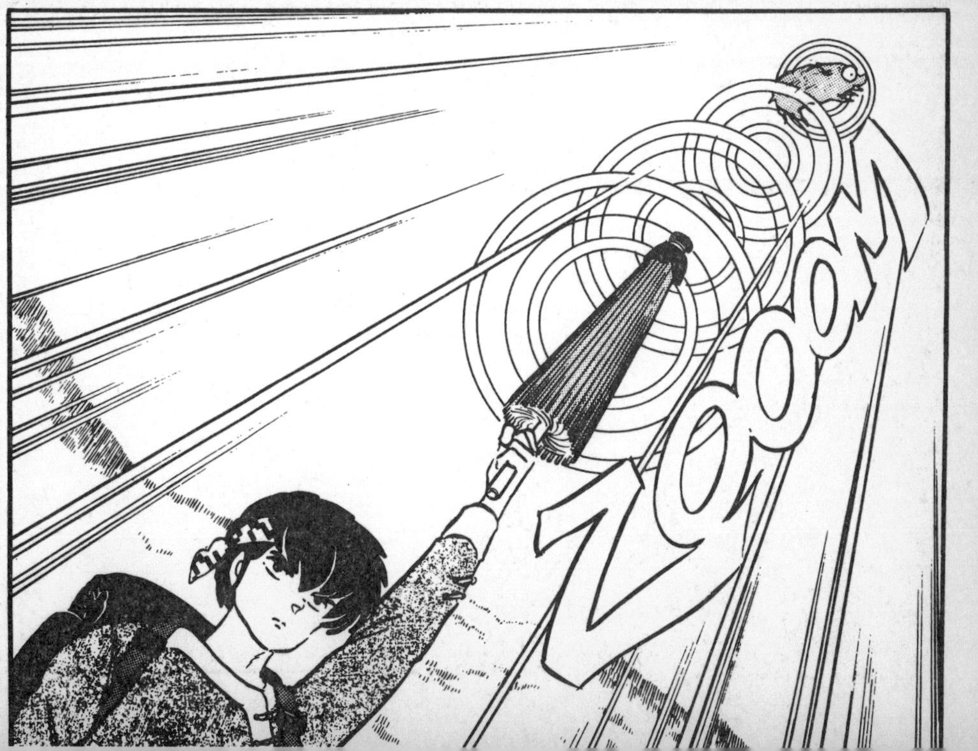
ZOOOOM

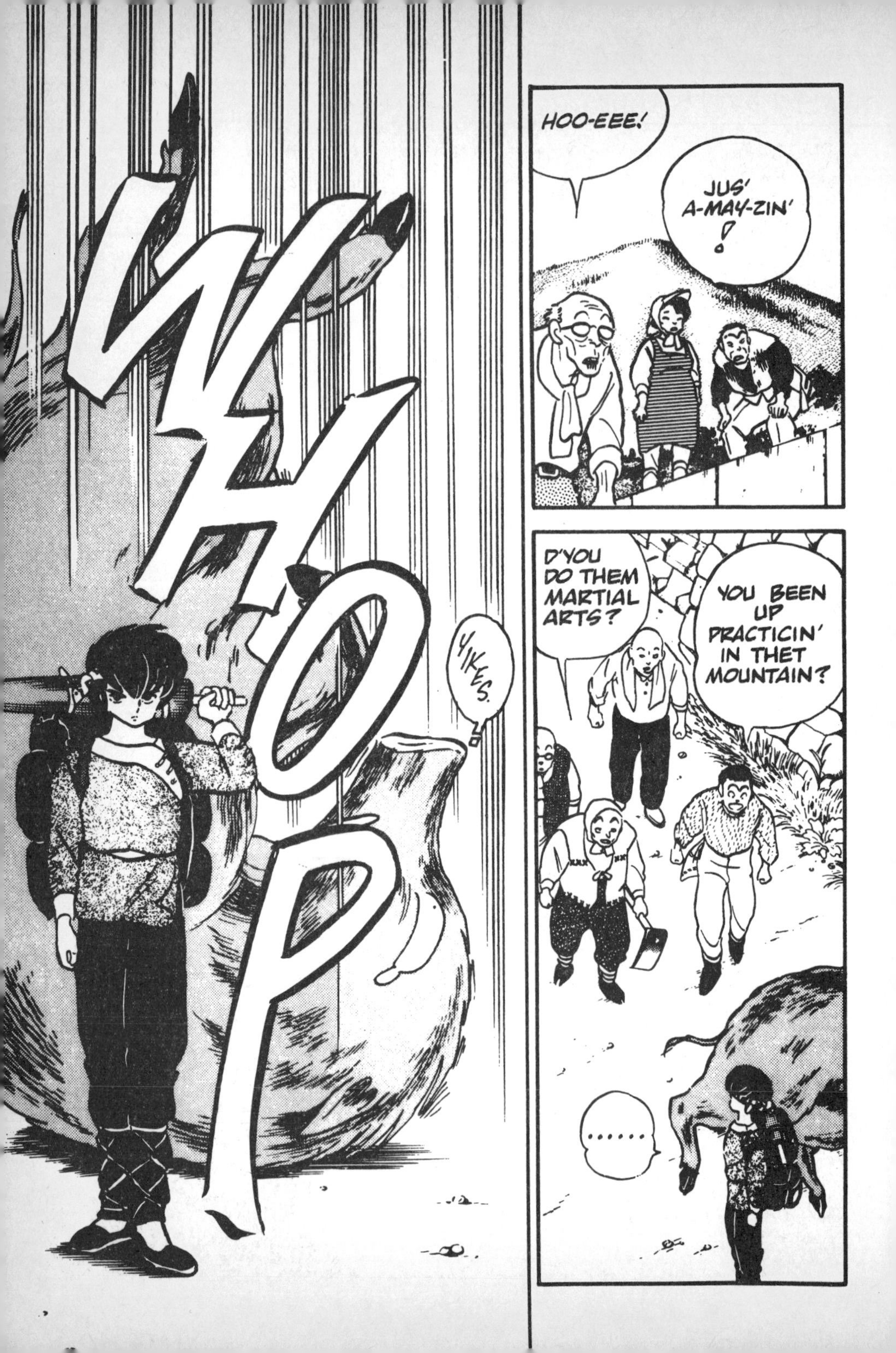
WHOOP
YIKES.
HOO-EEE!
JUS' A-MAY-ZIN'!
D'YOU DO THEM MARTIAL ARTS?
YOU BEEN UP PRACTICIN' IN THET MOUNTAIN?
......

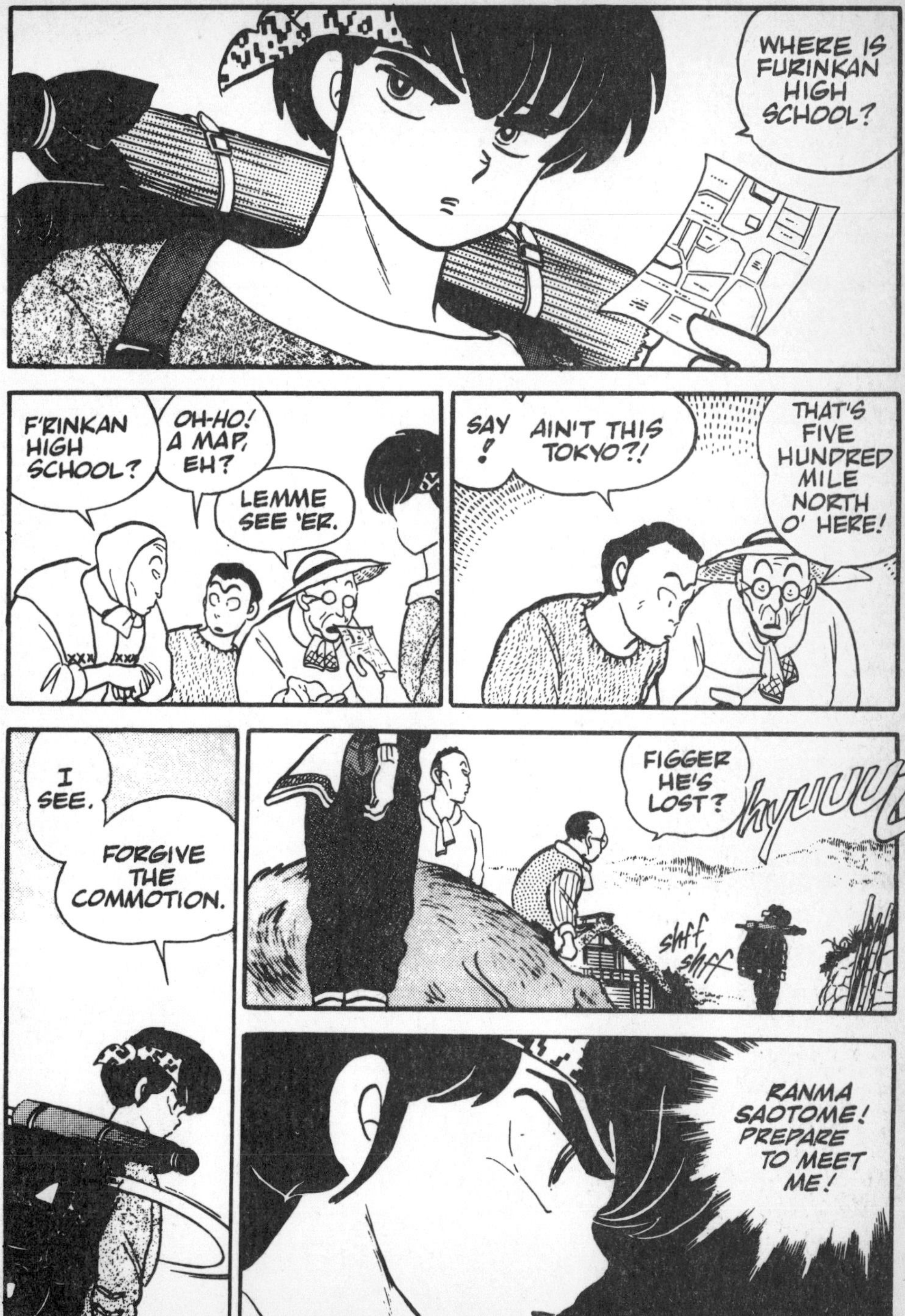
WHERE IS FURINKAN HIGH SCHOOL?
F'RINKAN HIGH SCHOOL?
OH-HO! A MAP, EH?
LEMME SEE 'ER.
SAY!
AIN'T THIS TOKYO?!
THAT'S FIVE HUNDRED MILE NORTH O' HERE!
I SEE.
FORGIVE THE COMMOTION.
FIGGER HE'S LOST?
hyuuuu
shff shff
RANMA SAOTOME! PREPARE TO MEET ME!

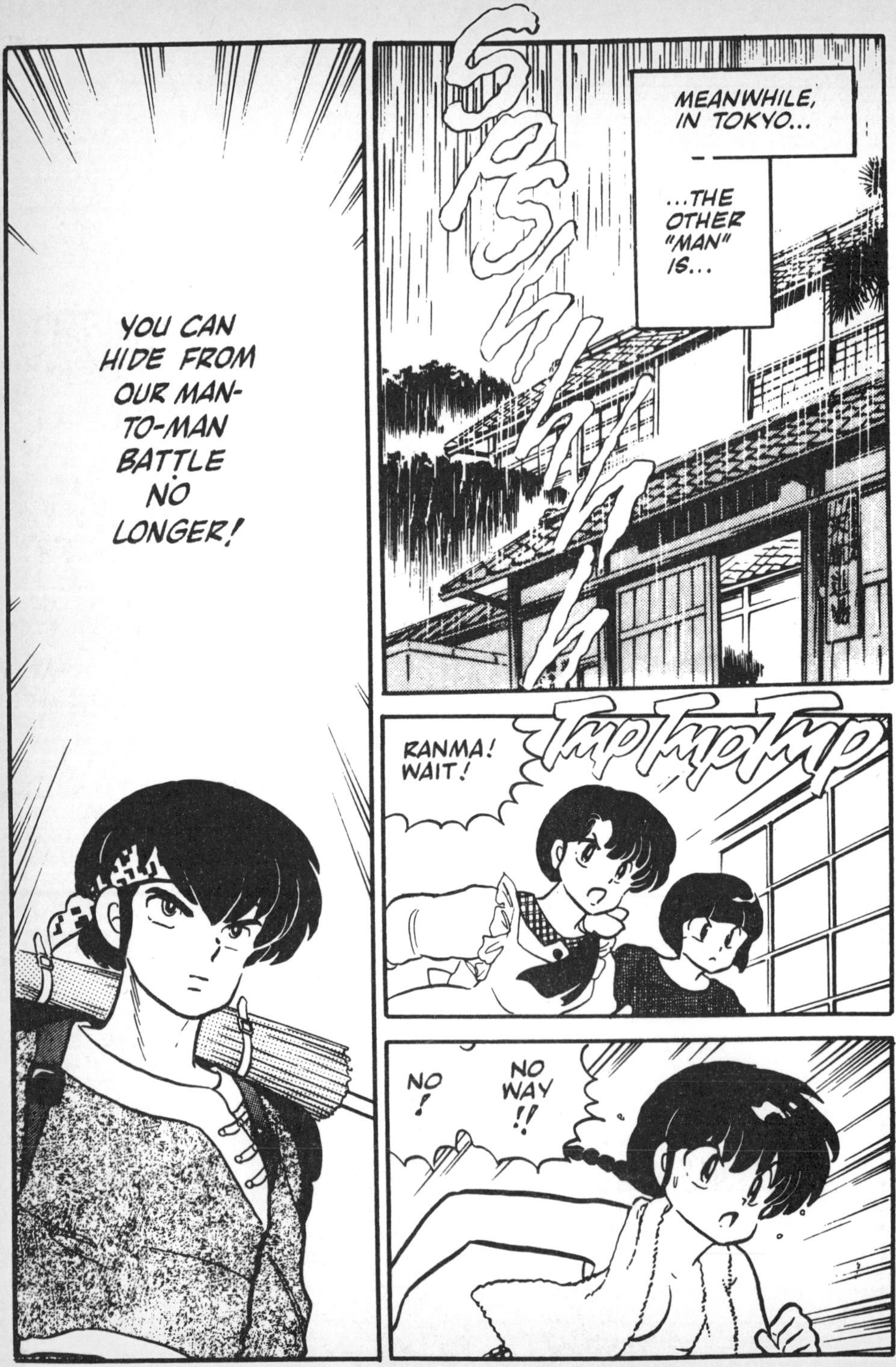
YOU CAN HIDE FROM OUR MAN-TO-MAN BATTLE NO LONGER!
MEANWHILE, IN TOKYO...
...THE OTHER "MAN" IS...
TMP TMP TMP
RANMA! WAIT!
NO!
NO WAY!!

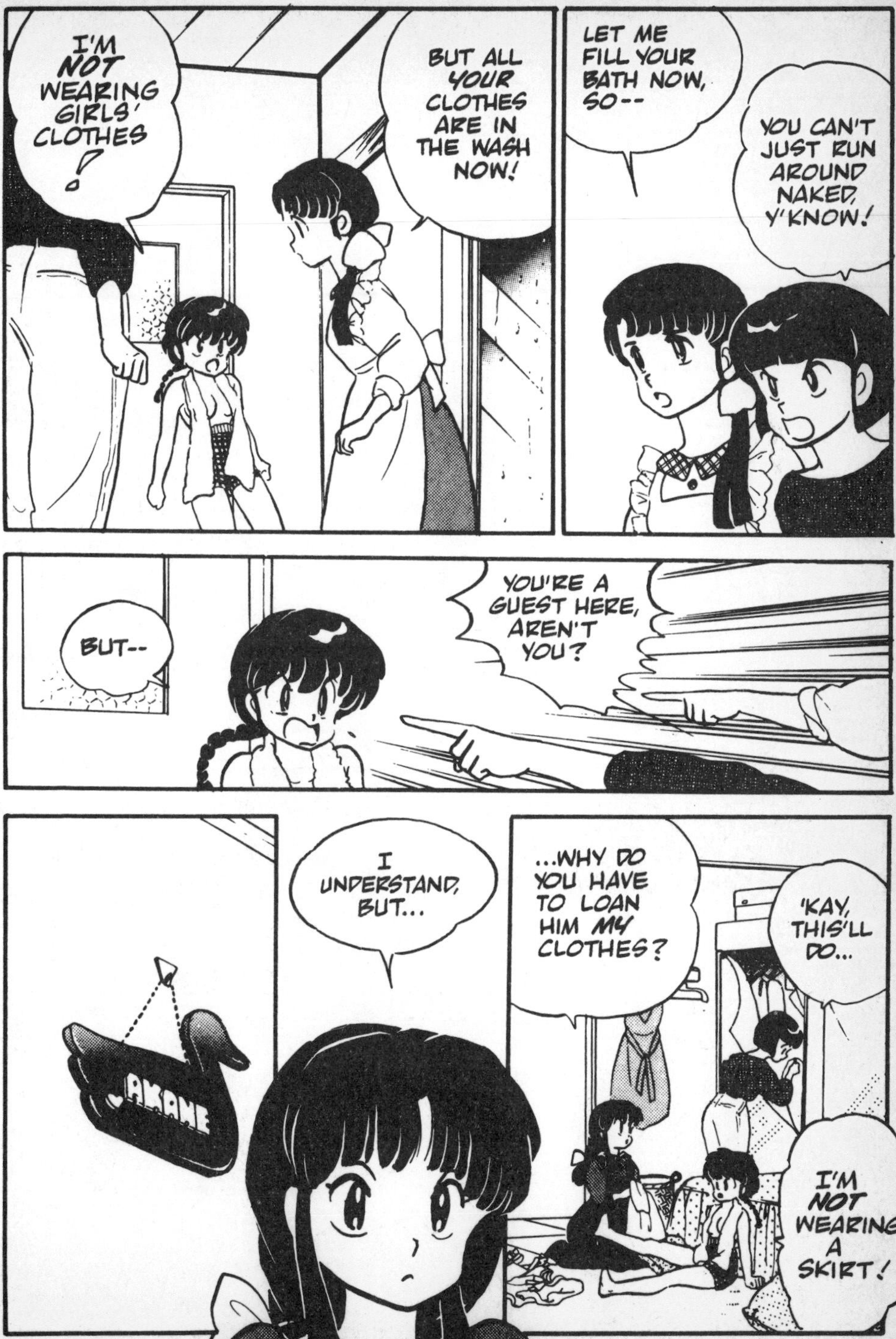
I'M NOT WEARING GIRLS' CLOTHES!
BUT ALL YOUR CLOTHES ARE IN THE WASH NOW!
LET ME FILL YOUR BATH NOW, SO--
YOU CAN'T JUST RUN AROUND NAKED, Y'KNOW!
BUT--
YOU'RE A GUEST HERE, AREN'T YOU?
AKANE
I UNDERSTAND, BUT...
...WHY DO YOU HAVE TO LOAN HIM MY CLOTHES?
'KAY, THIS'LL DO...
I'M NOT WEARING A SKIRT!

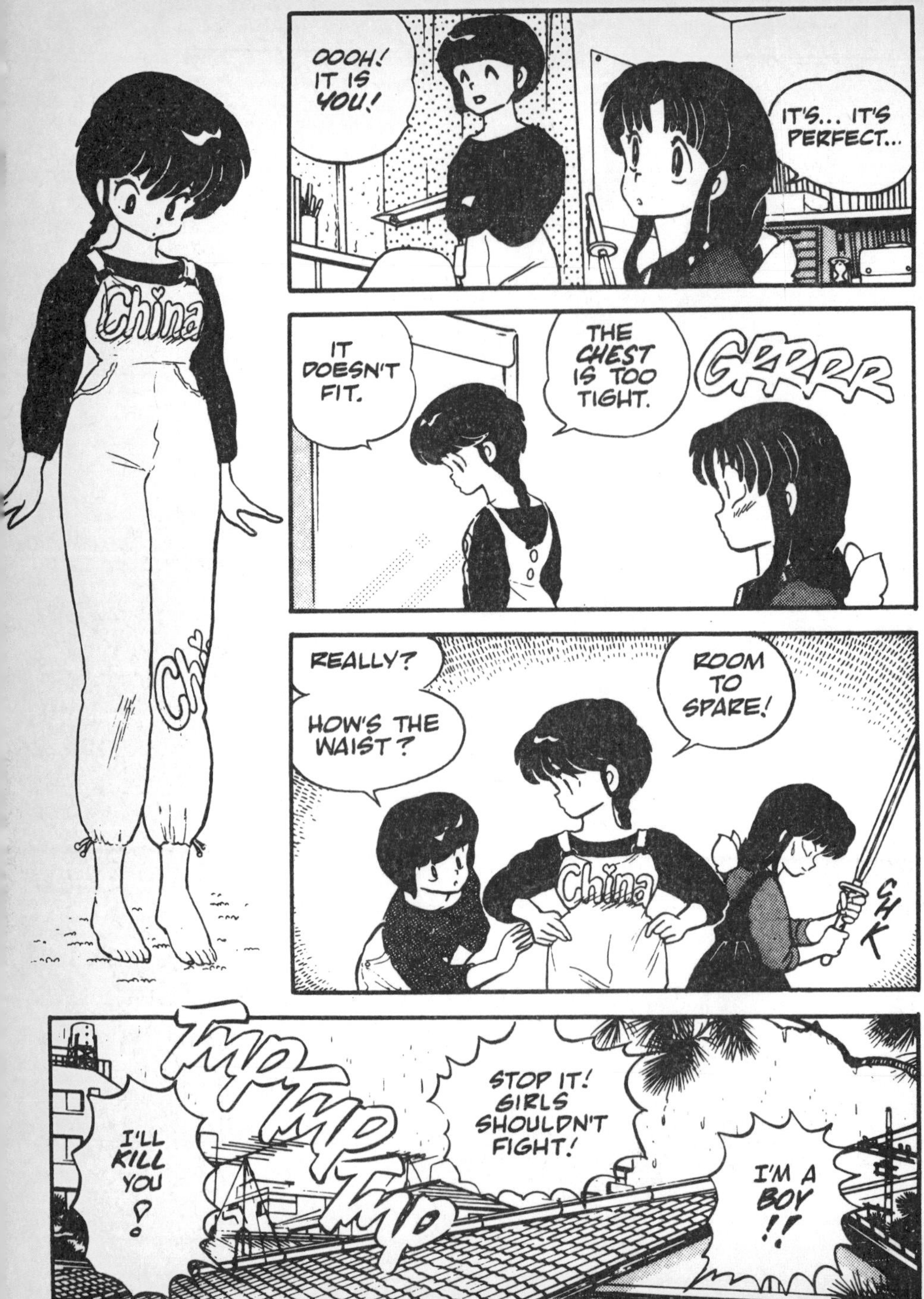
OOOH! IT IS YOU!
IT'S... IT'S PERFECT...
IT DOESN'T FIT.
THE CHEST IS TOO TIGHT.
GRRRR
REALLY?
HOW'S THE WAIST?
ROOM TO SPARE!
CHK
I'LL KILL YOU!
STOP IT! GIRLS SHOULDN'T FIGHT!
I'M A BOY!!
TMP TMP TMP TMP

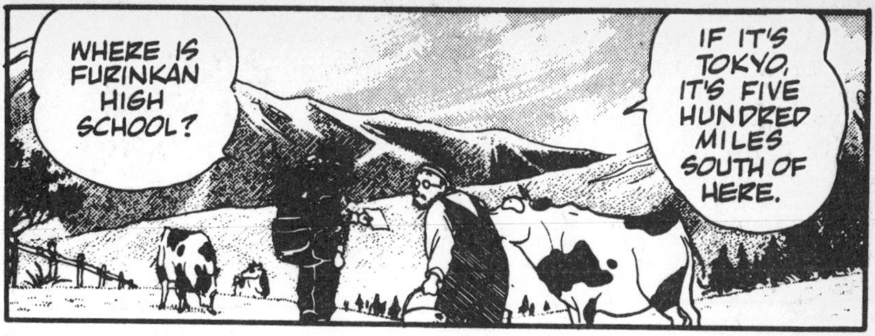
WHERE IS FURINKAN HIGH SCHOOL?
IF IT'S TOKYO, IT'S FIVE HUNDRED MILES SOUTH OF HERE.

ONE WEEK LATER...

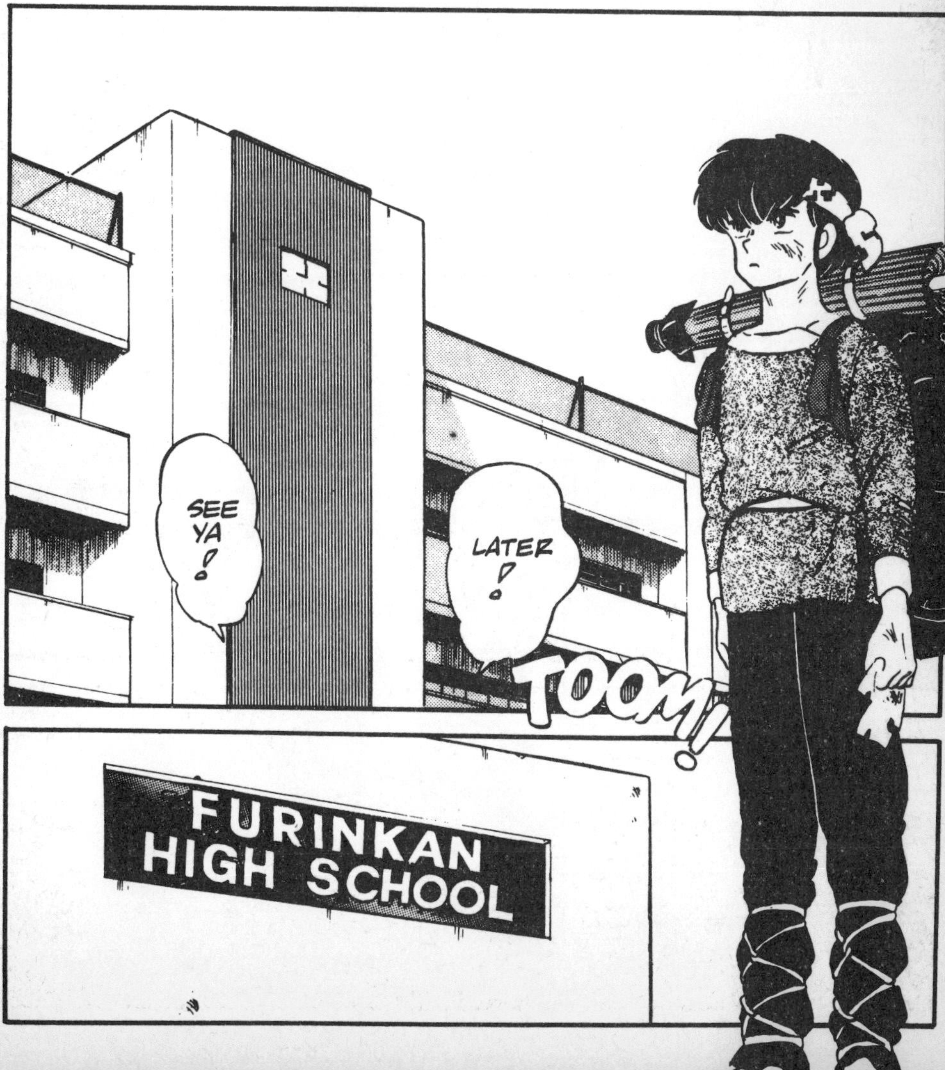
SEE YA!
LATER!
TOOM!
FURINKAN HIGH SCHOOL

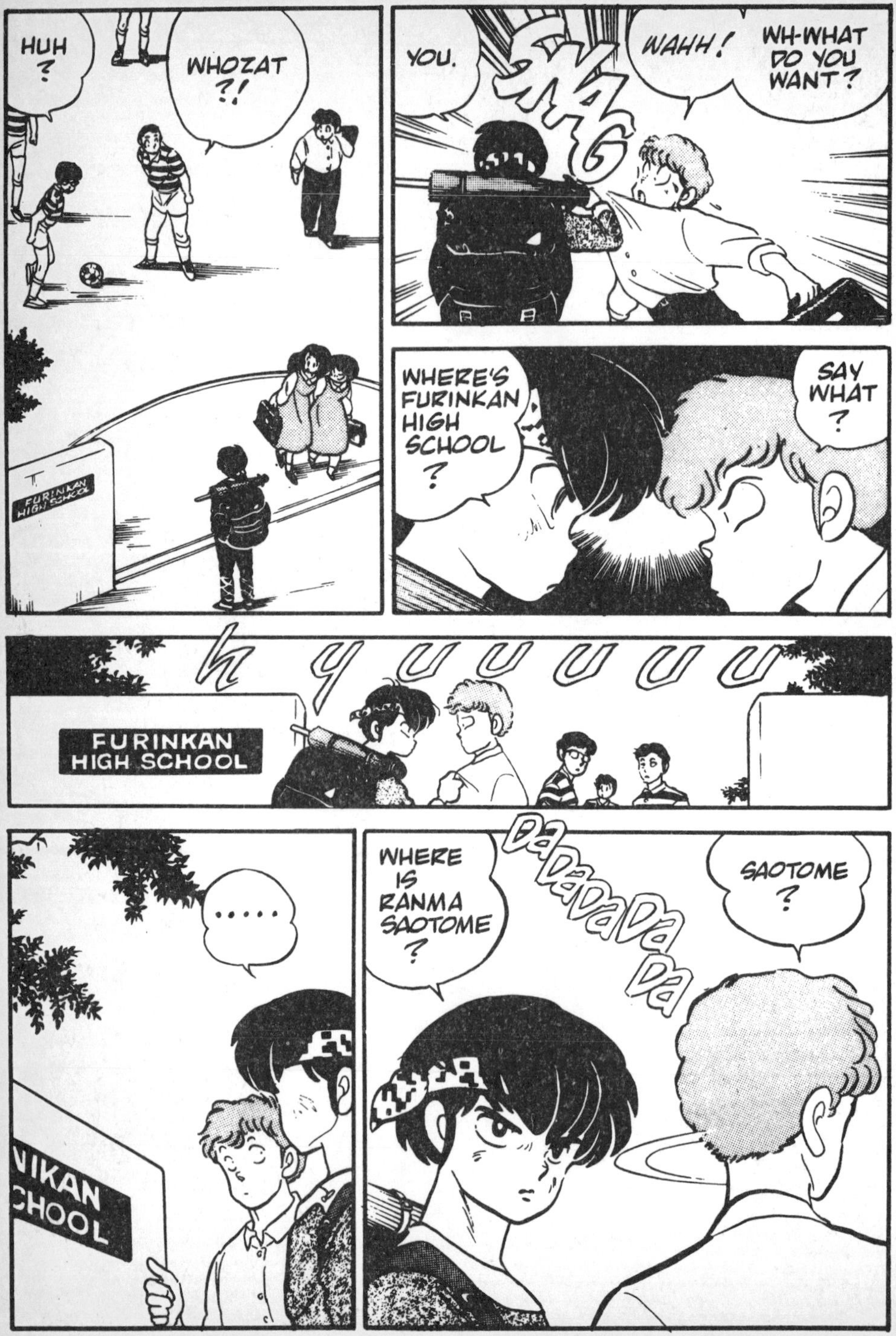
HUH ?
WHOZAT ?!
WH-WHAT DO YOU WANT?
WAHH!
YOU.
SMAG
FURINKAN HIGH SCHOOL
SAY WHAT ?
WHERE'S FURINKAN HIGH SCHOOL ?
hyuuuuuu
FURINKAN HIGH SCHOOL
SAOTOME ?
WHERE IS RANMA SAOTOME ?
DaDaDaDaDaDa
.....
NKAN SCHOOL

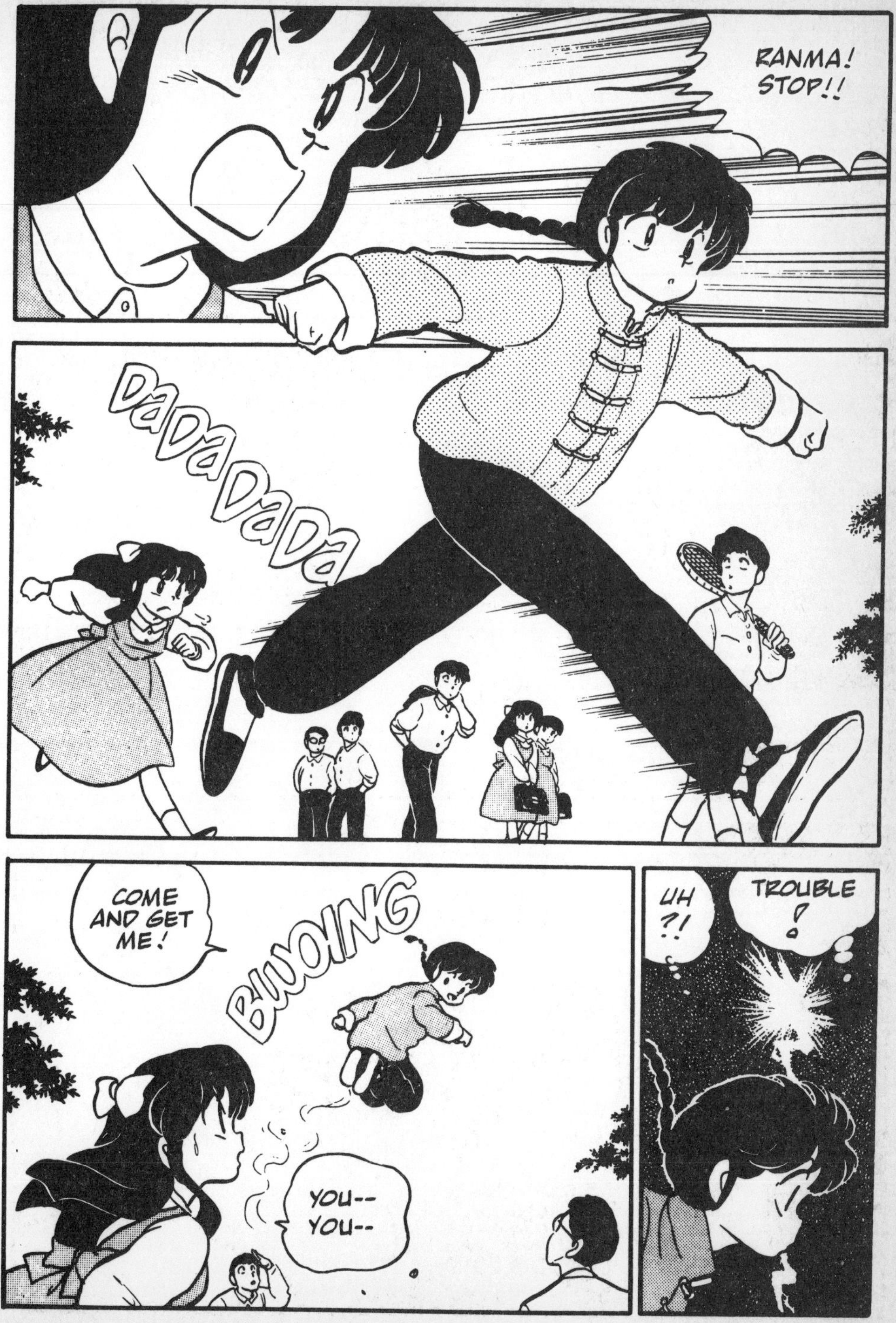
RANMA! STOP!!
DADADADADA
COME AND GET ME!
BWOING
YOU-- YOU--
TROUBLE!
UH ?!

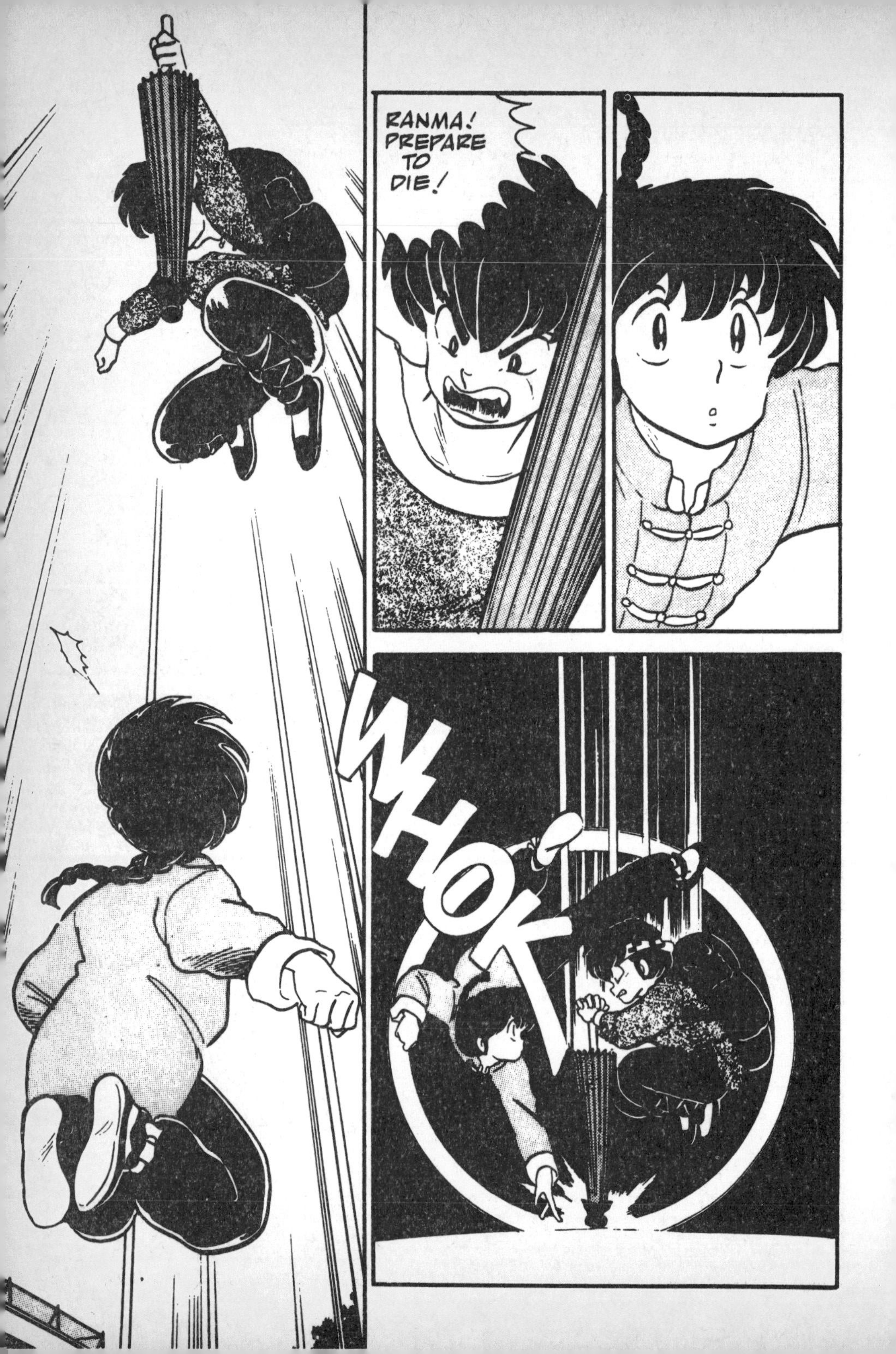
RANMA! PREPARE TO DIE!
WHOK

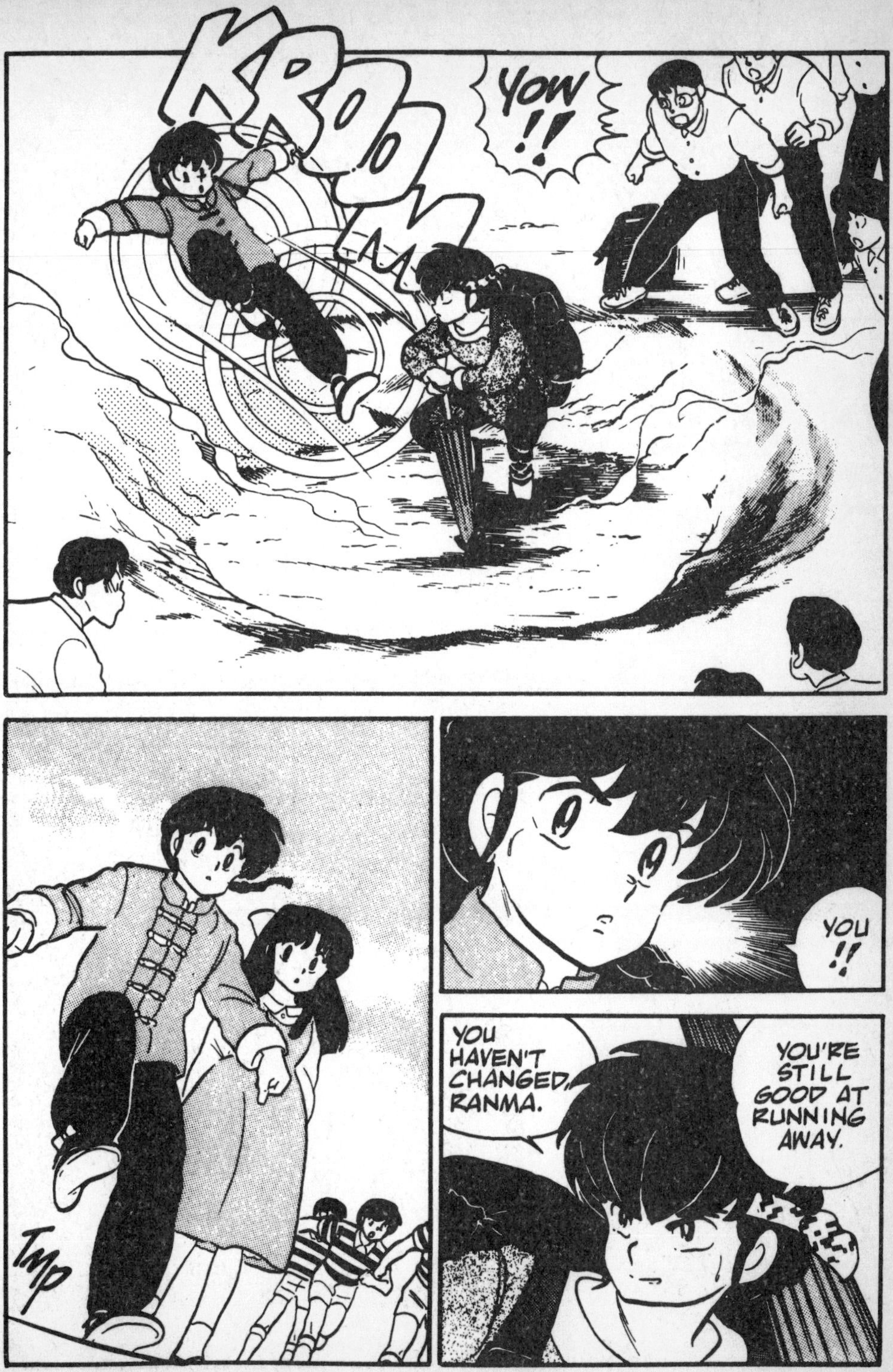
KROOOM
YOW!!
TMP
YOU!!
YOU HAVEN'T CHANGED, RANMA.
YOU'RE STILL GOOD AT RUNNING AWAY.

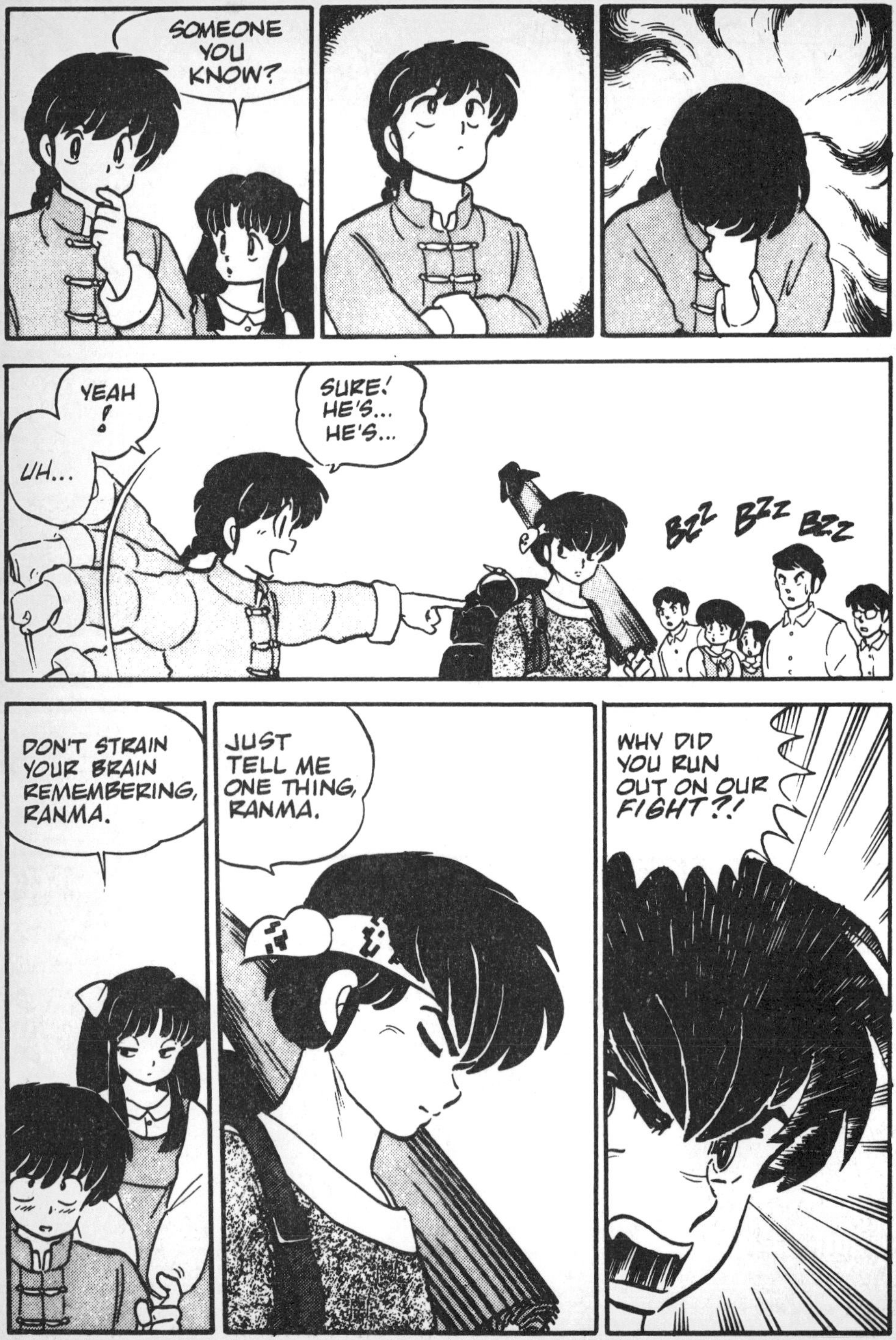
SOMEONE YOU KNOW?
YEAH!
UH...
SURE! HE'S... HE'S...
BZZ BZZ BZZ
DON'T STRAIN YOUR BRAIN REMEMBERING, RANMA.
JUST TELL ME ONE THING, RANMA.
WHY DID YOU RUN OUT ON OUR FIGHT?!

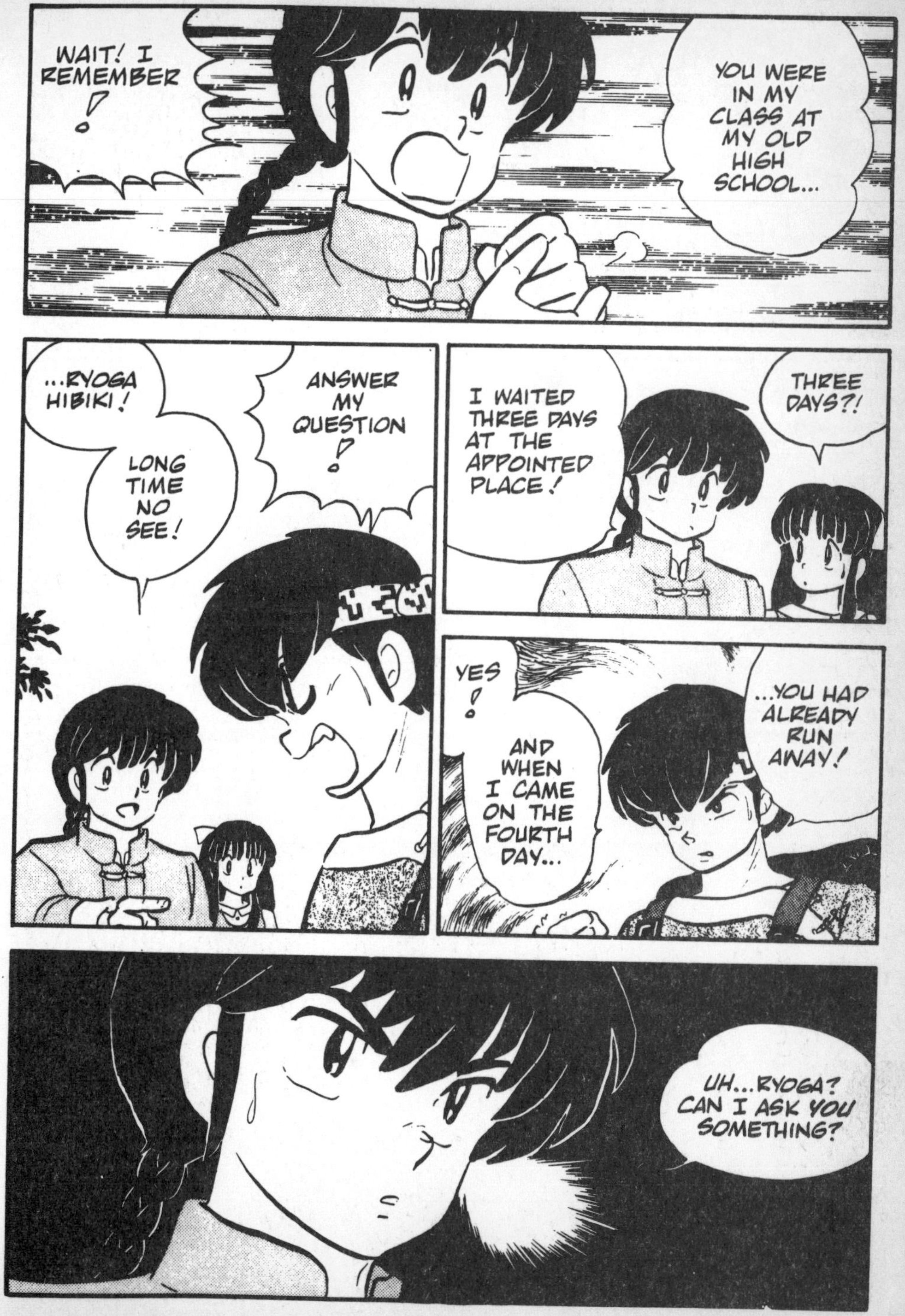
WAIT! I REMEMBER!
YOU WERE IN MY CLASS AT MY OLD HIGH SCHOOL...
...RYOGA HIBIKI!
LONG TIME NO SEE!
ANSWER MY QUESTION!
I WAITED THREE DAYS AT THE APPOINTED PLACE!
THREE DAYS?!
YES!
AND WHEN I CAME ON THE FOURTH DAY...
...YOU HAD ALREADY RUN AWAY!
UH...RYOGA? CAN I ASK YOU SOMETHING?

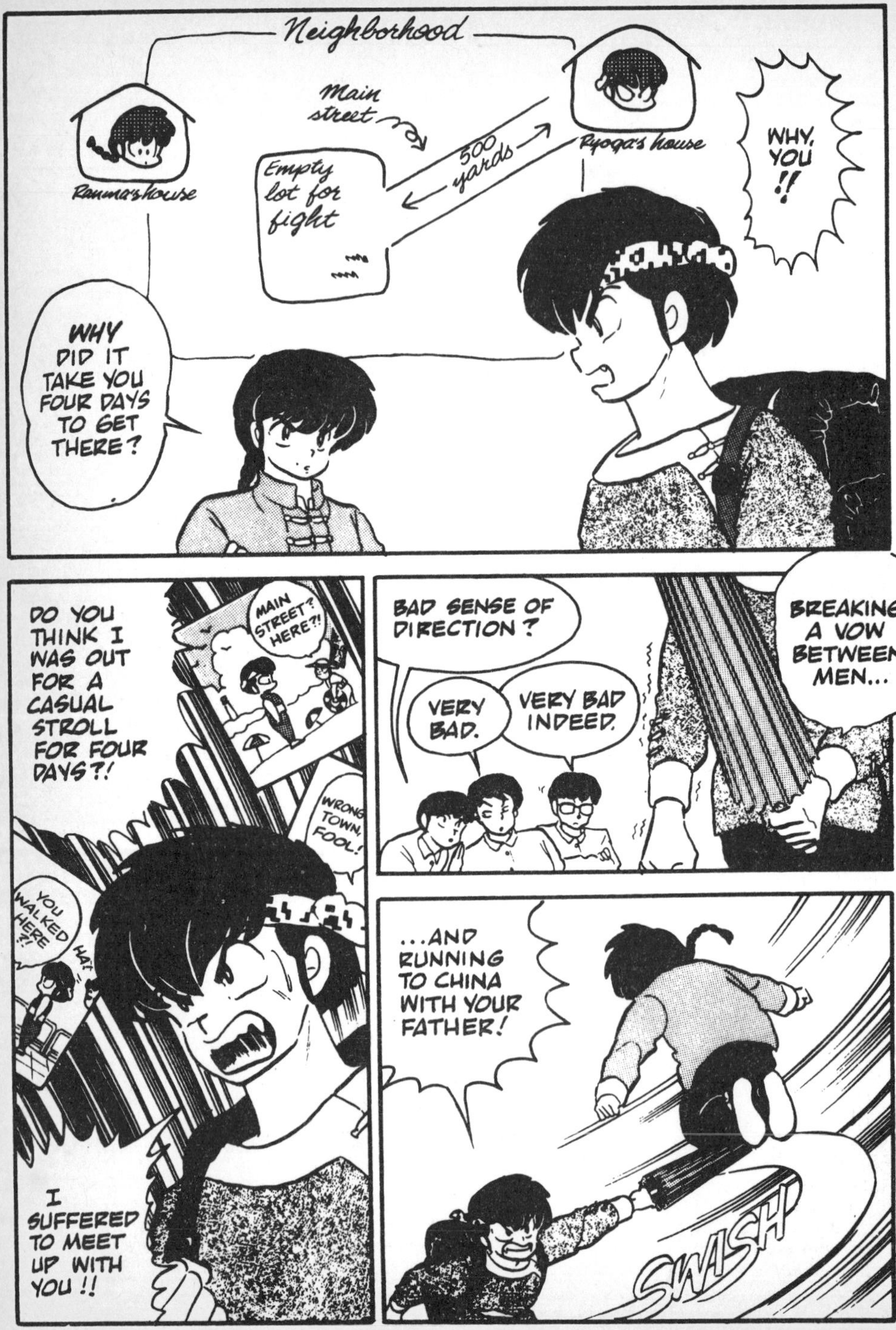

Neighborhood
Main street
500 yards
Empty lot for fight
Ranma's house
Ryoga's house
WHY, YOU !!
WHY DID IT TAKE YOU FOUR DAYS TO GET THERE?
DO YOU THINK I WAS OUT FOR A CASUAL STROLL FOR FOUR DAYS?!
MAIN STREET? HERE?!
WRONG TOWN, FOOL!
YOU WALKED HERE?!
HA!
I SUFFERED TO MEET UP WITH YOU!!
BAD SENSE OF DIRECTION?
VERY BAD.
VERY BAD INDEED.
BREAKING A VOW BETWEEN MEN...
...AND RUNNING TO CHINA WITH YOUR FATHER!
SWASH

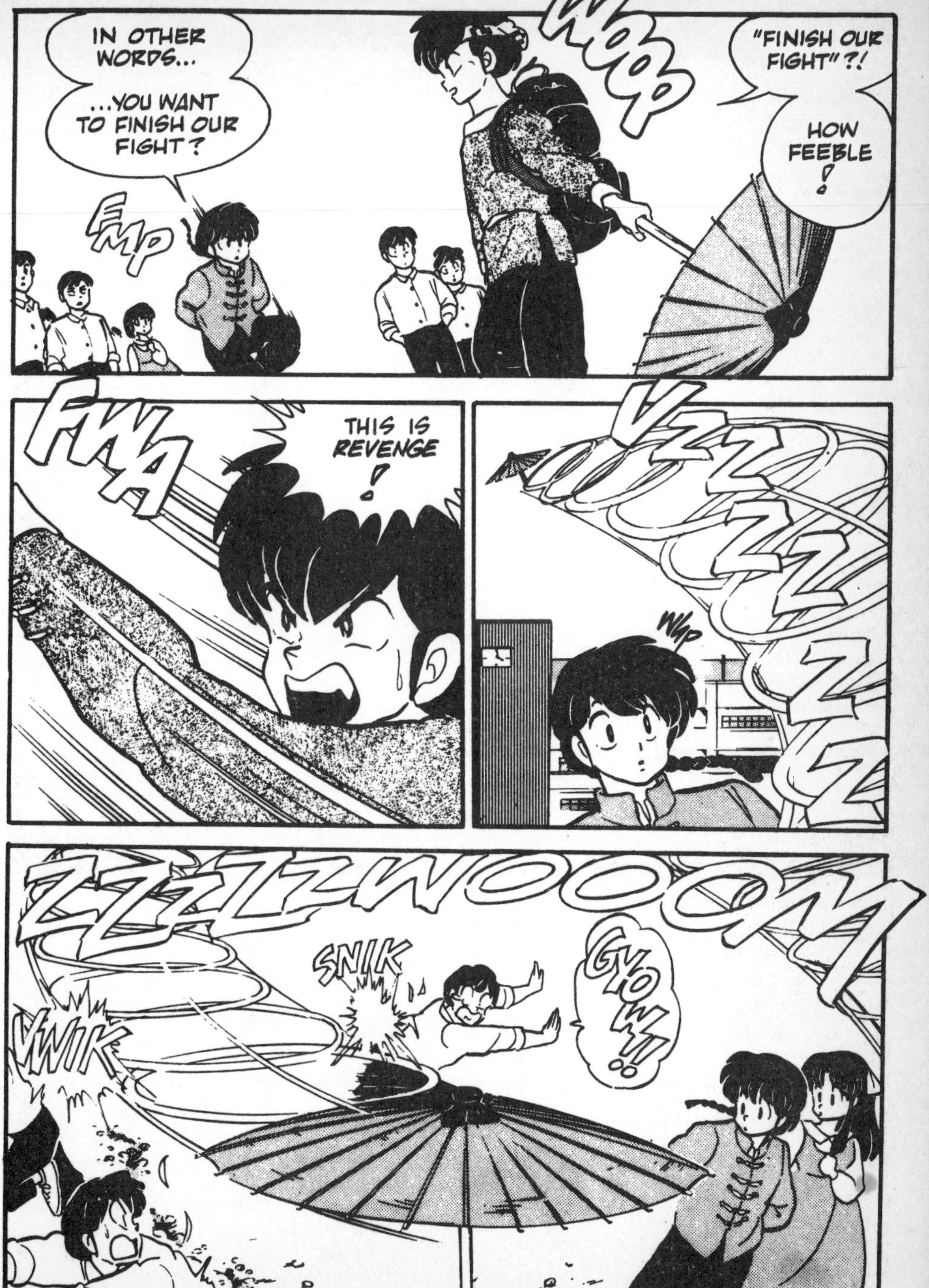
IN OTHER WORDS...
...YOU WANT TO FINISH OUR FIGHT?
FMP
WOOOP
"FINISH OUR FIGHT"?!
HOW FEEBLE!
FWA
THIS IS REVENGE!
VZZZZZZ
WHP
ZZZZWOOOOM
SNIK
VWIK
GYOW!!

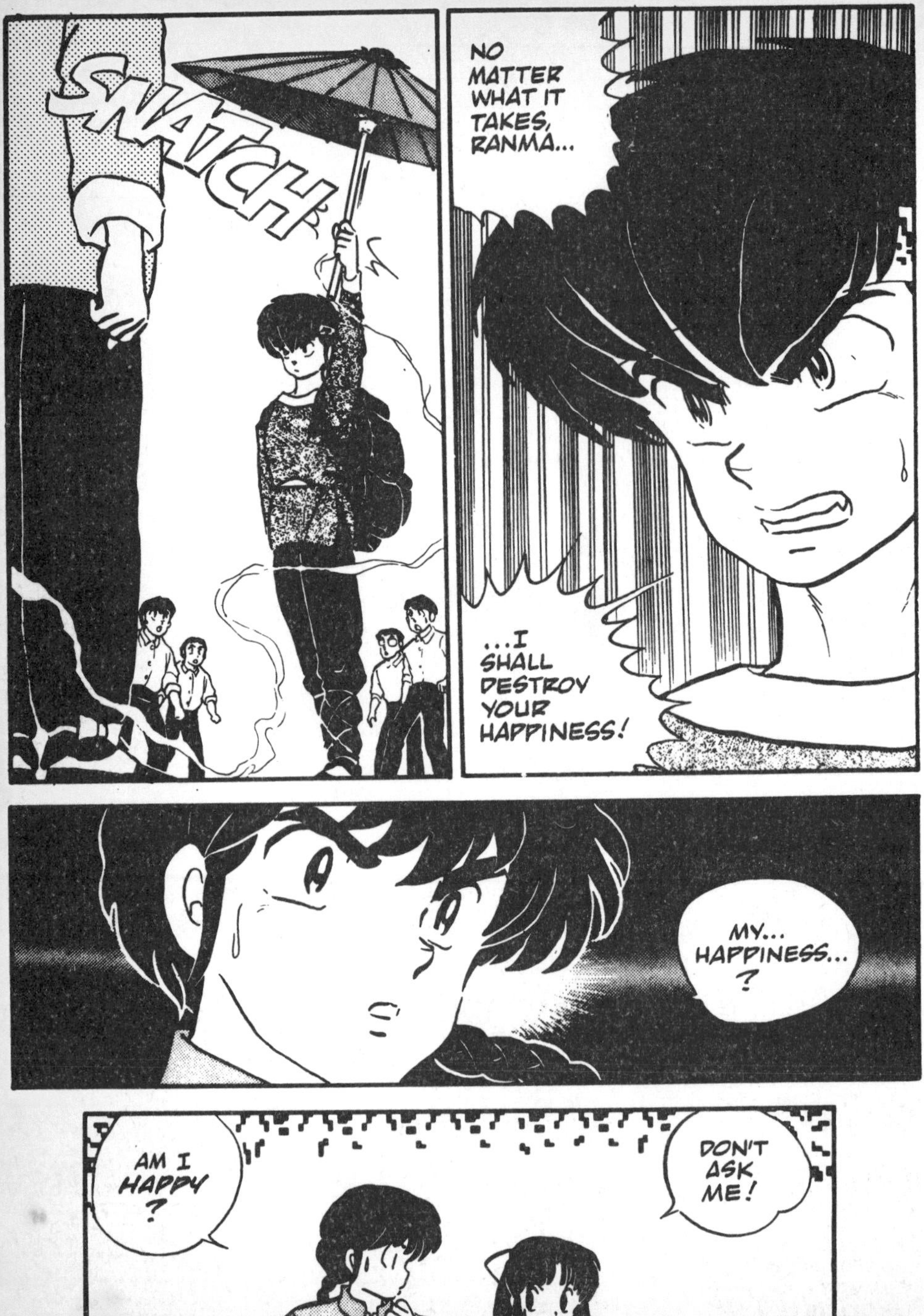
SNATCH
NO MATTER WHAT IT TAKES, RANMA...
...I SHALL DESTROY YOUR HAPPINESS!
MY... HAPPINESS...?
DON'T ASK ME!
AM I HAPPY?

PART ELEVEN
Bread Feud

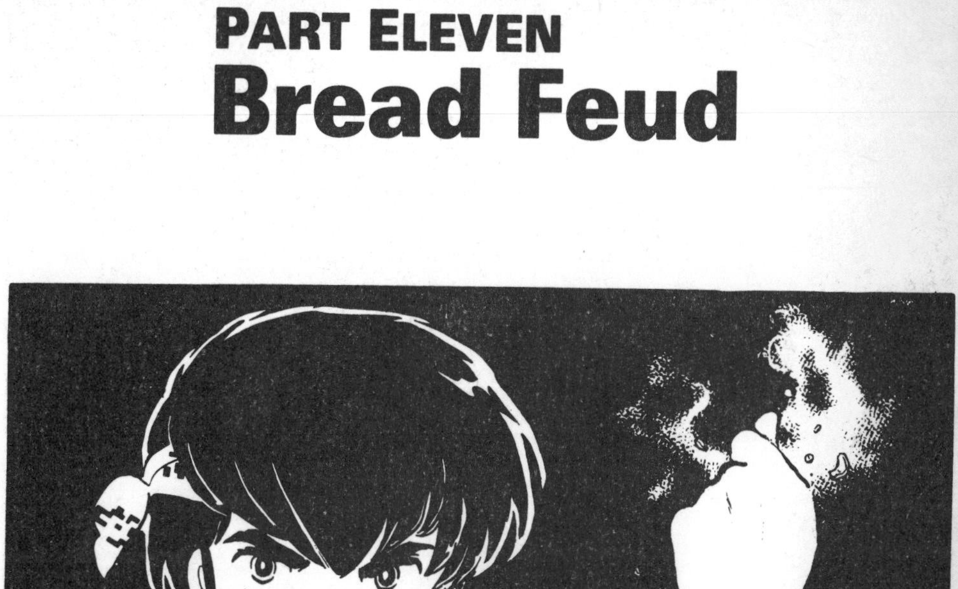

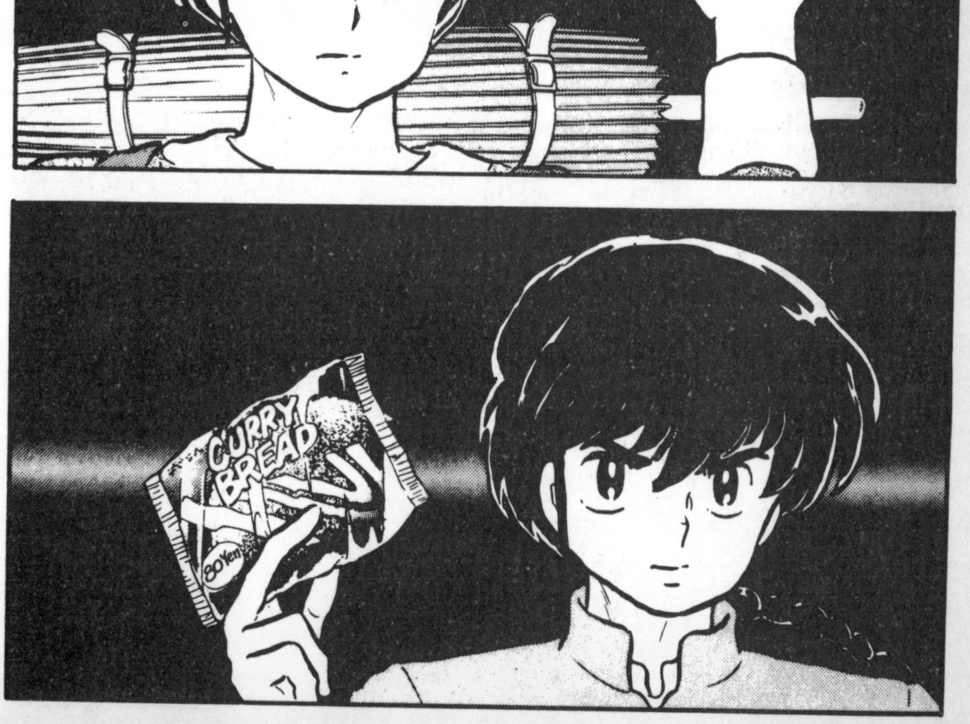
CURRY BREAD
80 Yen

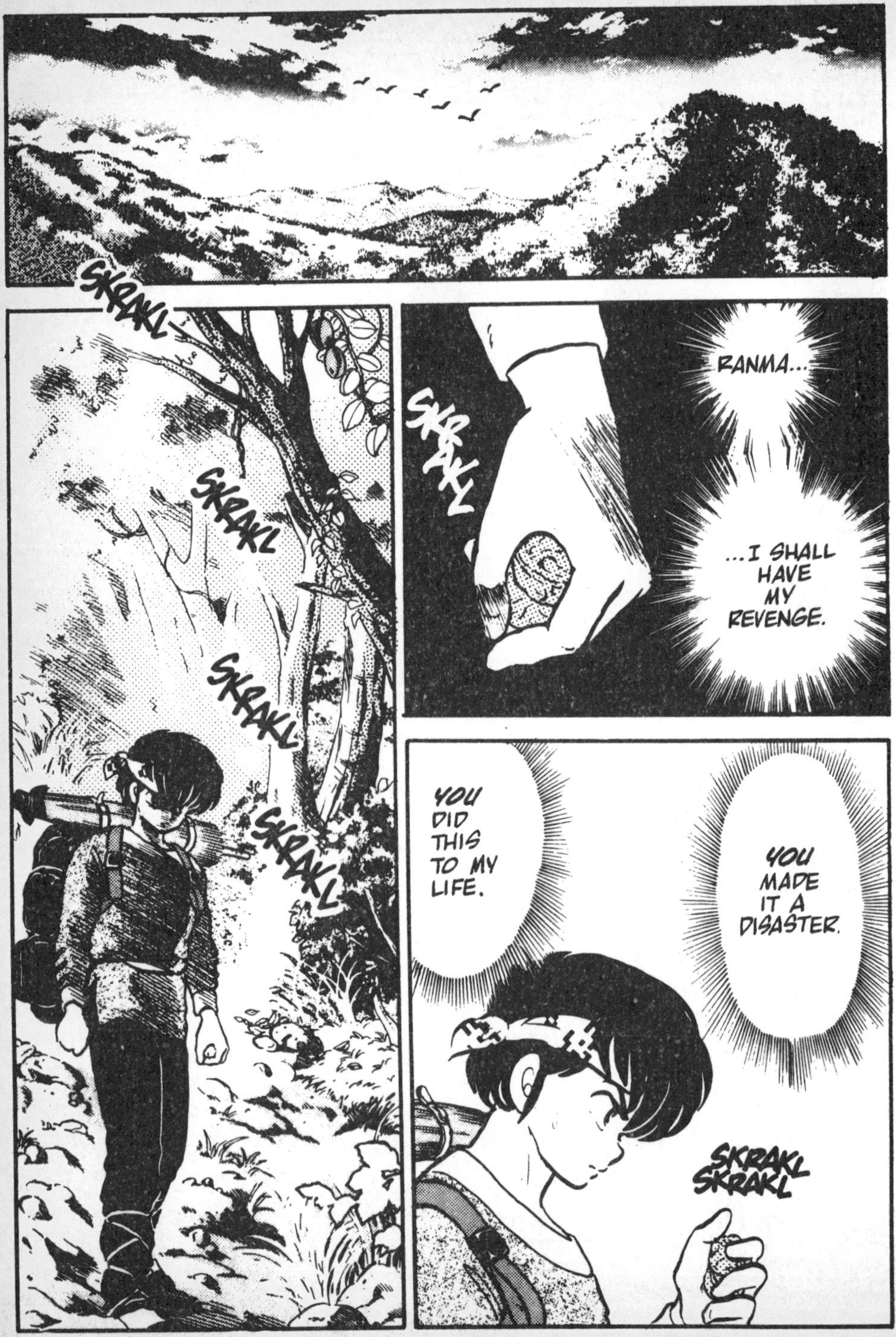
SKRAKL
SKRAKL
SKRAKL
SKRAKL
SKRAKL
RANMA...
...I SHALL HAVE MY REVENGE.
YOU MADE IT A DISASTER.
YOU DID THIS TO MY LIFE.
SKRAKL SKRAKL

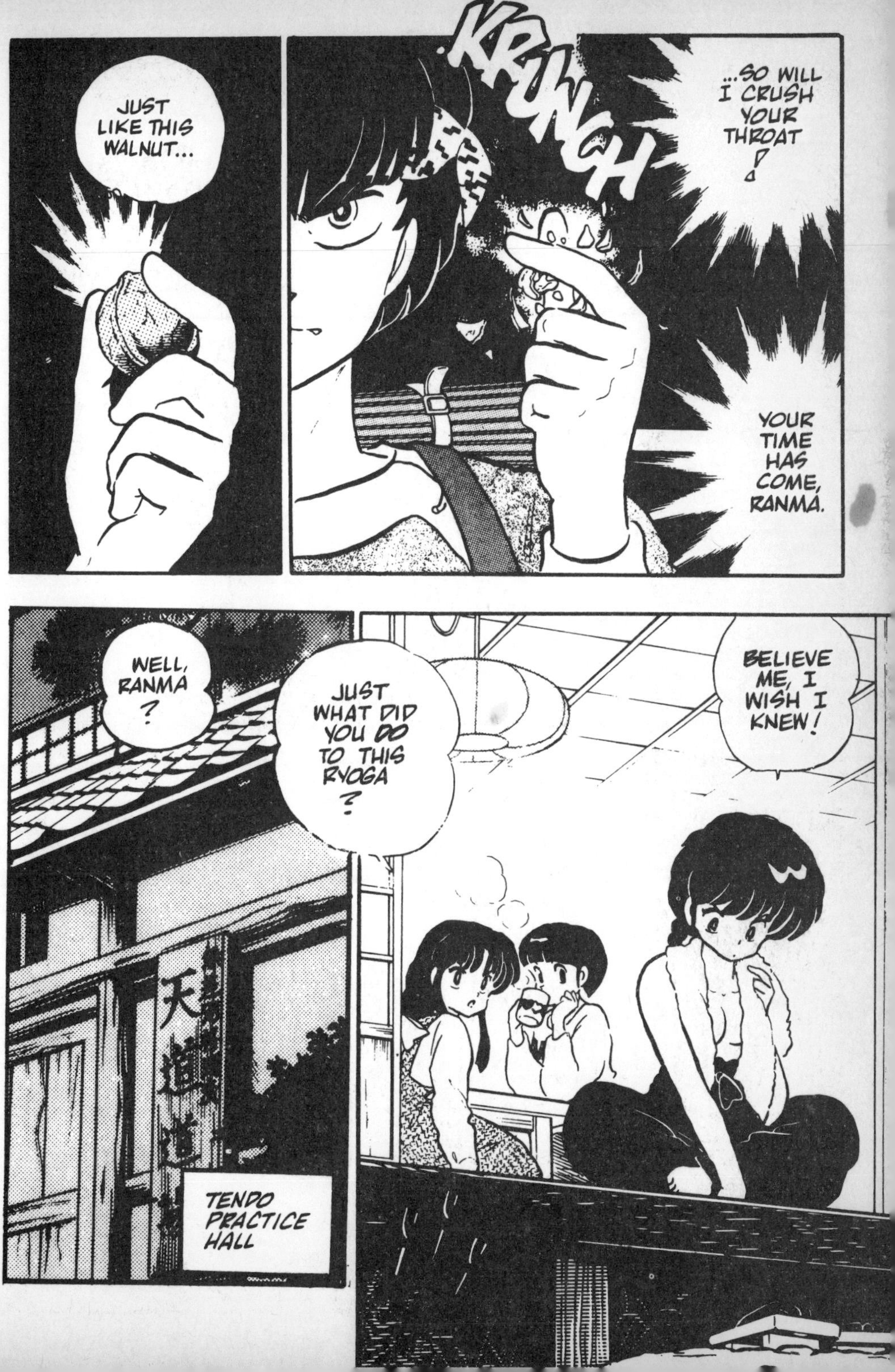

JUST LIKE THIS WALNUT...
KRUNCH
...SO WILL I CRUSH YOUR THROAT!
YOUR TIME HAS COME, RANMA.
WELL, RANMA?
JUST WHAT DID YOU DO TO THIS RYOGA?
TENDO PRACTICE HALL
BELIEVE ME, I WISH I KNEW!

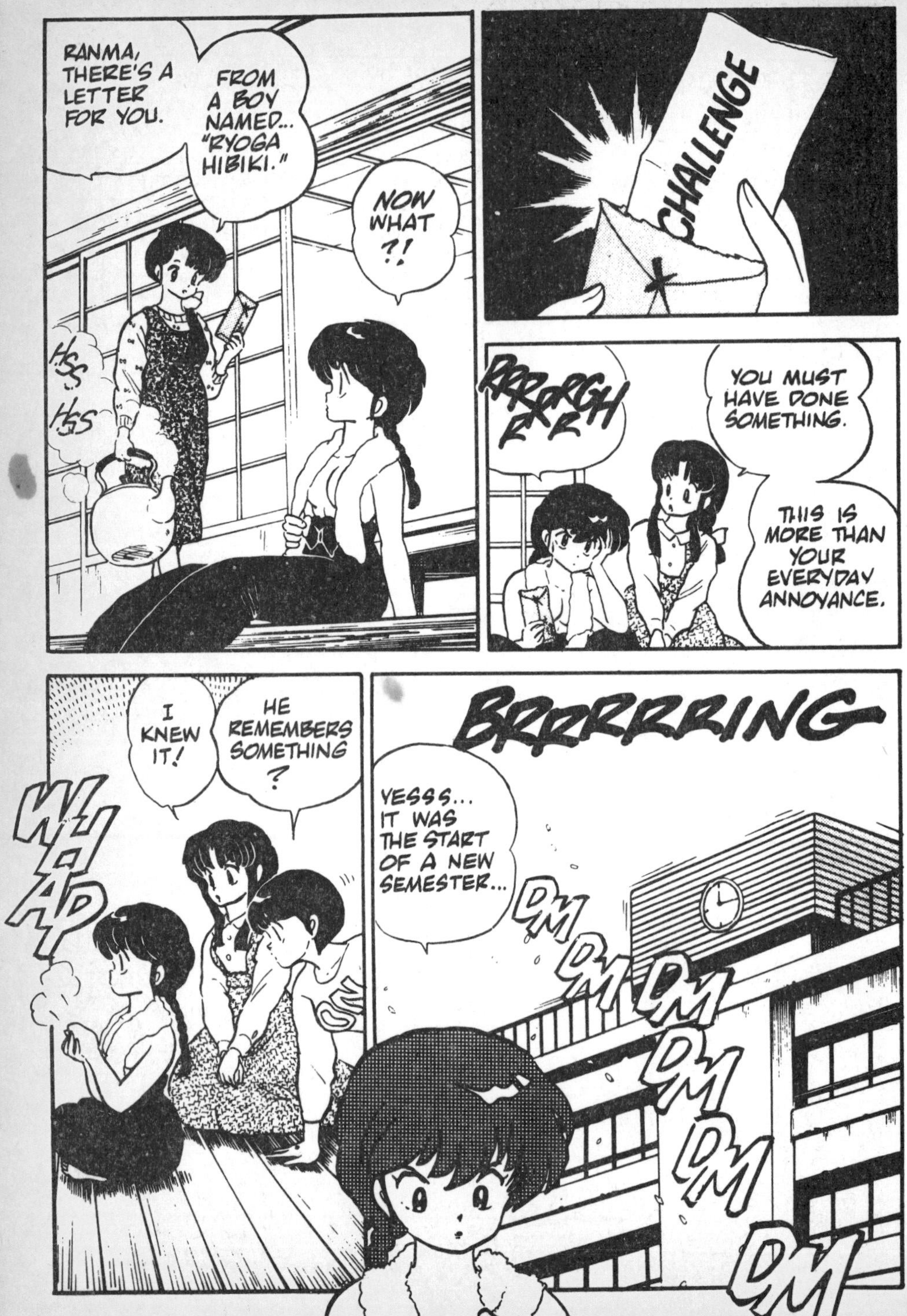
RANMA, THERE'S A LETTER FOR YOU.
FROM A BOY NAMED... "RYOGA HIBIKI."
NOW WHAT ?!
HSS HSS
CHALLENGE
BRRRRGH RRR
YOU MUST HAVE DONE SOMETHING.
THIS IS MORE THAN YOUR EVERYDAY ANNOYANCE.
I KNEW IT!
HE REMEMBERS SOMETHING ?
WHAP
BRRRRRING
YESSS... IT WAS THE START OF A NEW SEMESTER...
DM DM DM DM DM DM DM

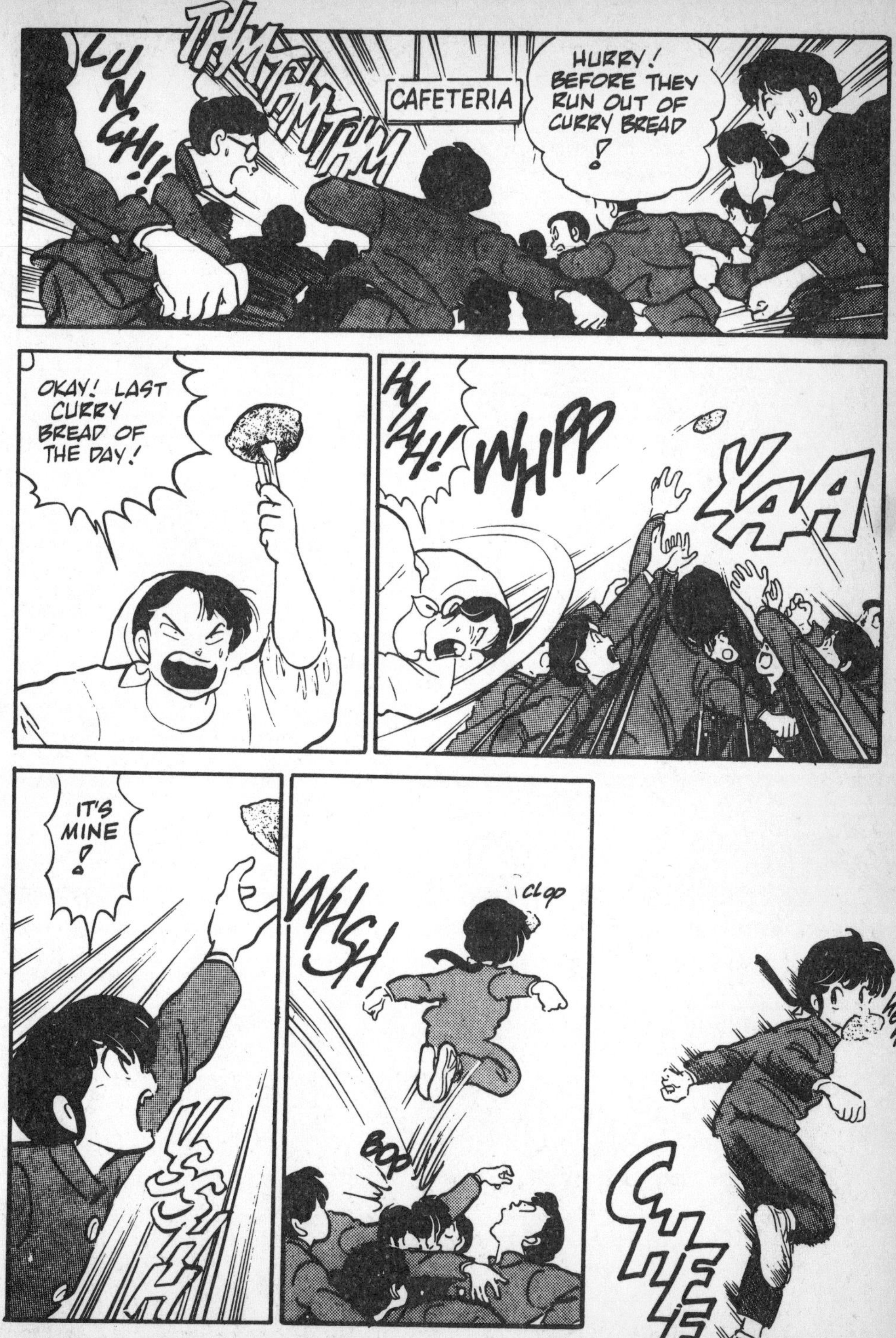
THMTHMTHM
LUNCH!!!
CAFETERIA
HURRY! BEFORE THEY RUN OUT OF CURRY BREAD!
OKAY! LAST CURRY BREAD OF THE DAY!
HYAAH!
WHPP
YAA
IT'S MINE!
WHSH
CLOP
BOP

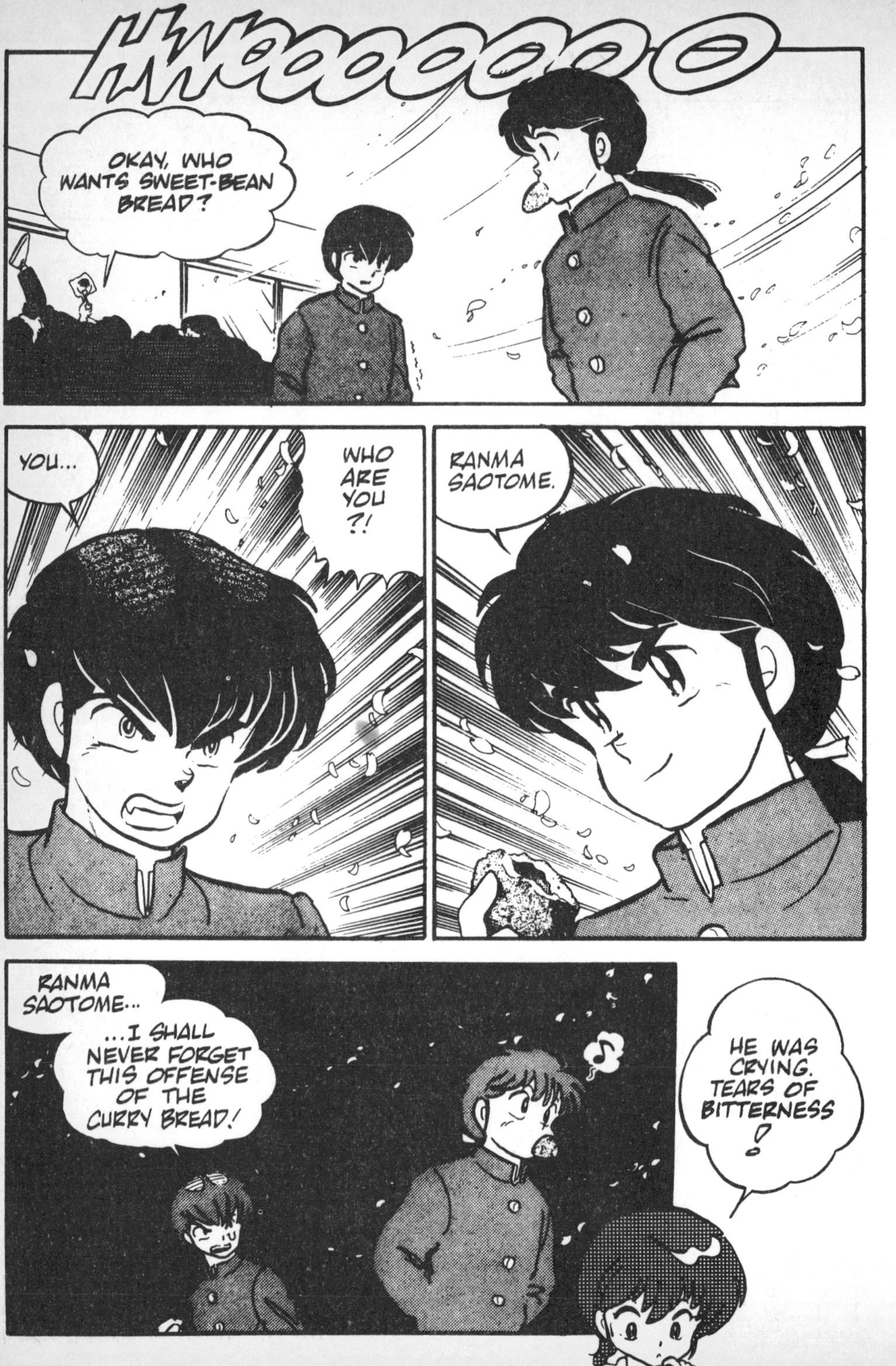
HWOOOOOOOO
OKAY, WHO WANTS SWEET-BEAN BREAD?
YOU...
WHO ARE YOU?!
RANMA SAOTOME.
RANMA SAOTOME...
...I SHALL NEVER FORGET THIS OFFENSE OF THE CURRY BREAD!
HE WAS CRYING. TEARS OF BITTERNESS?

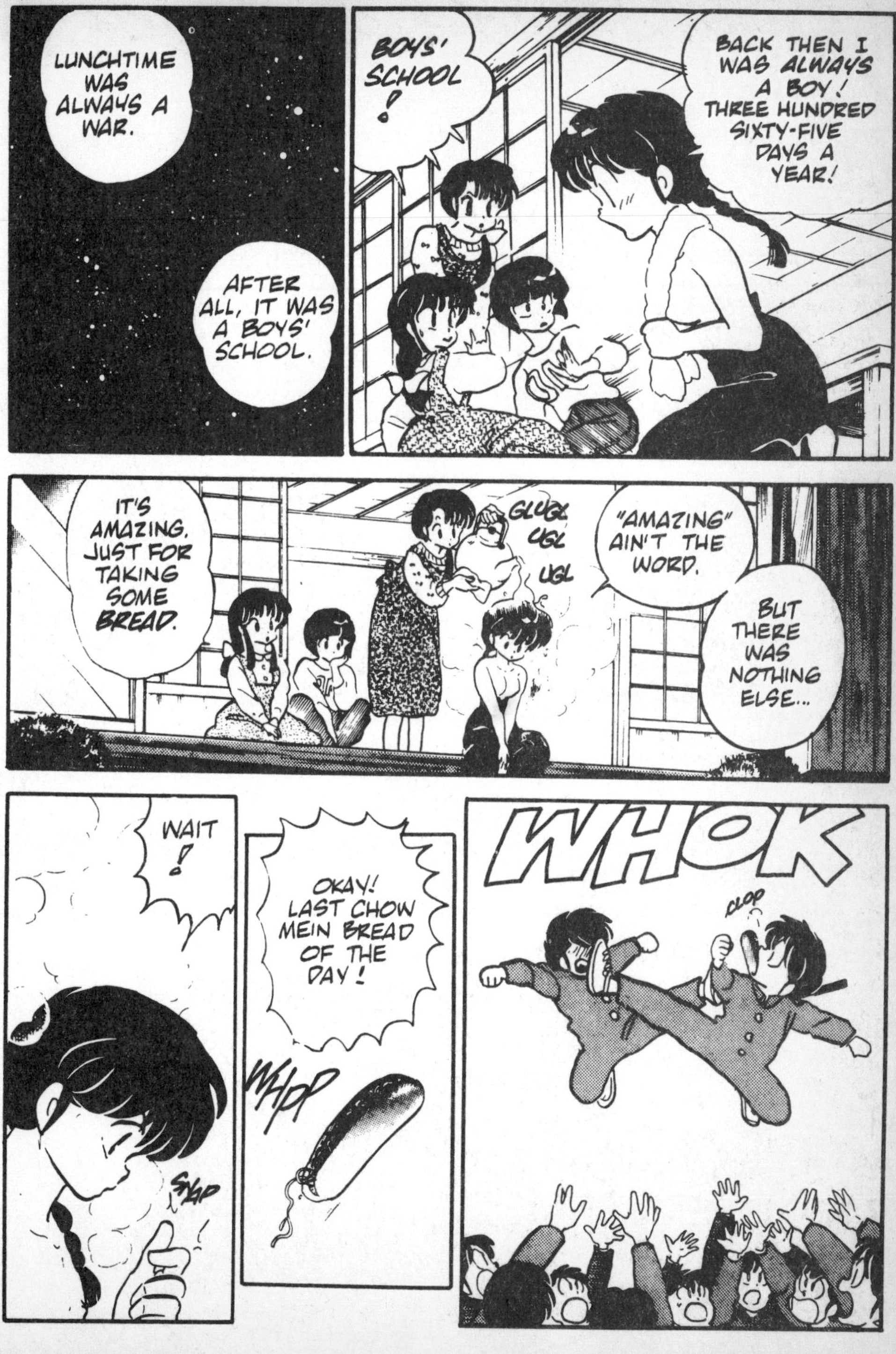
LUNCHTIME WAS ALWAYS A WAR.
AFTER ALL, IT WAS A BOYS' SCHOOL.
BACK THEN I WAS ALWAYS A BOY! THREE HUNDRED SIXTY-FIVE DAYS A YEAR!
BOYS' SCHOOL!
"AMAZING" AIN'T THE WORD.
BUT THERE WAS NOTHING ELSE...
GLUGL UGL UGL
IT'S AMAZING. JUST FOR TAKING SOME BREAD.
WHOK
CLOP
OKAY! LAST CHOW MEIN BREAD OF THE DAY!
WHOP
WAIT!
SLURP

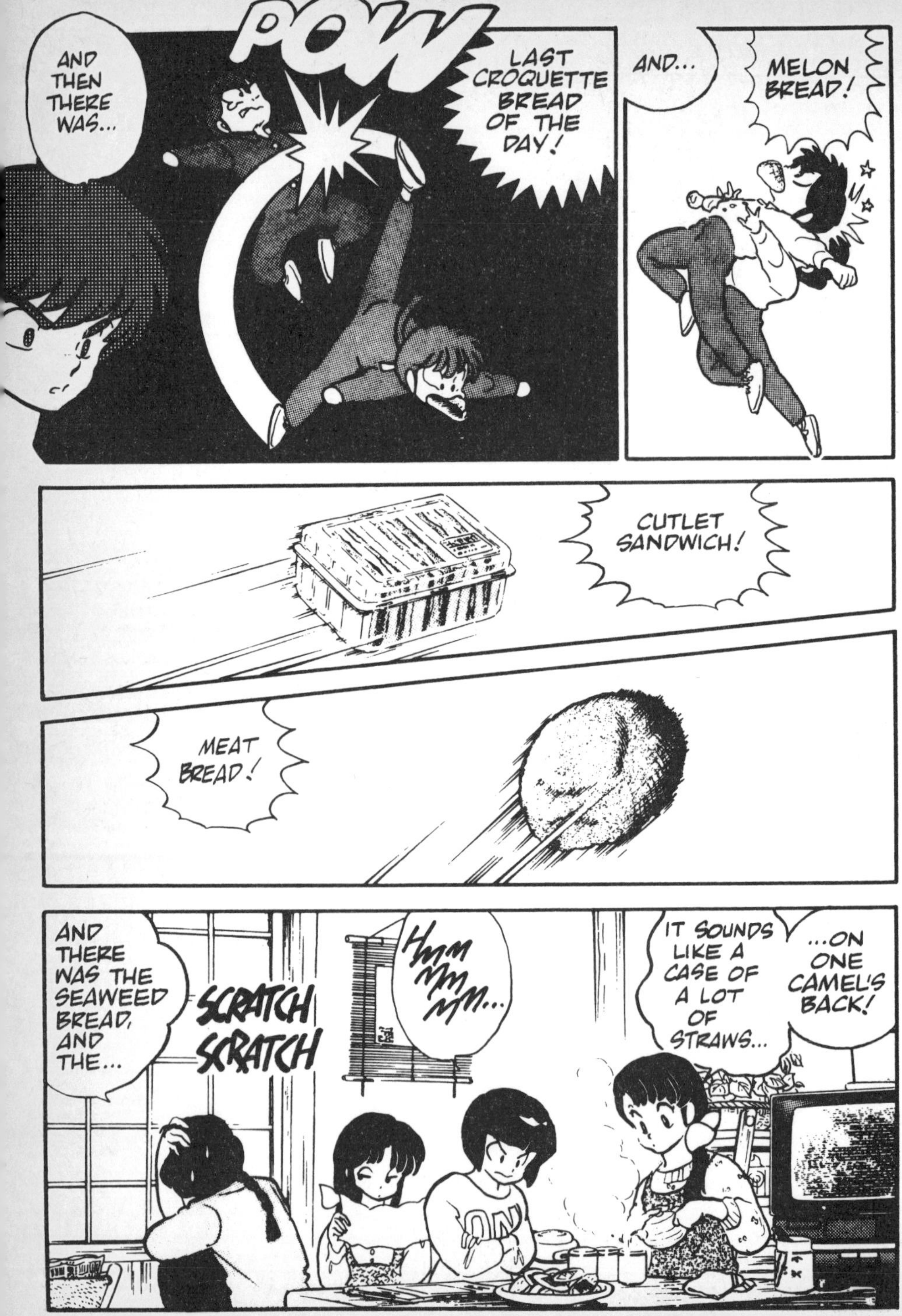
AND THEN THERE WAS...
POW
LAST CROQUETTE BREAD OF THE DAY!
AND...
MELON BREAD!
CUTLET SANDWICH!
MEAT BREAD!
AND THERE WAS THE SEAWEED BREAD, AND THE...
SCRATCH SCRATCH
HMM MM MM...
IT SOUNDS LIKE A CASE OF A LOT OF STRAWS...
...ON ONE CAMEL'S BACK!

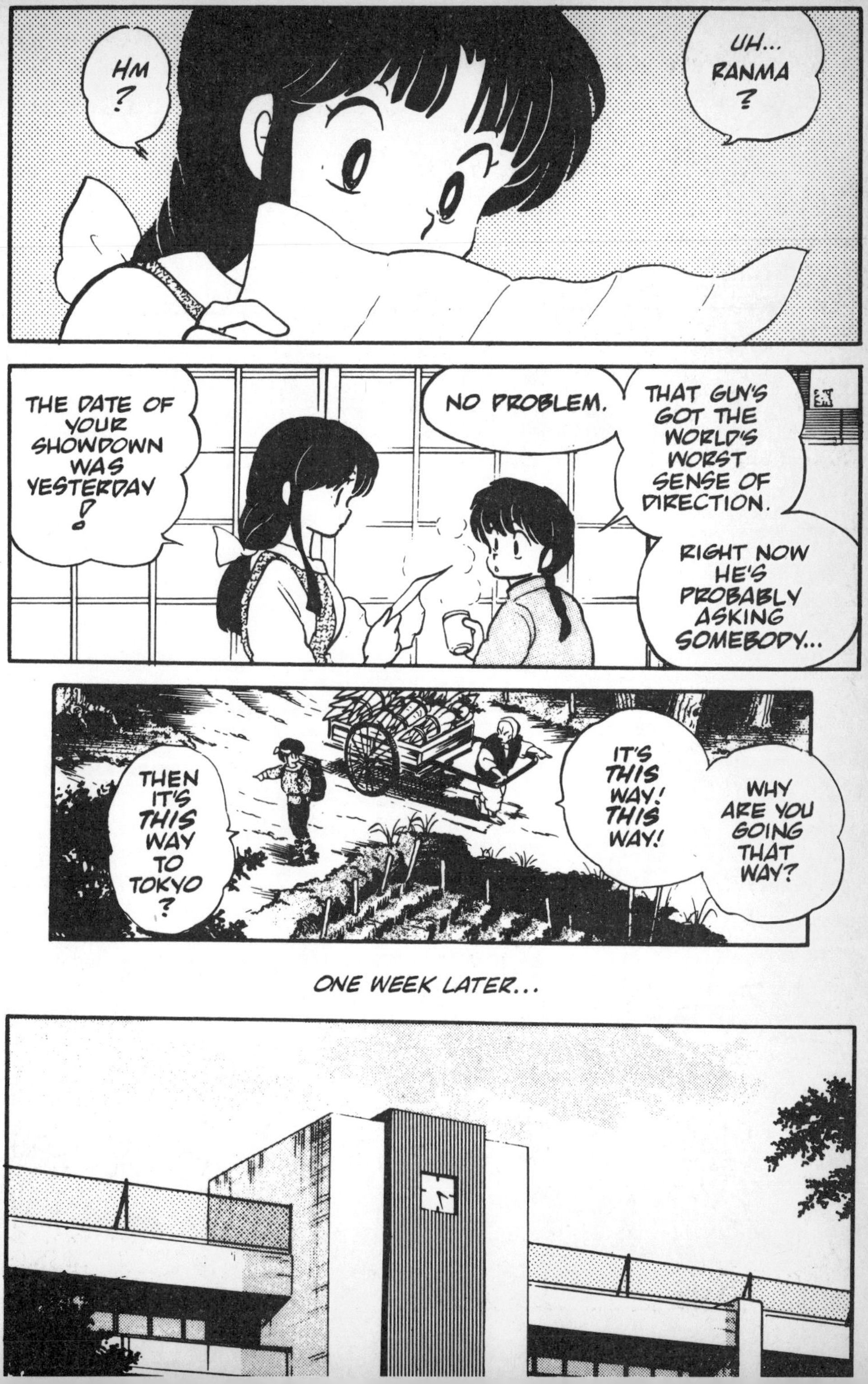
HM?
UH... RANMA?
THE DATE OF YOUR SHOWDOWN WAS YESTERDAY!
NO PROBLEM.
THAT GUY'S GOT THE WORLD'S WORST SENSE OF DIRECTION.
RIGHT NOW HE'S PROBABLY ASKING SOMEBODY...
THEN IT'S THIS WAY TO TOKYO?
IT'S THIS WAY! THIS WAY!
WHY ARE YOU GOING THAT WAY?
ONE WEEK LATER...

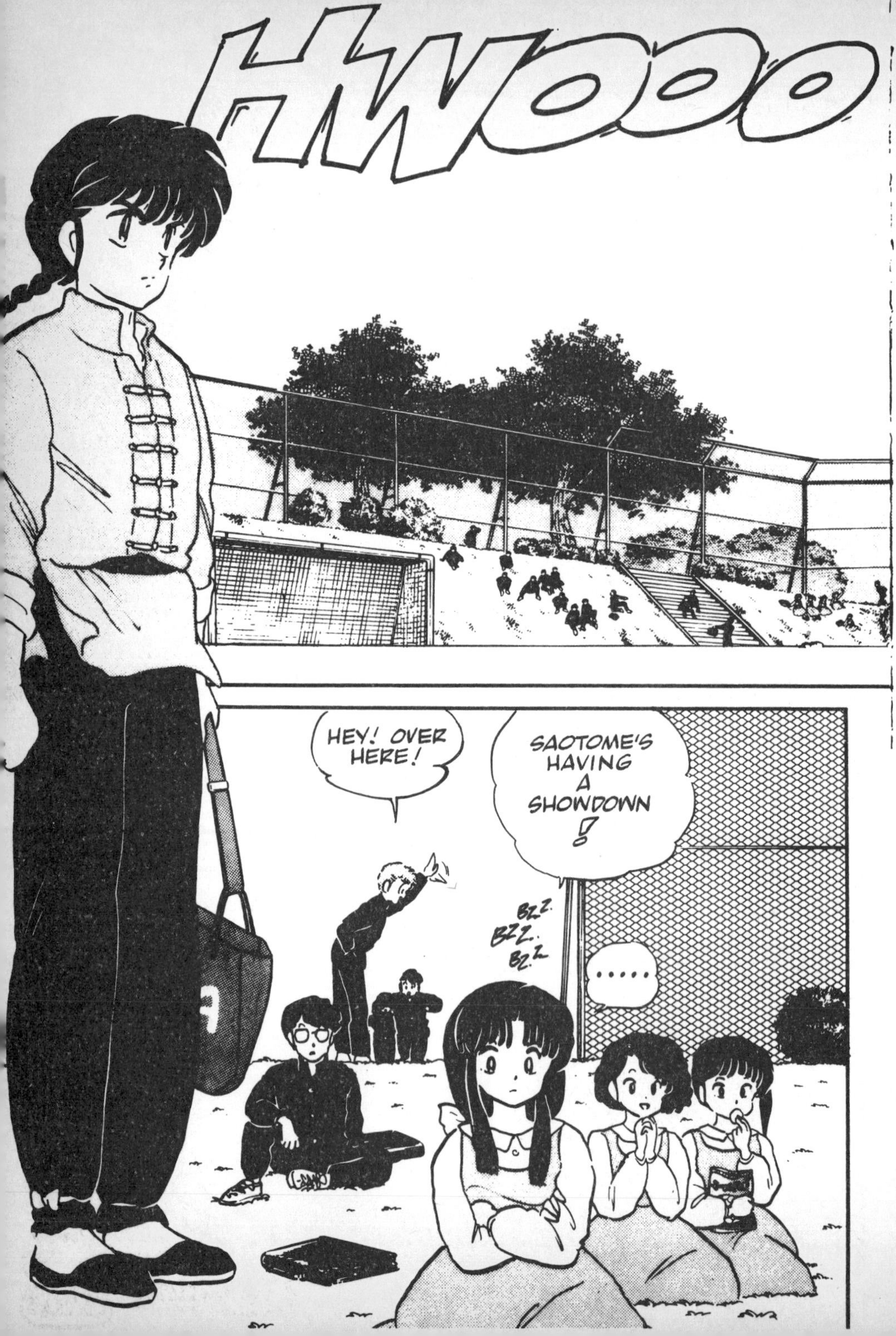
HWOOO
HEY! OVER HERE!
SAOTOME'S HAVING A SHOWDOWN!
BZZ. BZZ. BZZ
.....

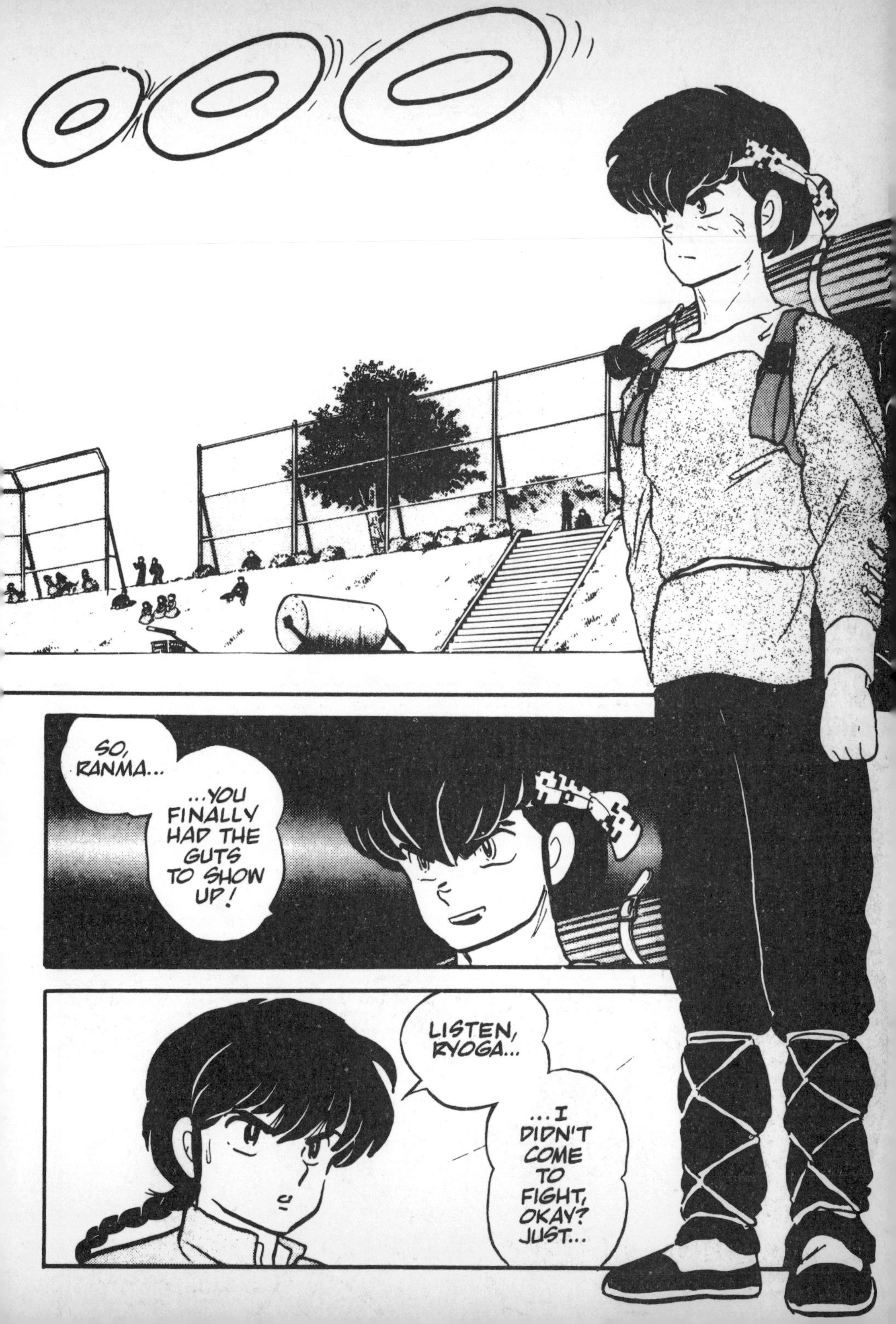
SO, RANMA...
...YOU FINALLY HAD THE GUTS TO SHOW UP!
LISTEN, RYOGA...
...I DIDN'T COME TO FIGHT, OKAY? JUST...

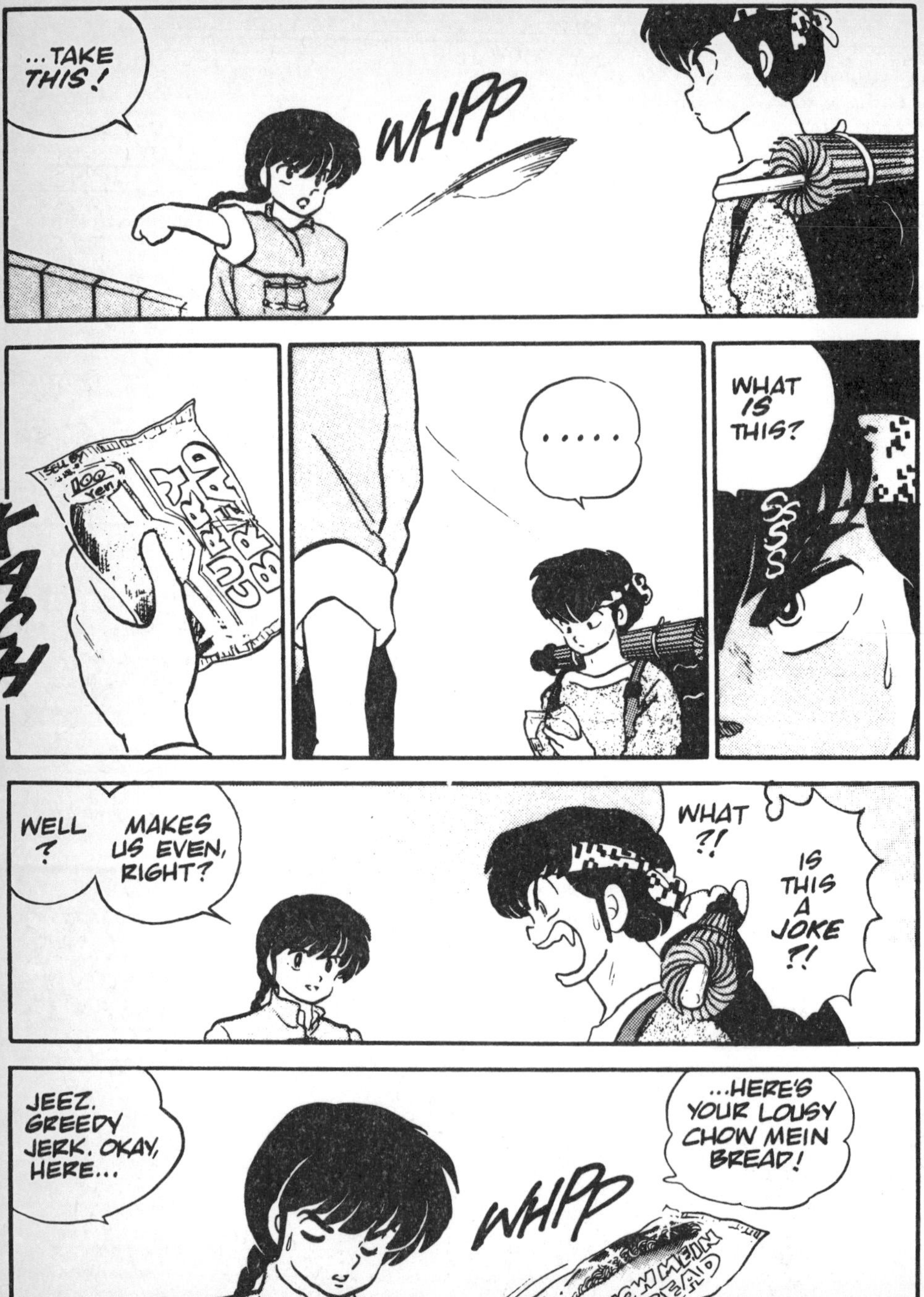

...TAKE THIS!
WHPP
KACH
100 Yen
CURRANT BREAD
.....
WHAT IS THIS?
WELL?
MAKES US EVEN, RIGHT?
WHAT?!
IS THIS A JOKE?!
JEEZ. GREEDY JERK. OKAY, HERE...
...HERE'S YOUR LOUSY CHOW MEIN BREAD!
WHPP
CHOW MEIN BREAD

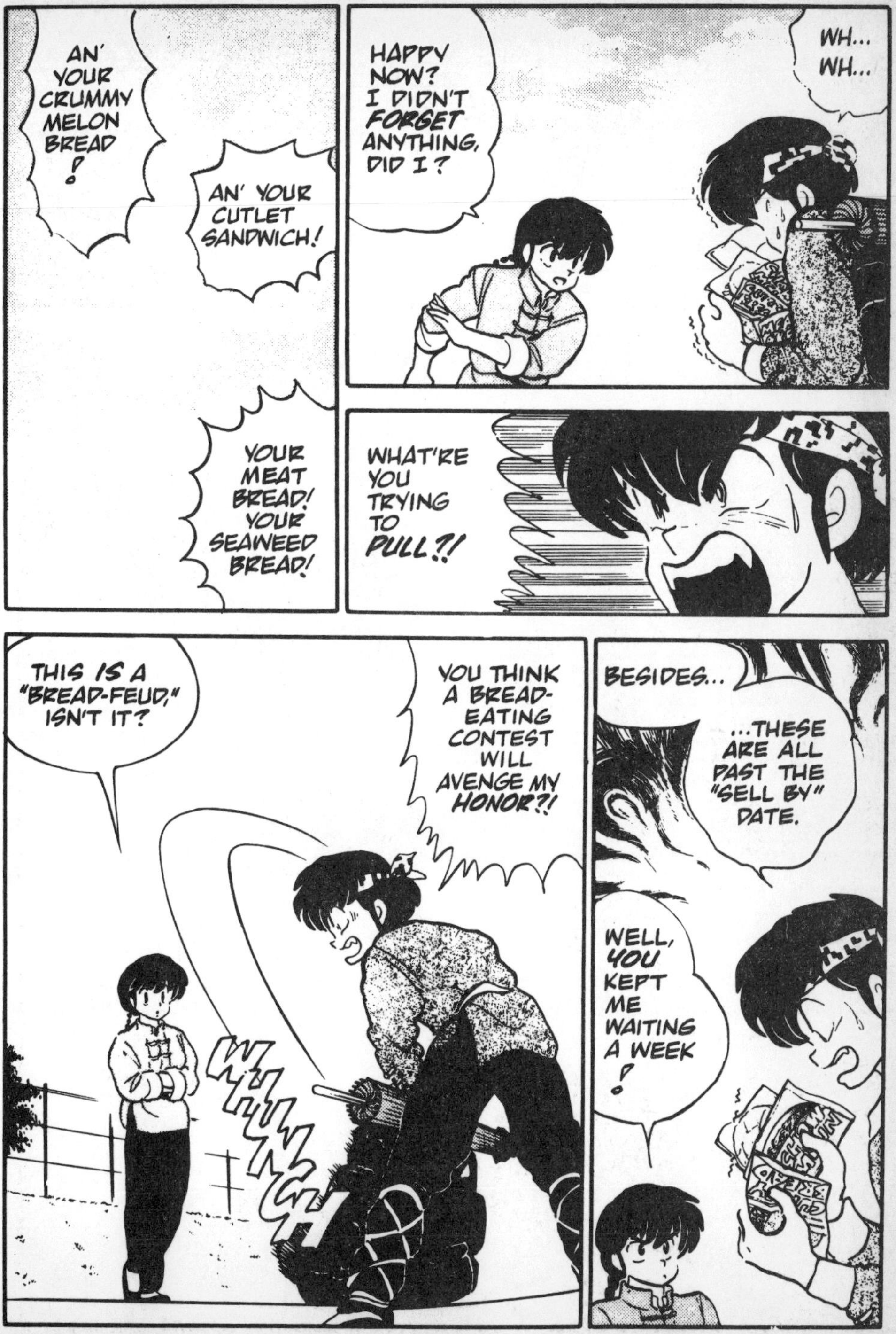
AN' YOUR CRUMMY MELON BREAD!
AN' YOUR CUTLET SANDWICH!
YOUR MEAT BREAD! YOUR SEAWEED BREAD!
HAPPY NOW? I DIDN'T FORGET ANYTHING, DID I?
WH... WH...
WHAT'RE YOU TRYING TO PULL?!
THIS IS A "BREAD-FEUD," ISN'T IT?
YOU THINK A BREAD-EATING CONTEST WILL AVENGE MY HONOR?!
WHUNCH
BESIDES...
...THESE ARE ALL PAST THE "SELL BY" DATE.
WELL, YOU KEPT ME WAITING A WEEK!

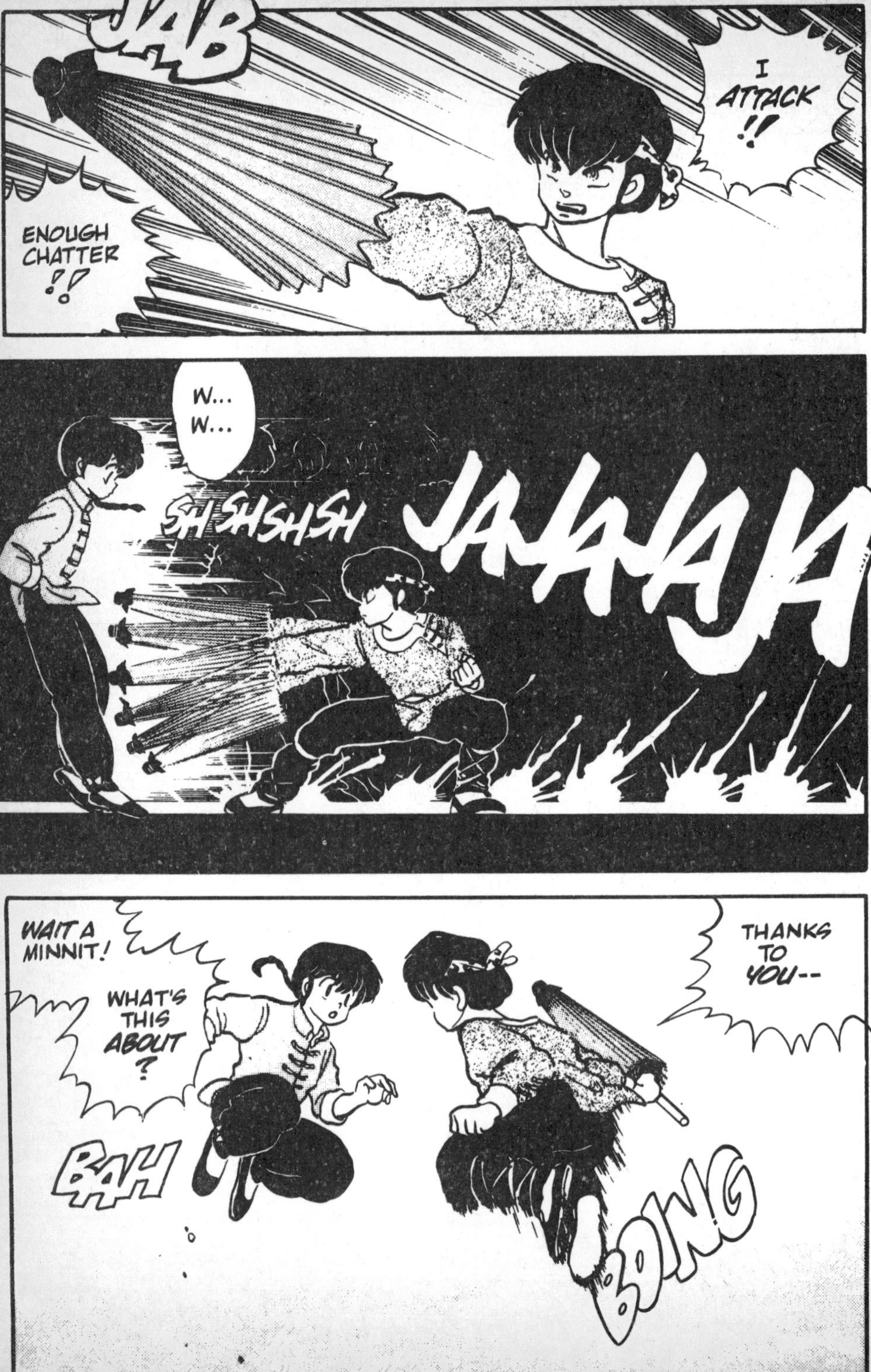
JAB
ENOUGH CHATTER !!
I ATTACK !!
W... W...
SH SHSHSH
JAJAJAJA
WAIT A MINNIT!
WHAT'S THIS ABOUT ?
THANKS TO YOU--
BAH
BOING

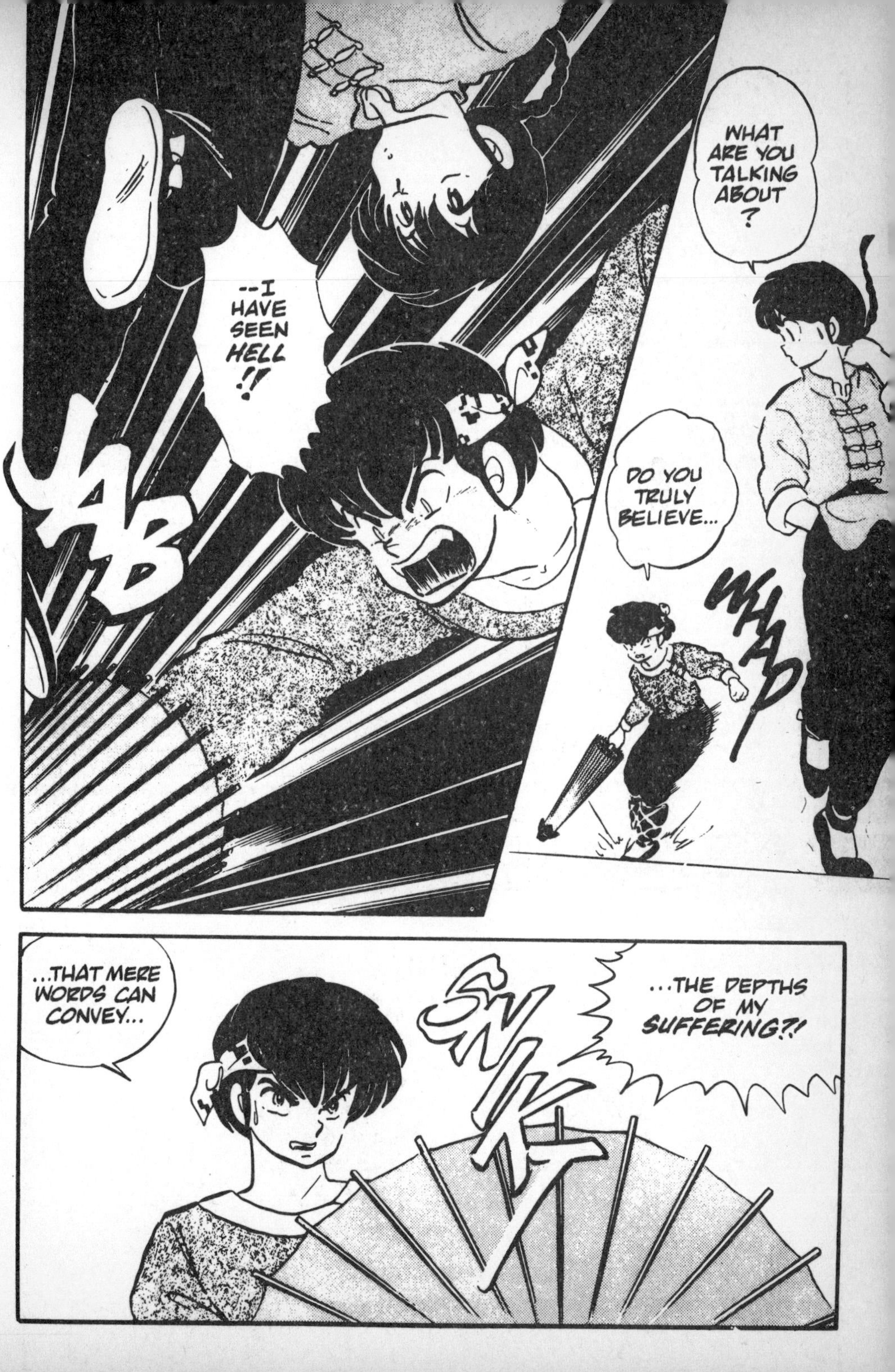
WHAT ARE YOU TALKING ABOUT?
DO YOU TRULY BELIEVE...
WHAM
--I HAVE SEEN HELL!!
JAB
...THAT MERE WORDS CAN CONVEY...
SNIKT
...THE DEPTHS OF MY SUFFERING?!

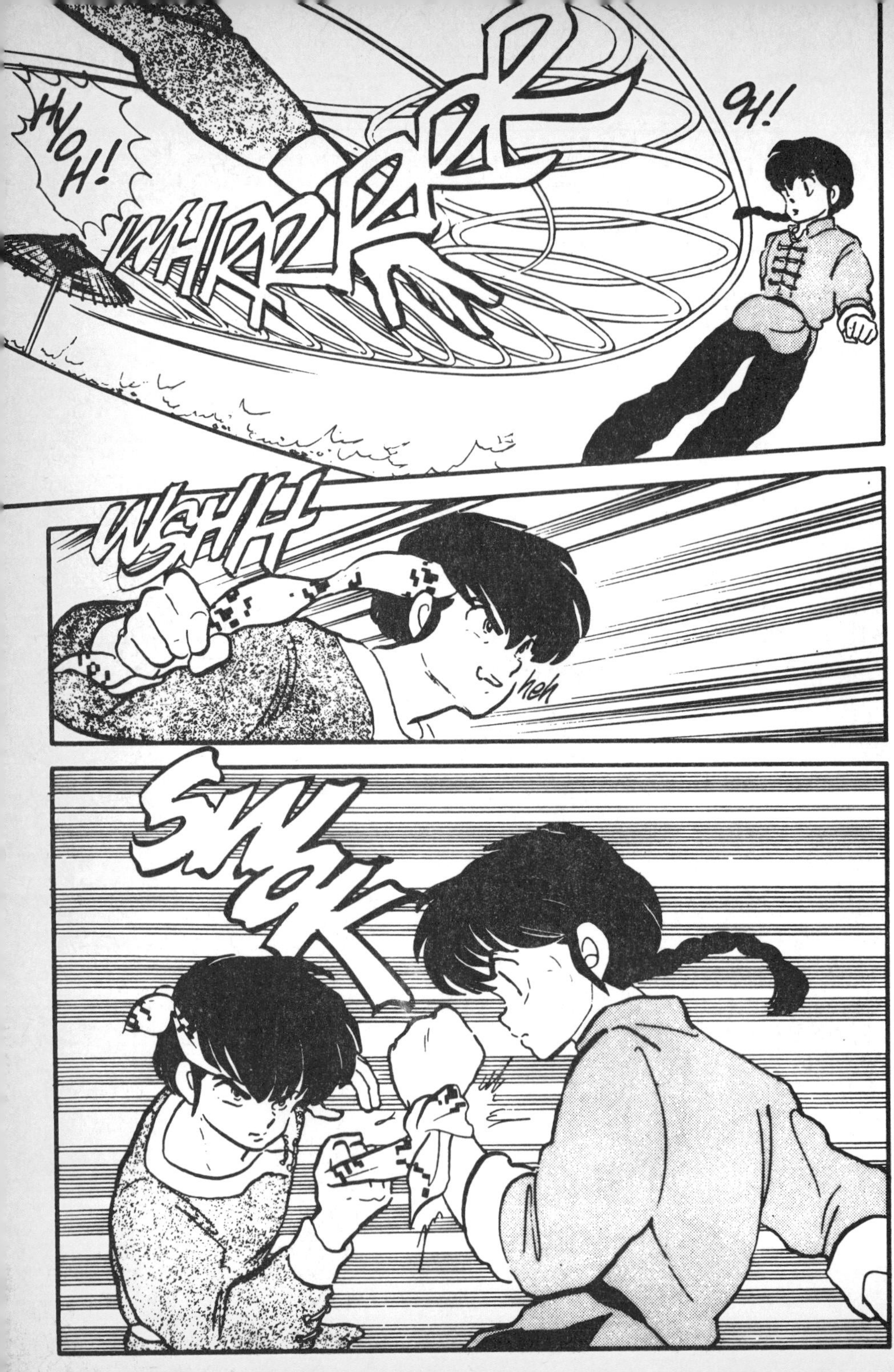
OH!
HYOH!
WHRRRRR
WSHH
heh
SMACK

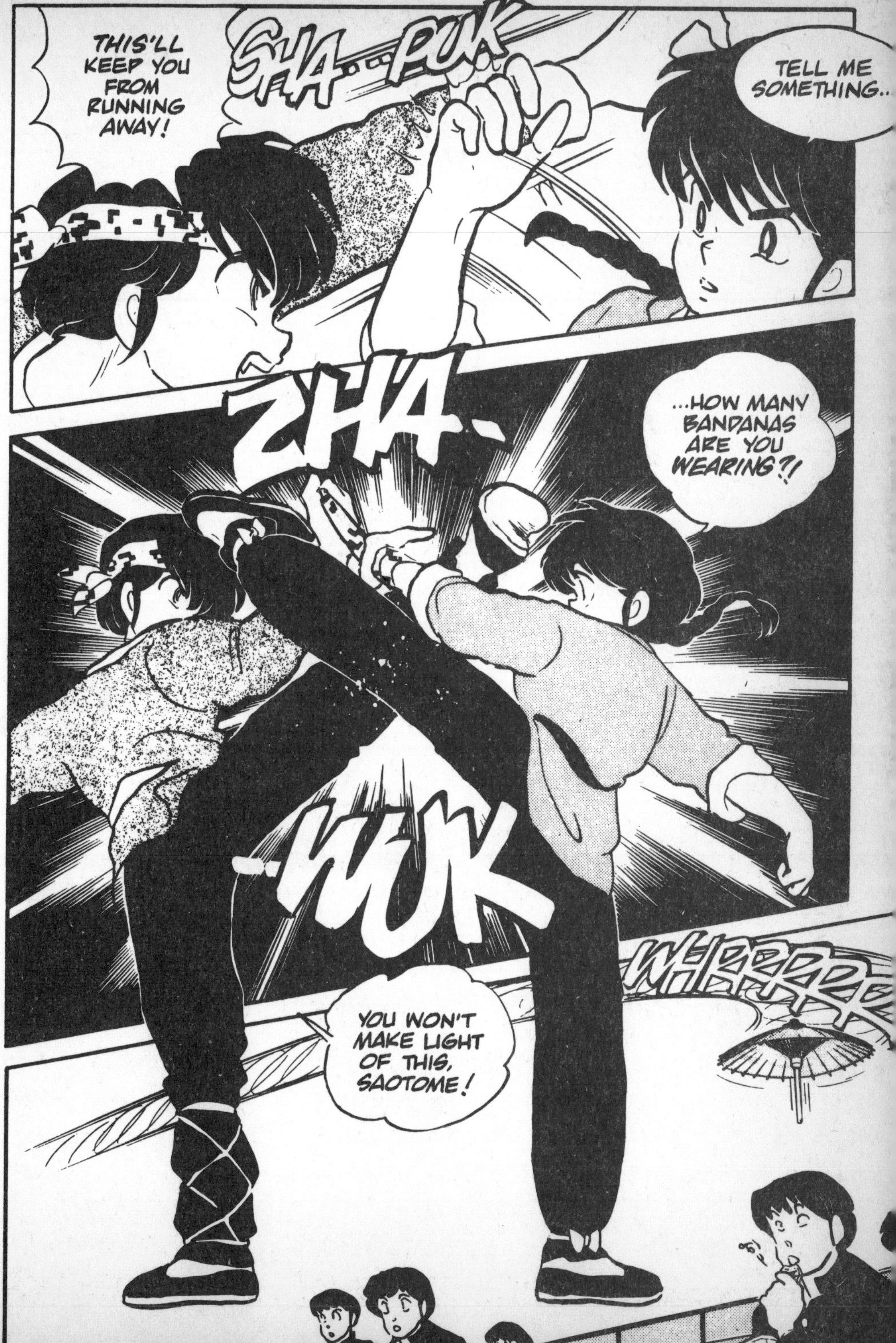
TELL ME SOMETHING...
SHA...PUK
THIS'LL KEEP YOU FROM RUNNING AWAY!
...HOW MANY BANDANAS ARE YOU WEARING?!
ZHA
WUK
WHRRRRR
YOU WON'T MAKE LIGHT OF THIS, SAOTOME!

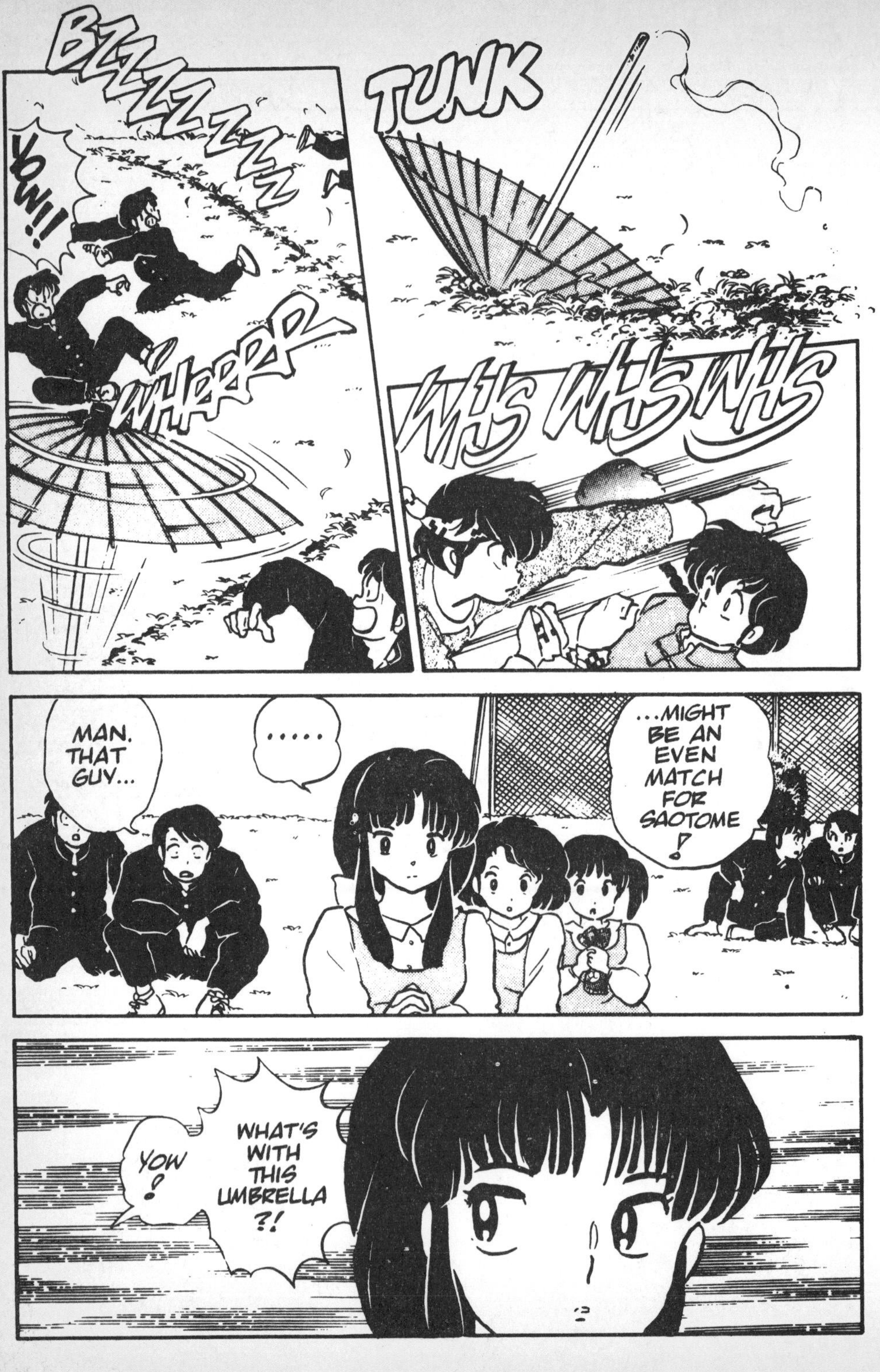
BZZZZZZ
YOW!!!
WHRRRR
TUNK
WHS WHS WHS
MAN. THAT GUY...
.....
...MIGHT BE AN EVEN MATCH FOR SAOTOME!
YOW!
WHAT'S WITH THIS UMBRELLA?!

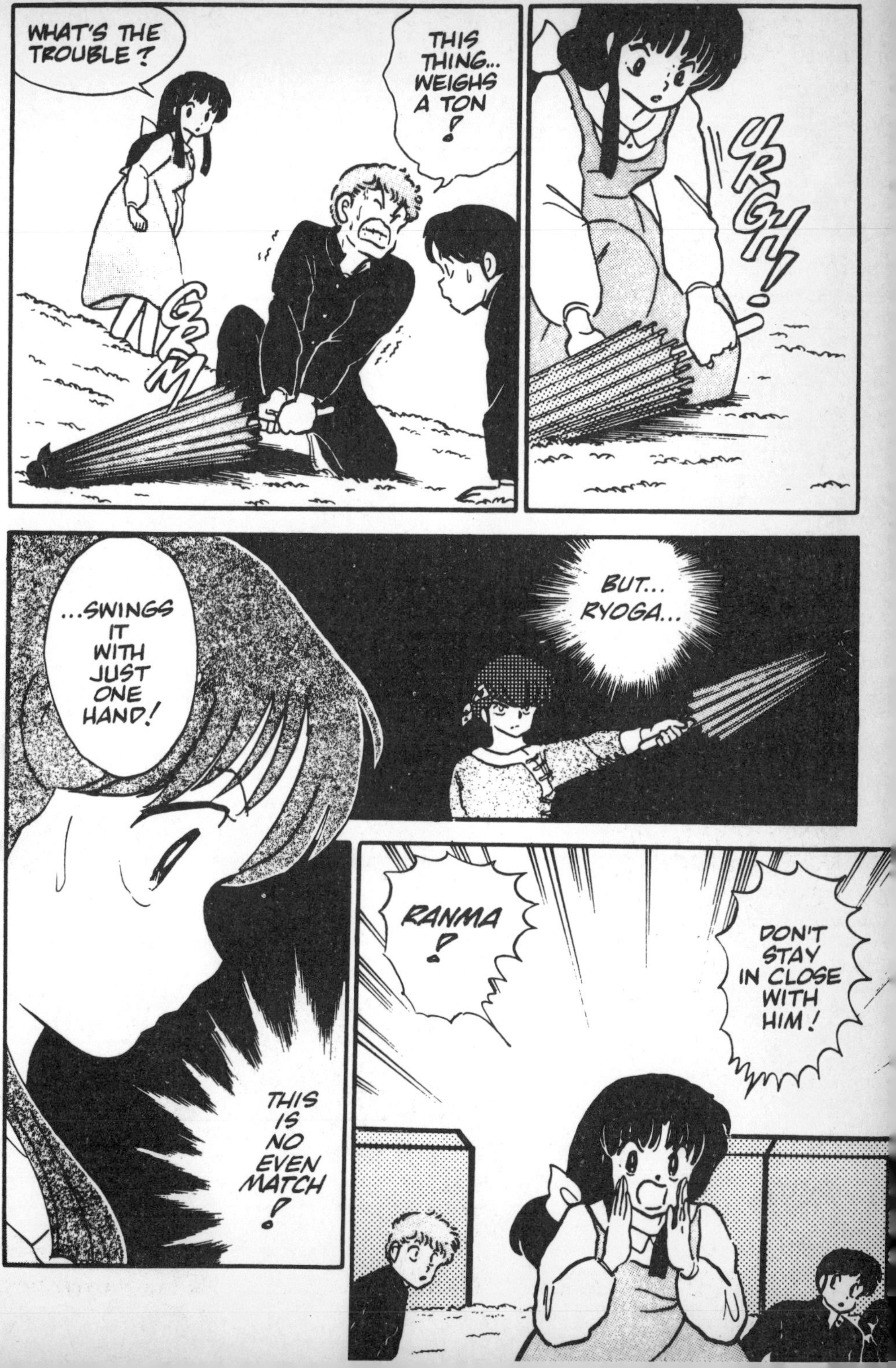

WHAT'S THE TROUBLE?
THIS THING... WEIGHS A TON!
GRRM
URGH!
BUT... RYOGA...
...SWINGS IT WITH JUST ONE HAND!
THIS IS NO EVEN MATCH!
RANMA!
DON'T STAY IN CLOSE WITH HIM!

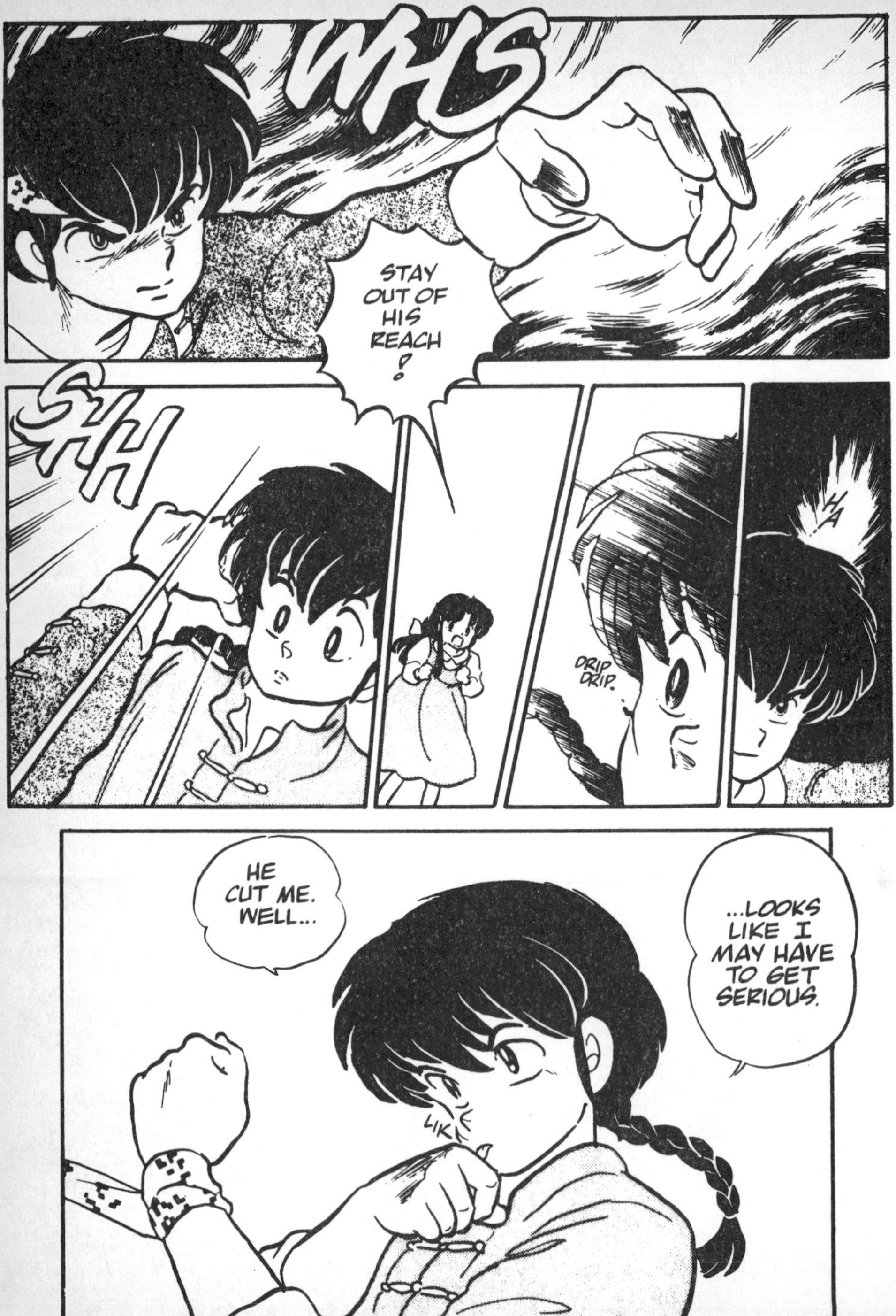
WHS
STAY OUT OF HIS REACH!
SHH
DRIP DRIP.
HA
HE CUT ME. WELL...
...LOOKS LIKE I MAY HAVE TO GET SERIOUS.
LIK

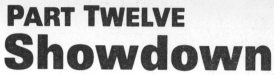

PART TWELVE
Showdown

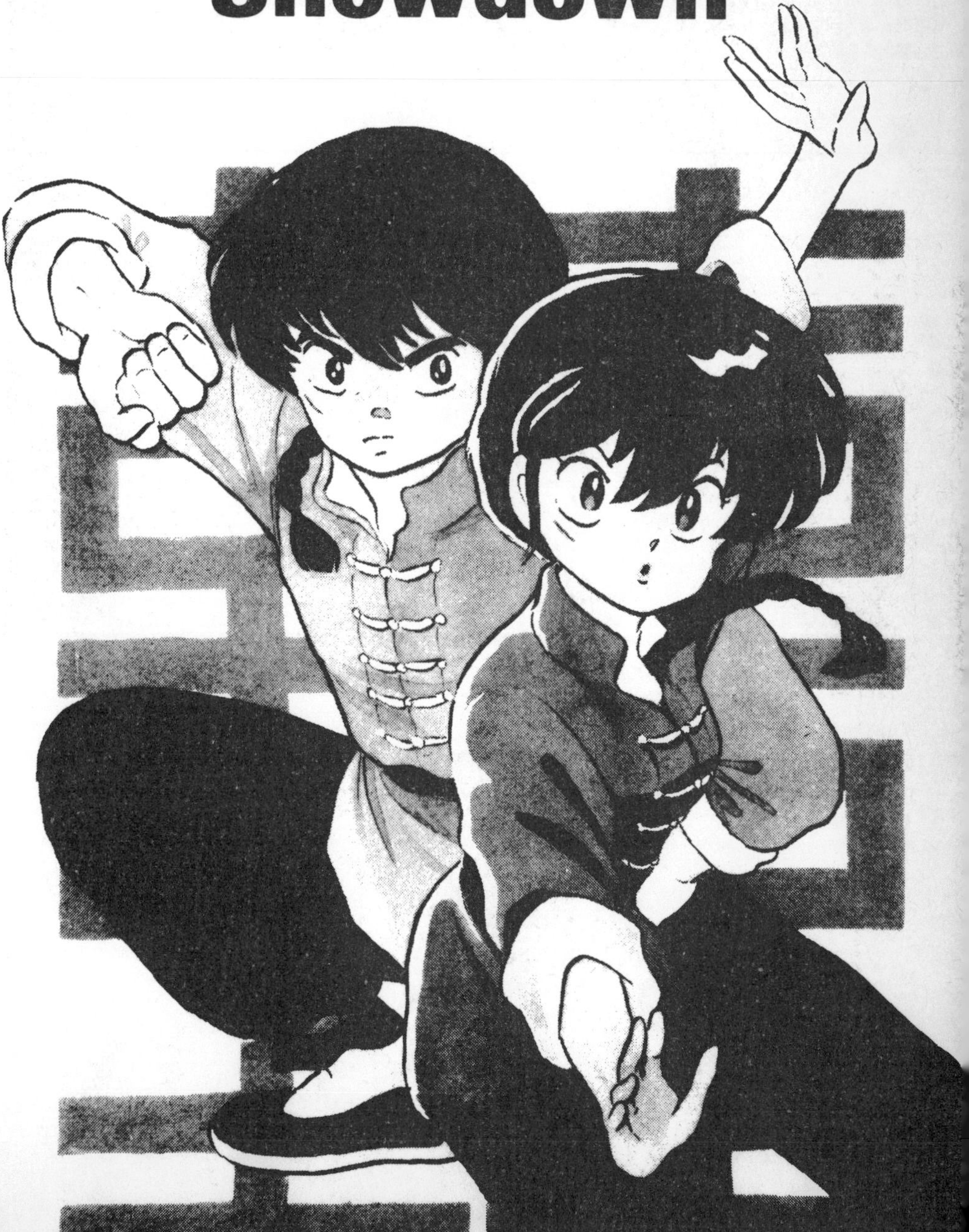

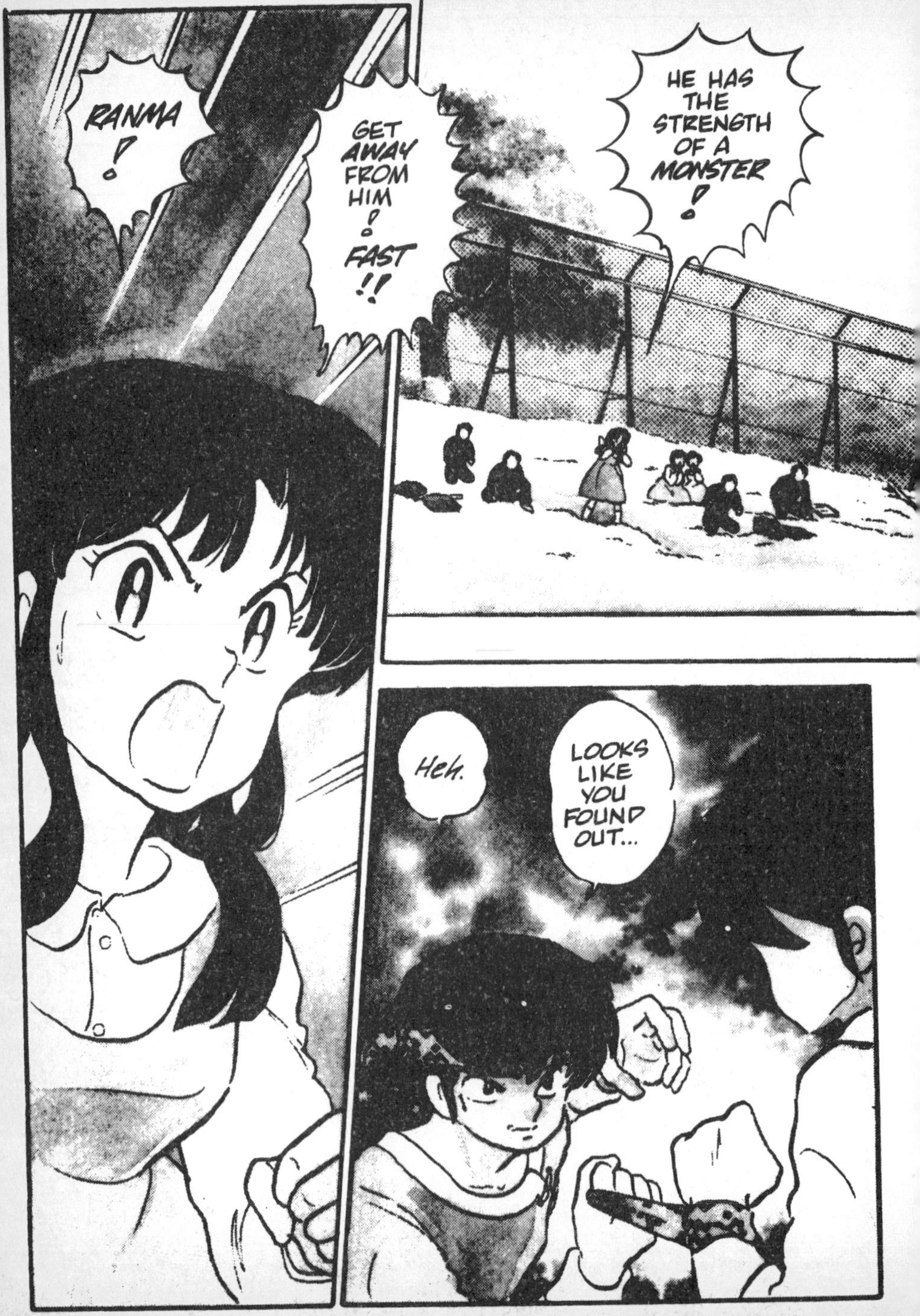
RANMA!
GET AWAY FROM HIM! FAST!!
HE HAS THE STRENGTH OF A MONSTER!
Heh.
LOOKS LIKE YOU FOUND OUT...

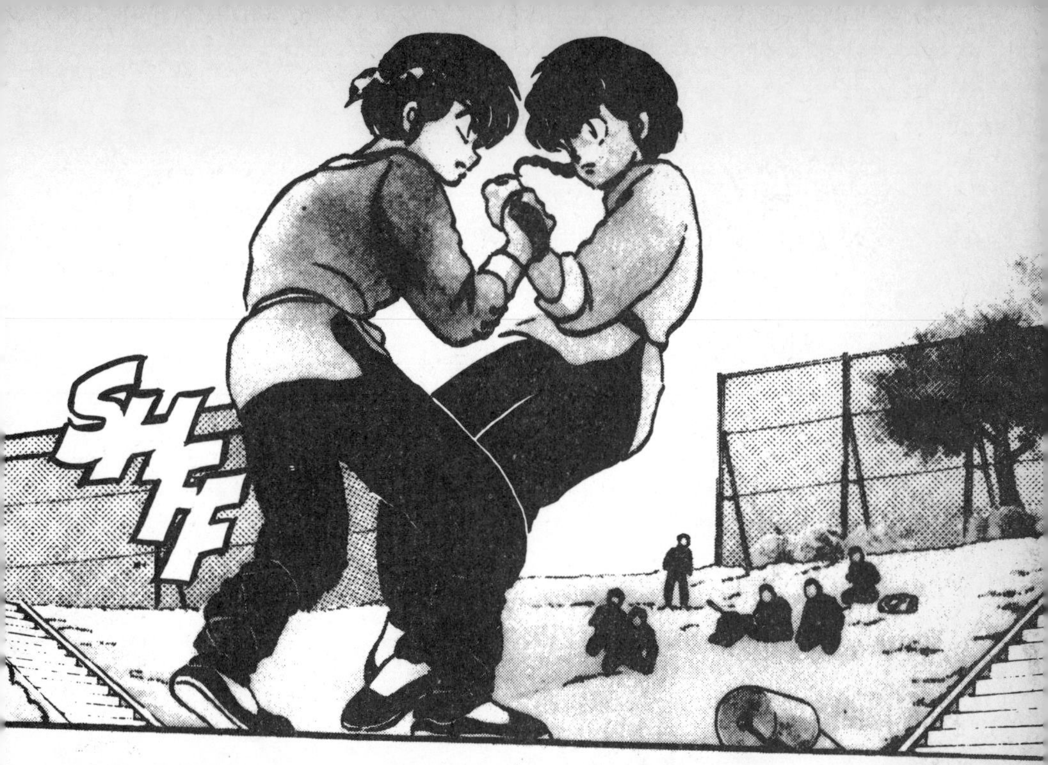
SHFF

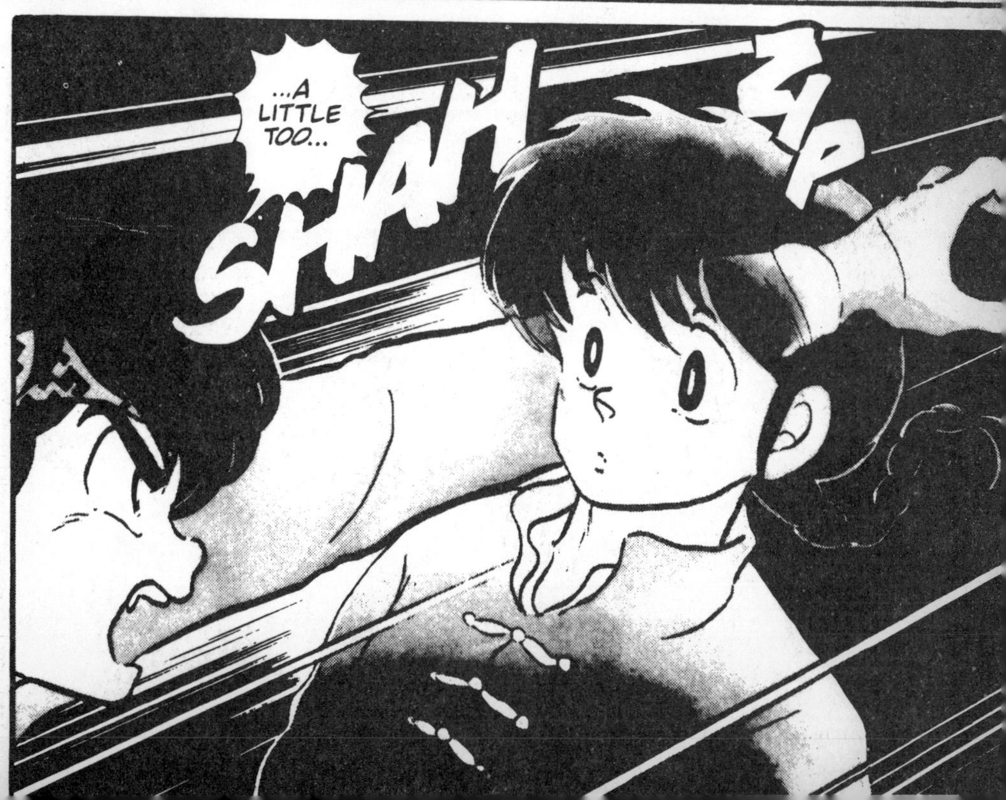
ZIP
SHAH
...A LITTLE TOO...

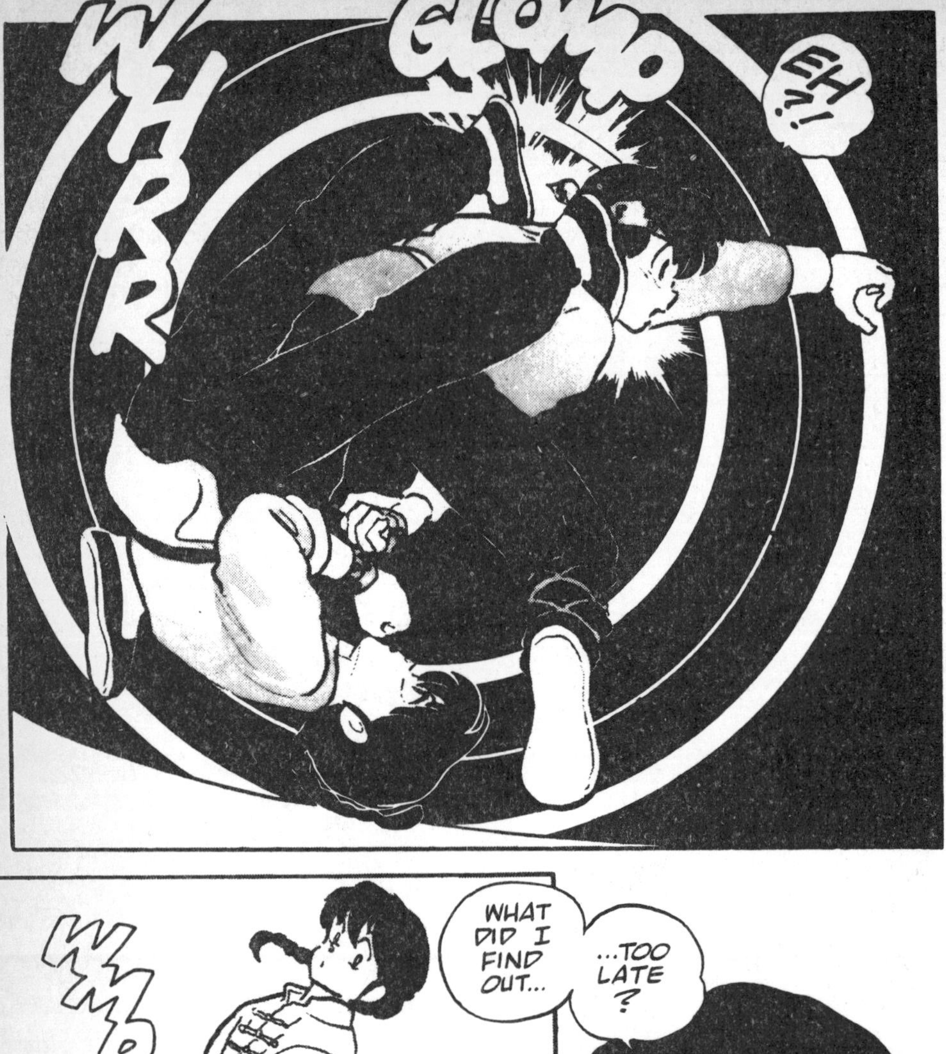
WHRR
GLOMP
EH?!
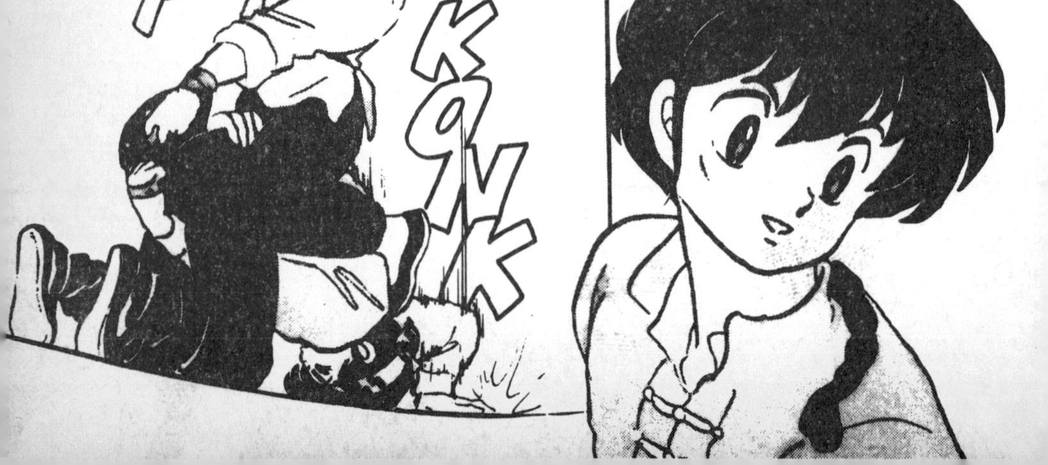
WMP
KONK
WHAT DID I FIND OUT...
...TOO LATE?

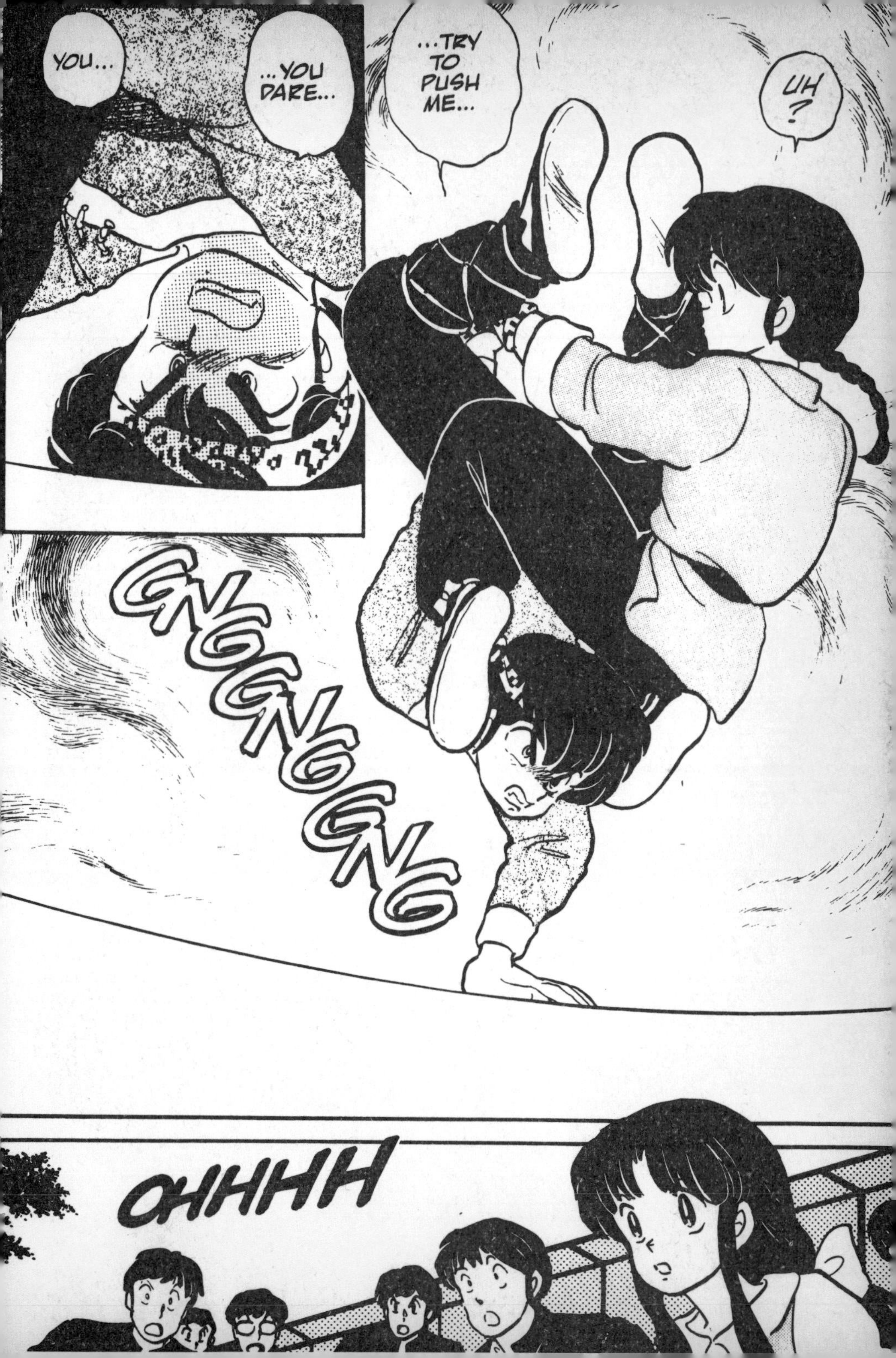
YOU...
...YOU DARE...
...TRY TO PUSH ME...
UH?
GNGNGNGNG
OHHHH

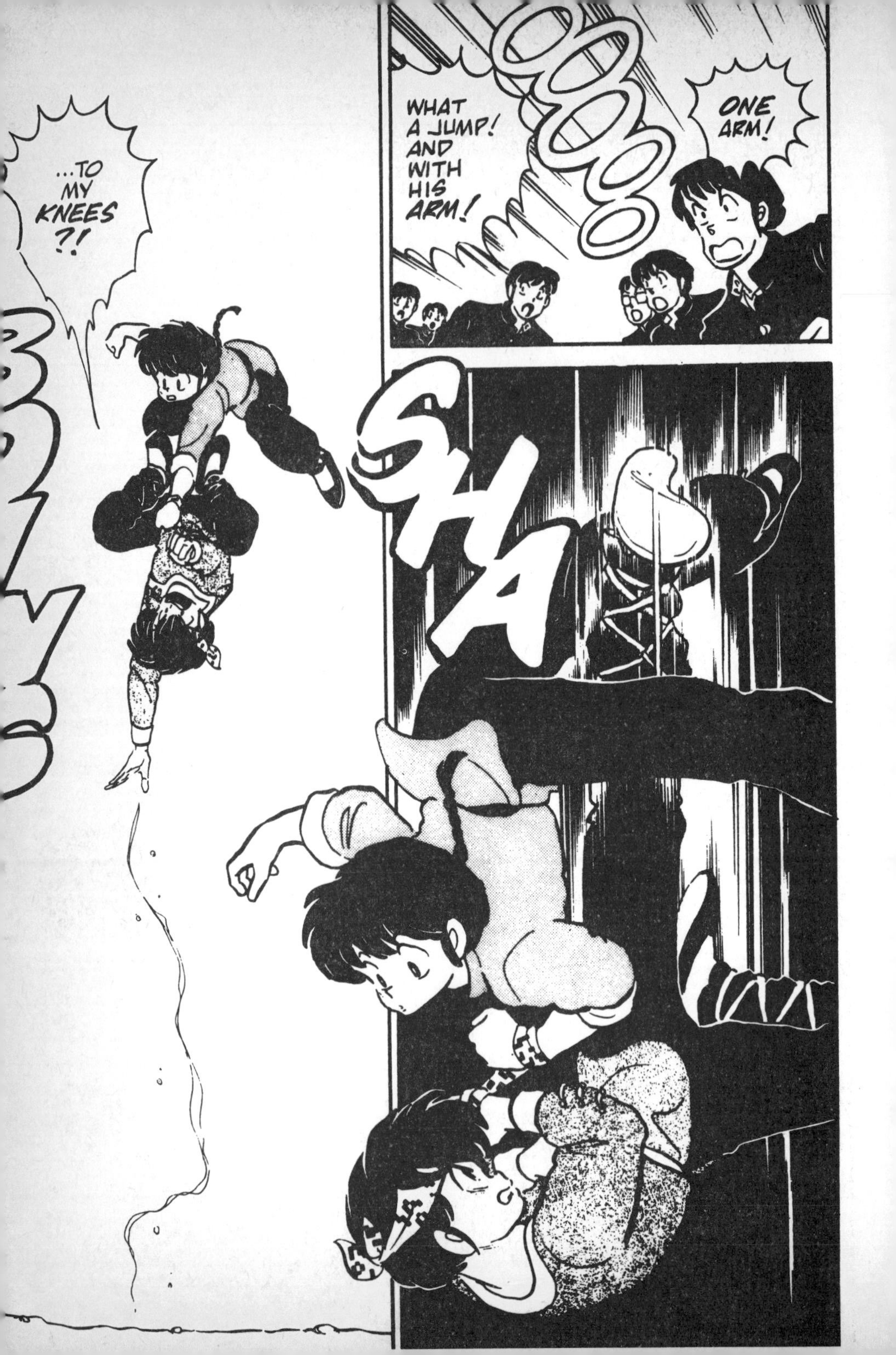
ONE ARM!
WHAT A JUMP! AND WITH HIS ARM!
OOOOO
SHA
...TO MY KNEES ?!

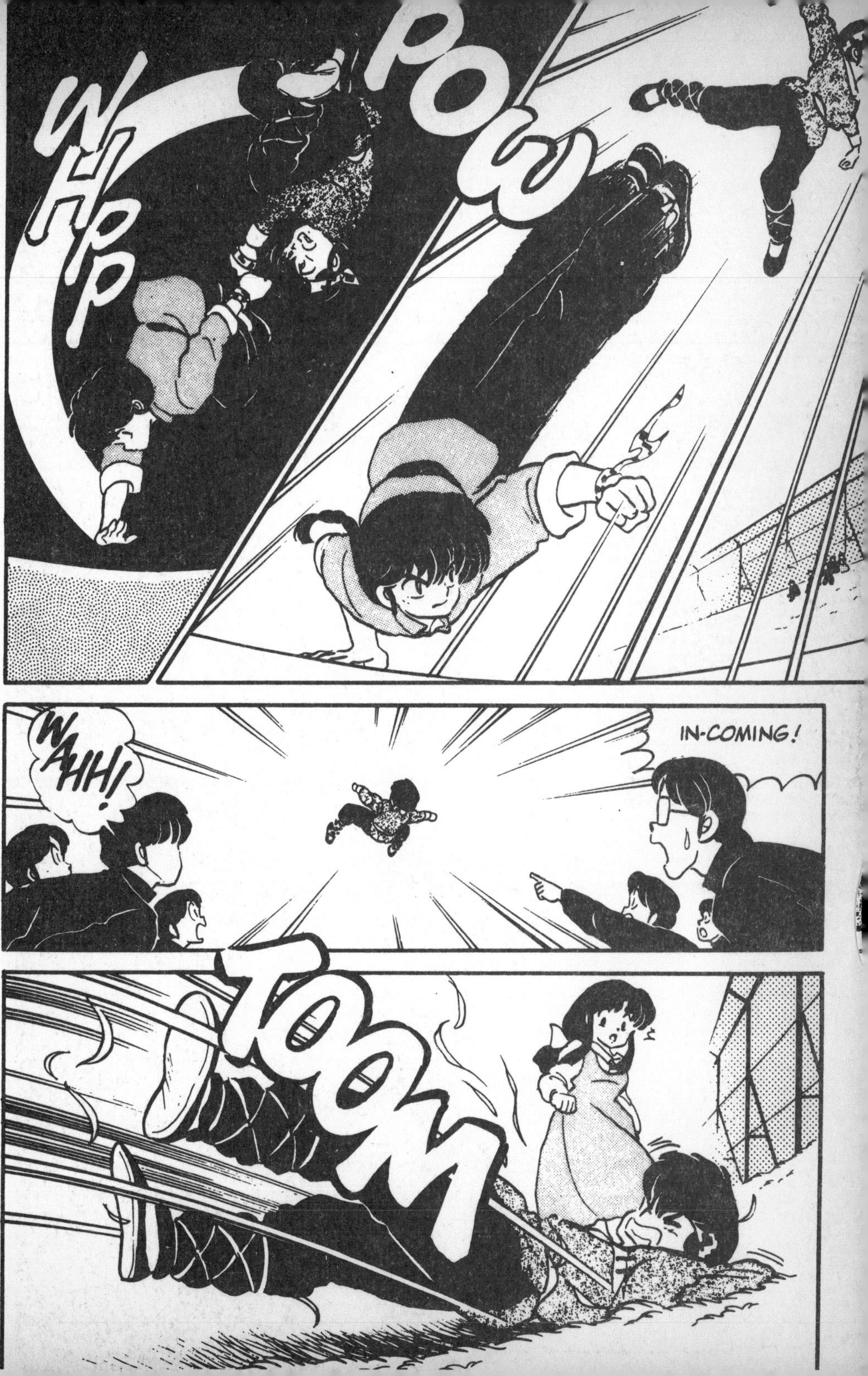
POW
WHIP
IN-COMING!
WAHH!
TOOM

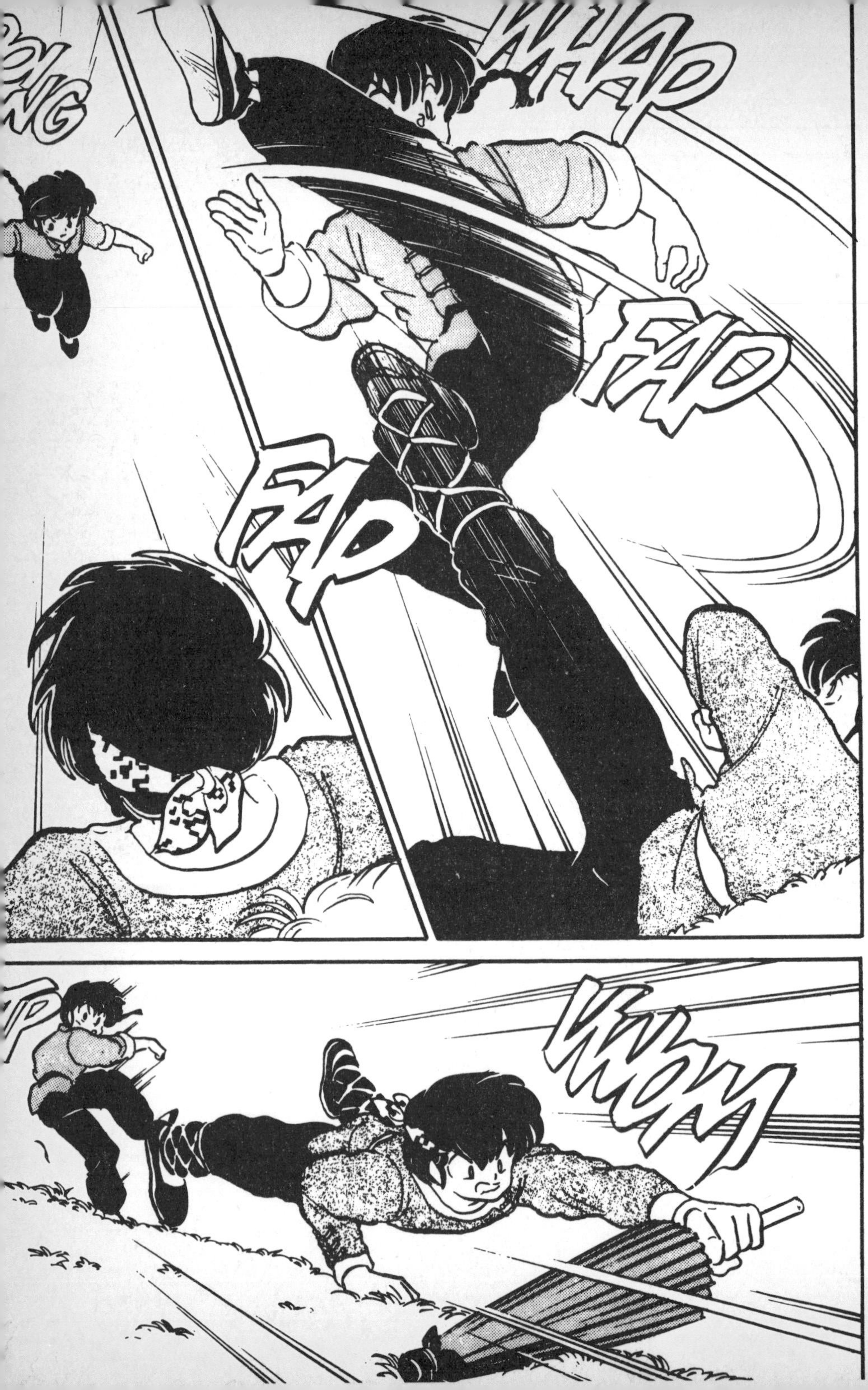
WHAP
FAP
FAP
VWOM

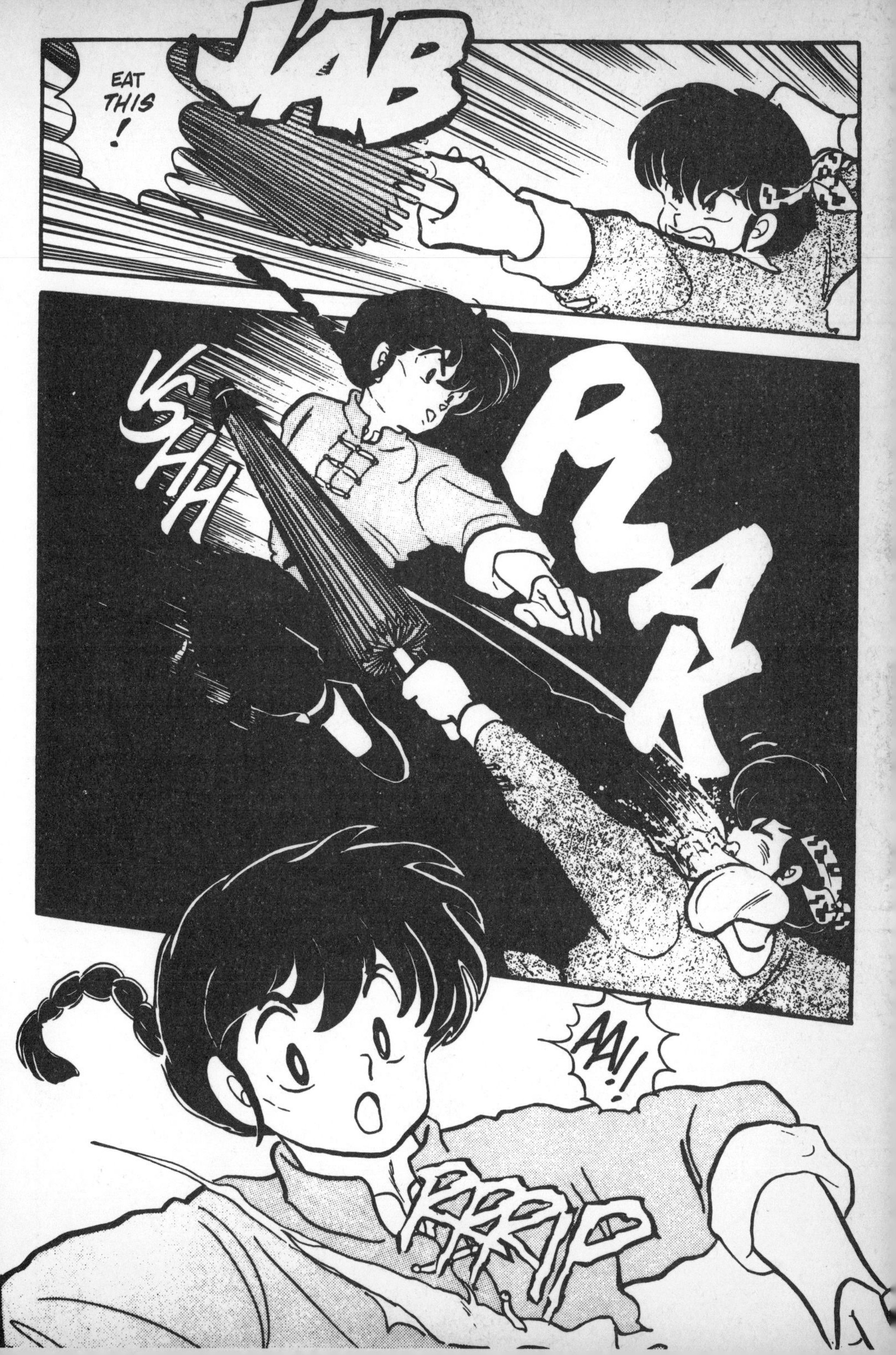
JAB
EAT THIS !
VSHHH
PLAK
AAA!!
RRRIP

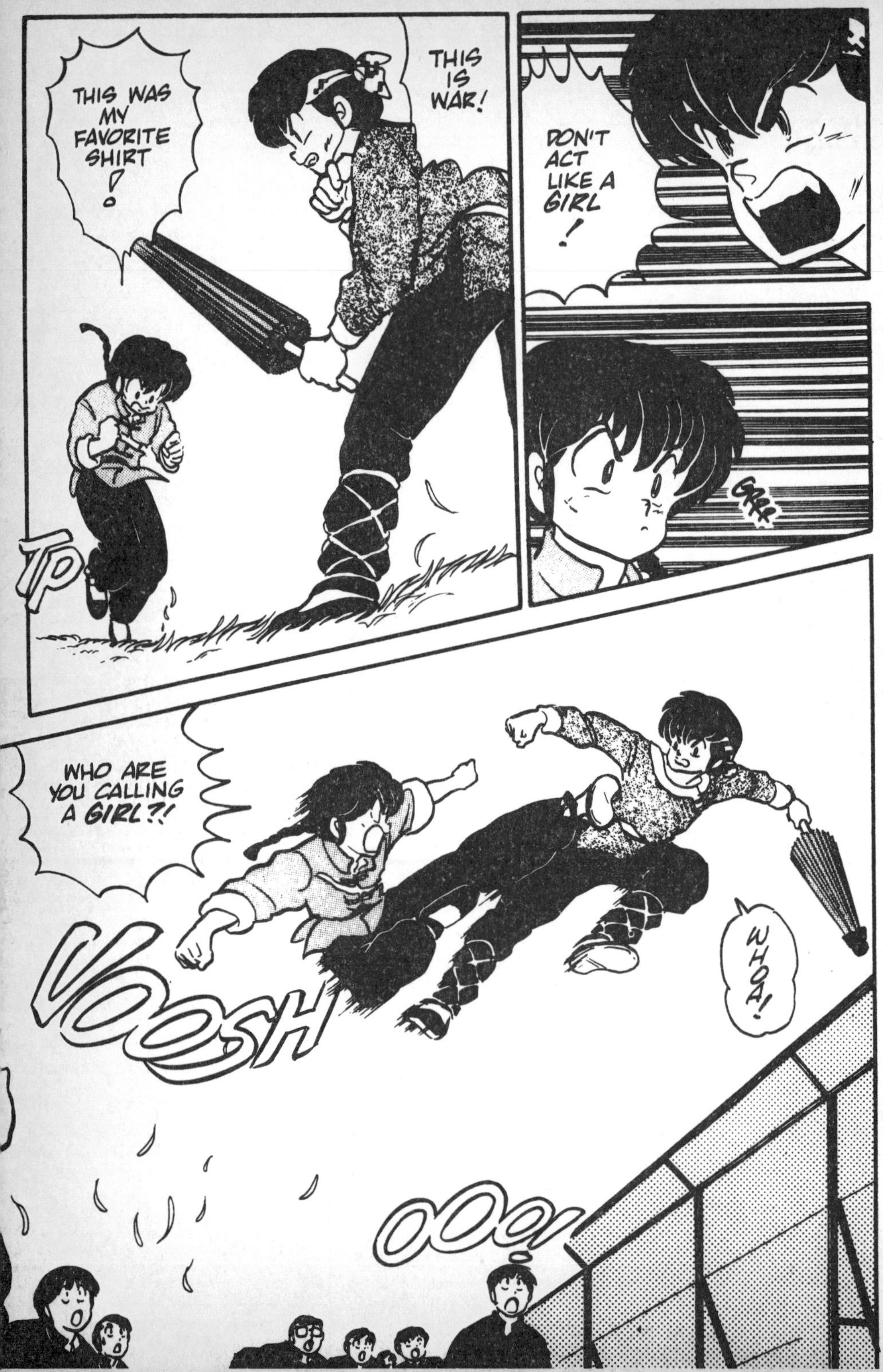
DON'T ACT LIKE A GIRL!
GRRR
THIS IS WAR!
THIS WAS MY FAVORITE SHIRT!
TP
WHO ARE YOU CALLING A GIRL?!
WHOA!
VOOSH
OOO!

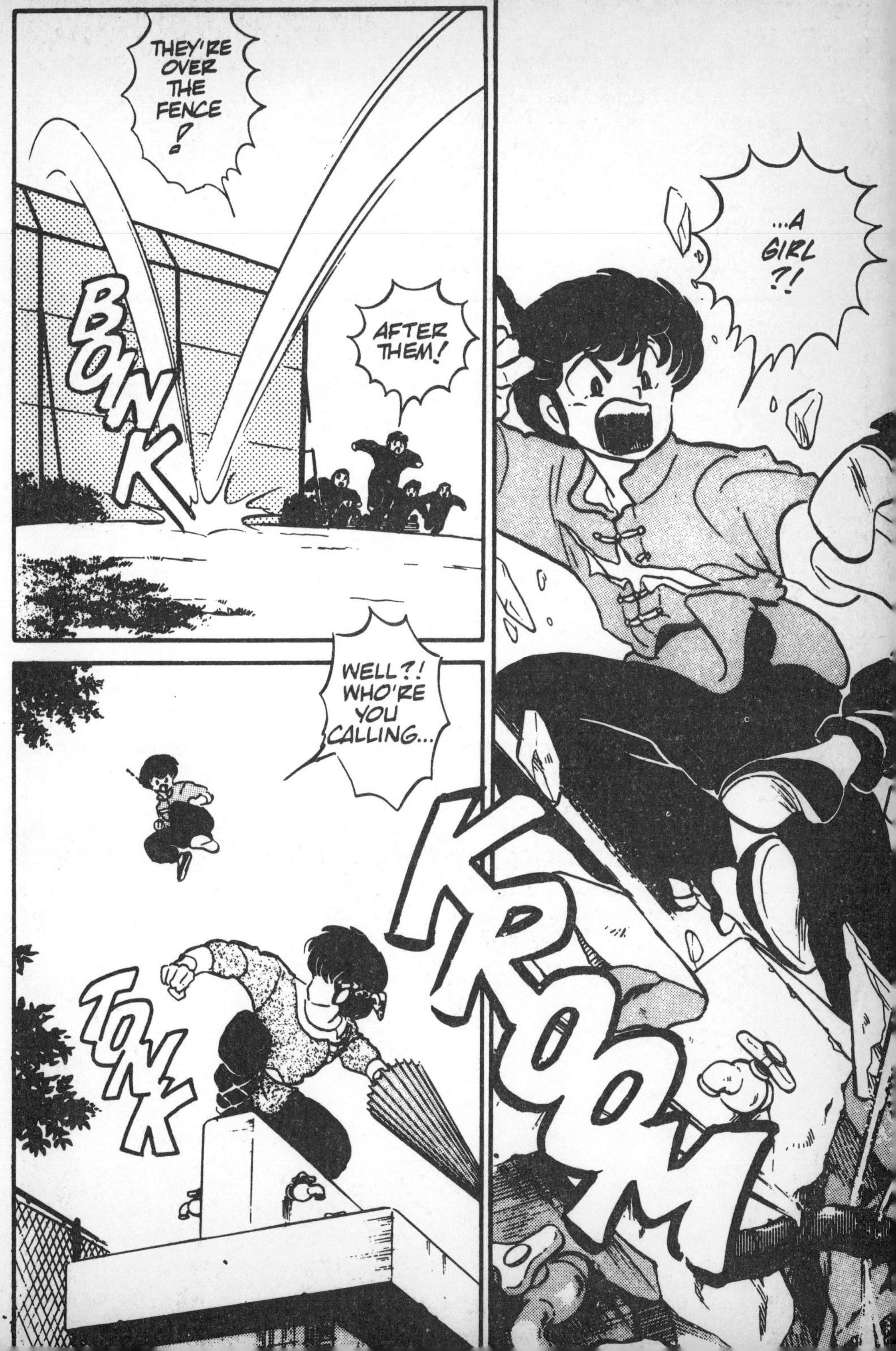
THEY'RE OVER THE FENCE!
BONK
AFTER THEM!
WELL?! WHO'RE YOU CALLING...
TONK
...A GIRL ?!
KROOM

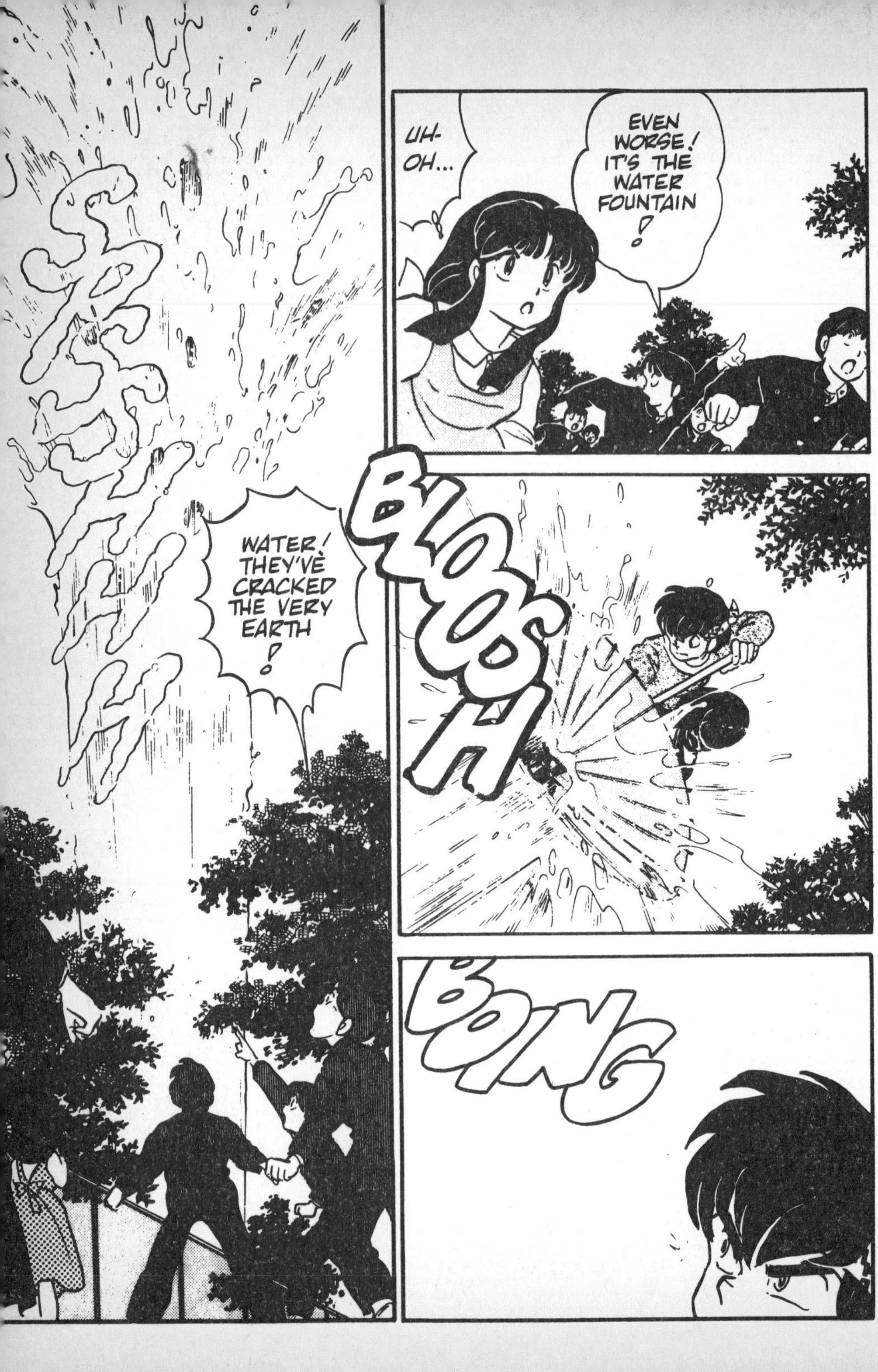
WATER! THEY'VE CRACKED THE VERY EARTH!
UH-OH...
EVEN WORSE! IT'S THE WATER FOUNTAIN!
BLOOSH
BOING

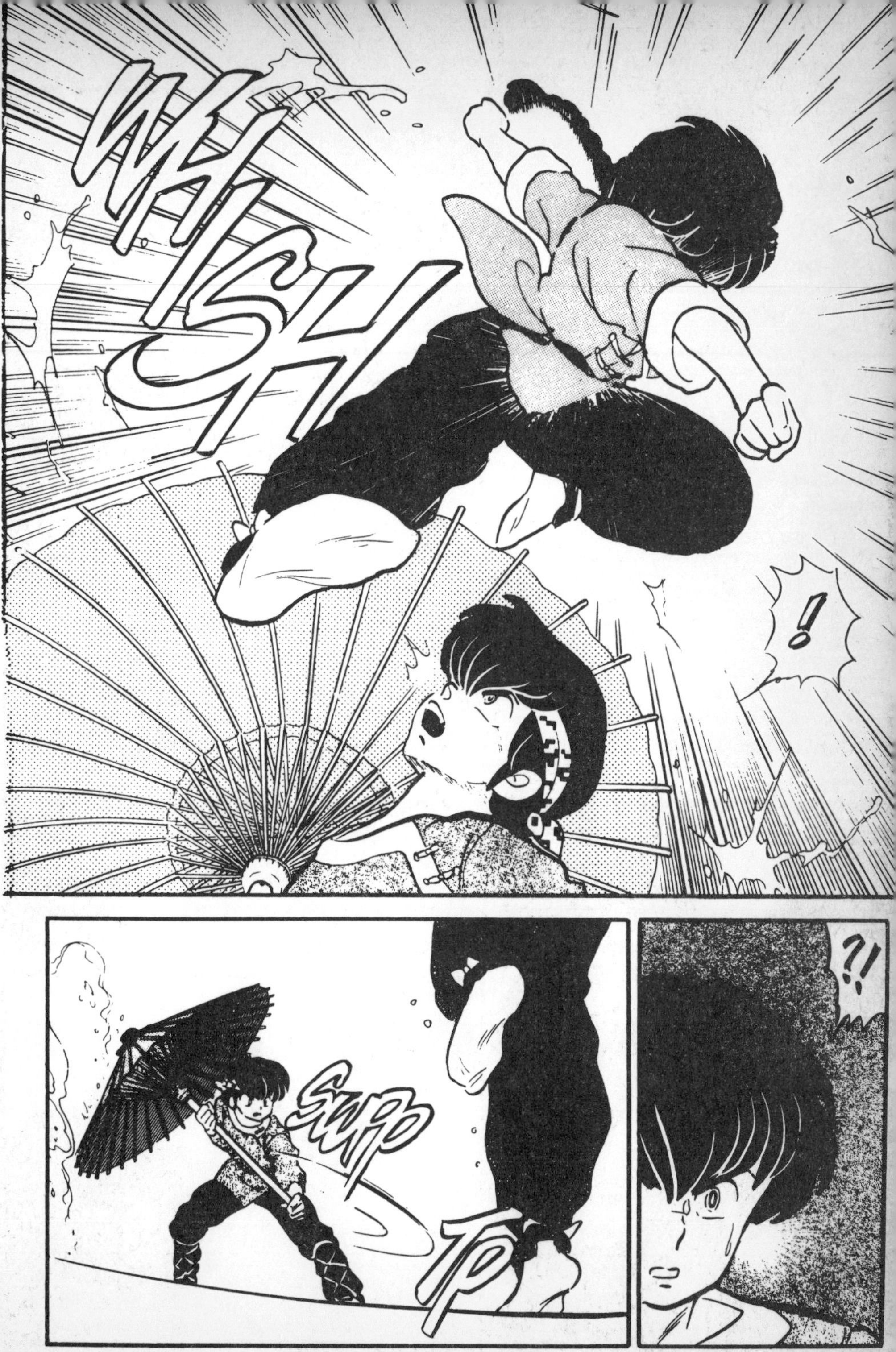
WHISH
!
?!
Swip
Tp

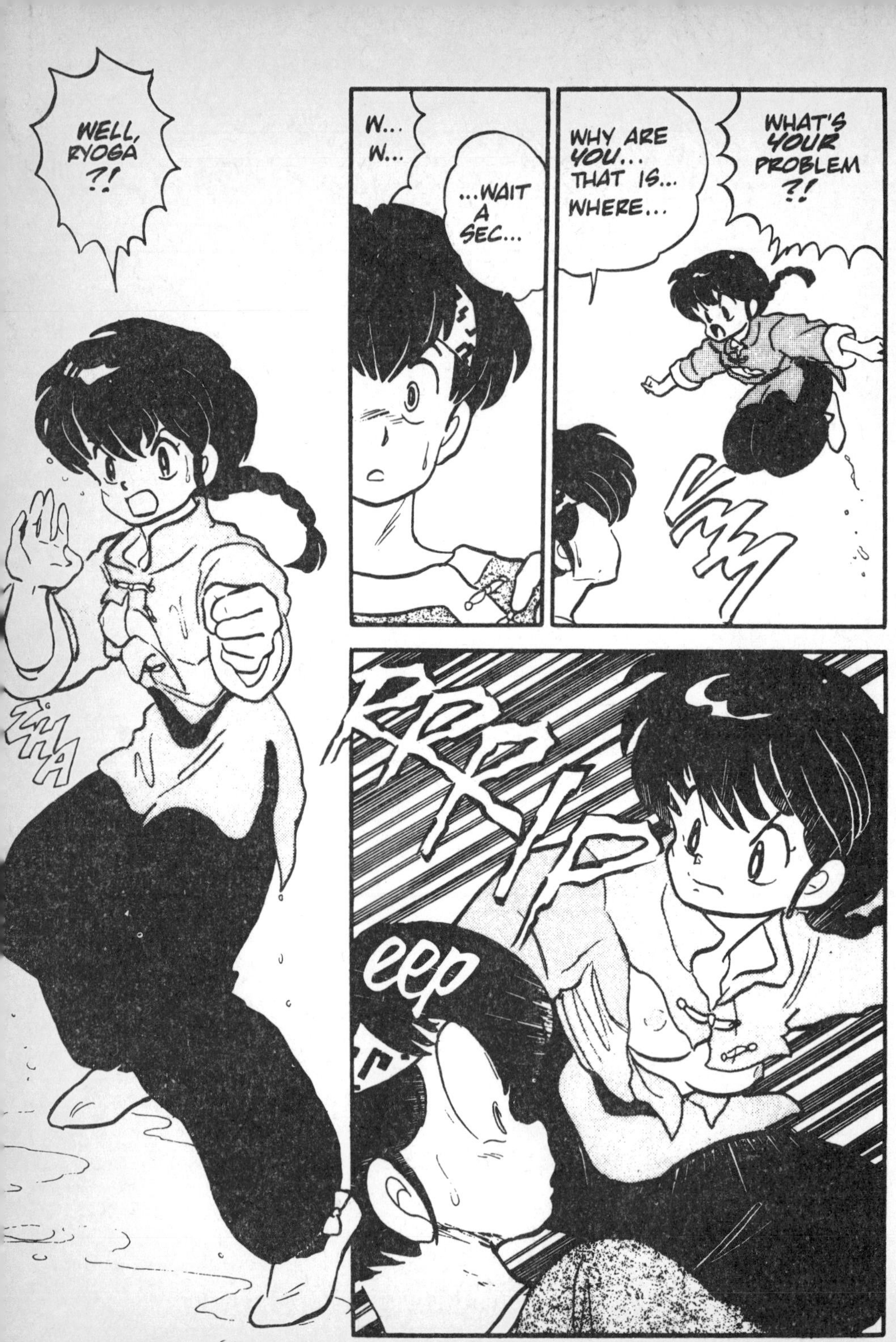
WELL, RYOGA ?!
W... W...
...WAIT A SEC...
WHY ARE YOU... THAT IS... WHERE...
WHAT'S YOUR PROBLEM ?!
eep

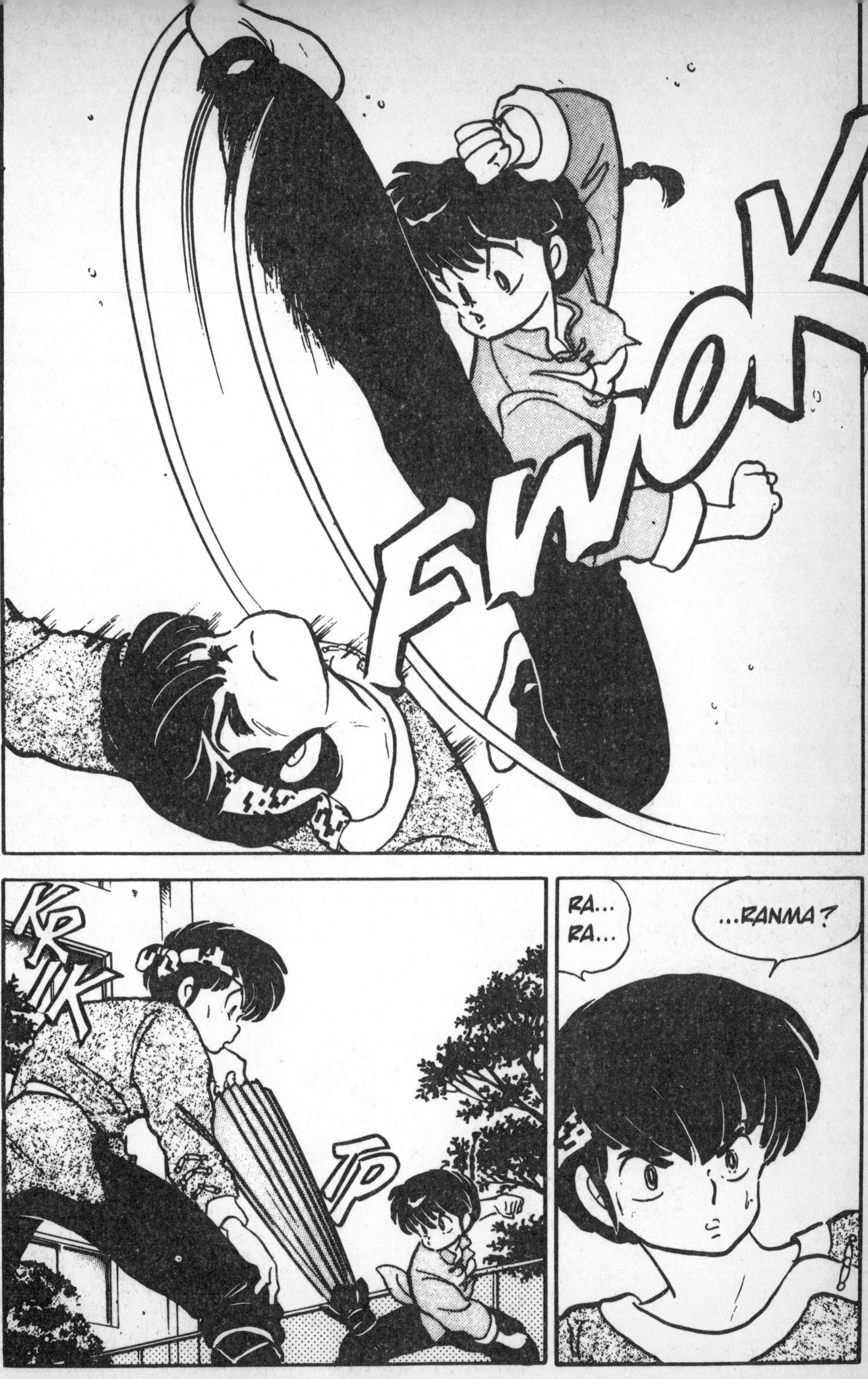
FWOK
KRIK
TP
RA... RA...
...RANMA?

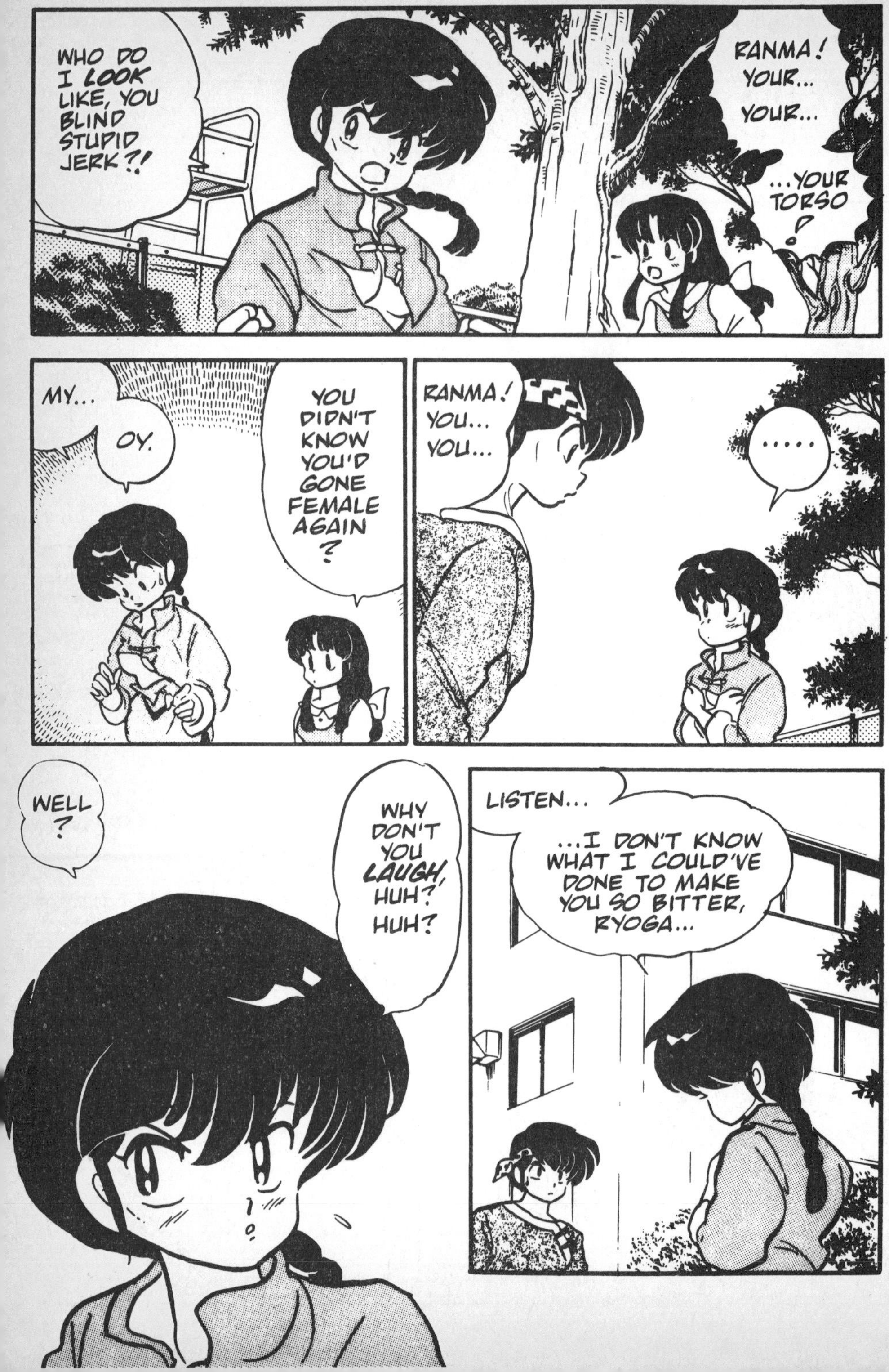
WHO DO I *LOOK* LIKE, YOU BLIND STUPID JERK?!
RANMA! YOUR... YOUR...
...YOUR TORSO?
MY...
OY.
YOU DIDN'T KNOW YOU'D GONE FEMALE AGAIN?
RANMA! YOU... YOU...
.....
WELL?
WHY DON'T YOU *LAUGH*, HUH? HUH?
LISTEN...
...I DON'T KNOW WHAT I COULD'VE DONE TO MAKE YOU SO BITTER, RYOGA...

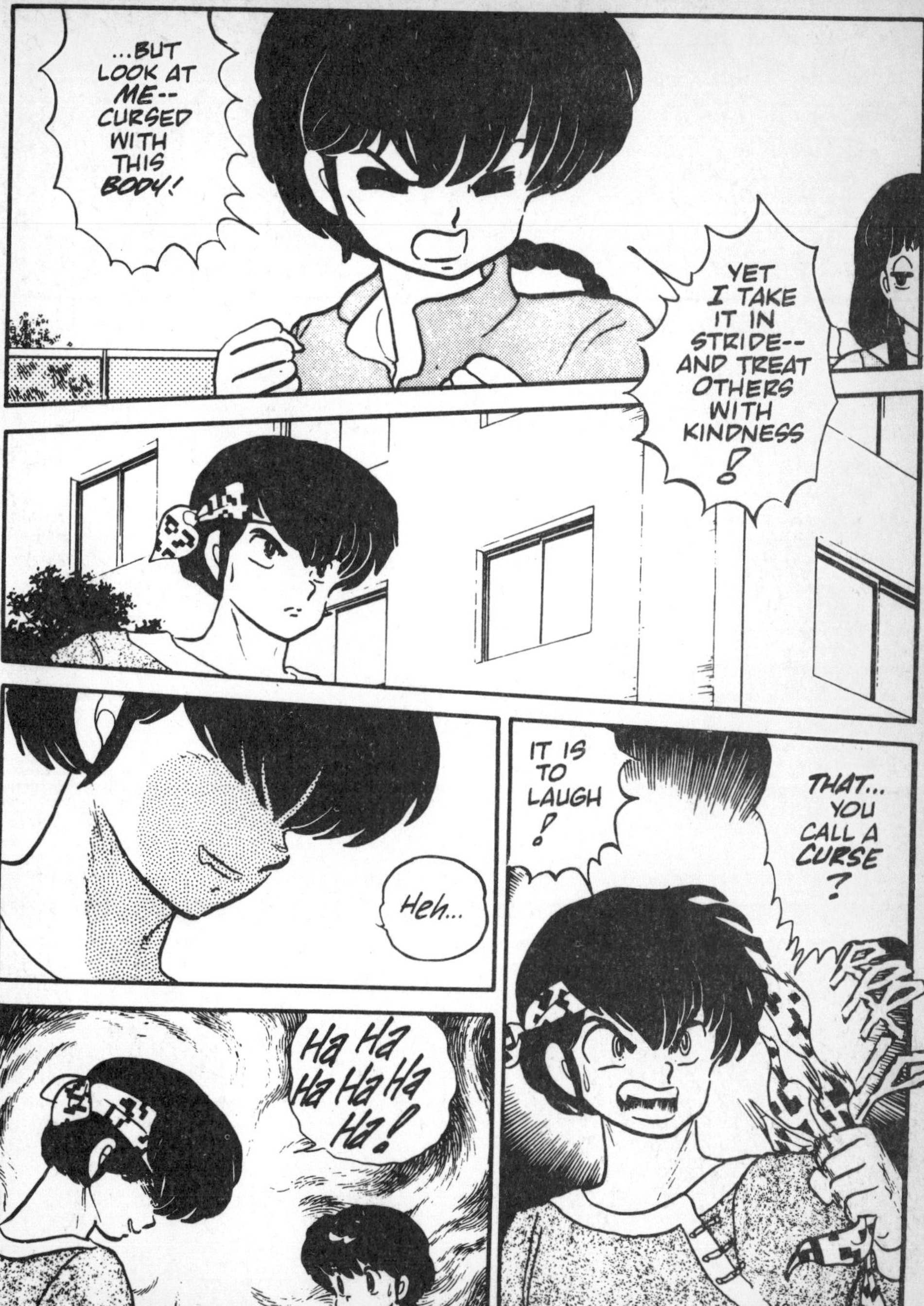
...BUT LOOK AT ME-- CURSED WITH THIS BODY!
YET I TAKE IT IN STRIDE-- AND TREAT OTHERS WITH KINDNESS!
Heh...
IT IS TO LAUGH!
THAT... YOU CALL A CURSE?
Ha Ha Ha Ha Ha Ha!

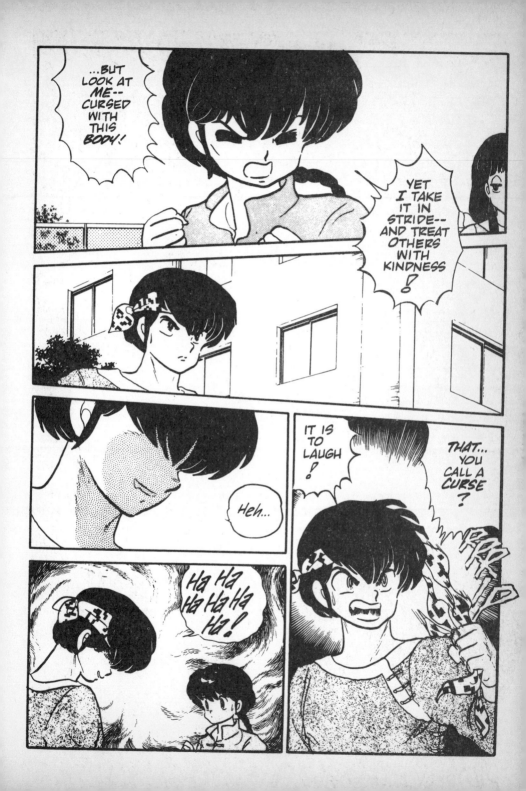

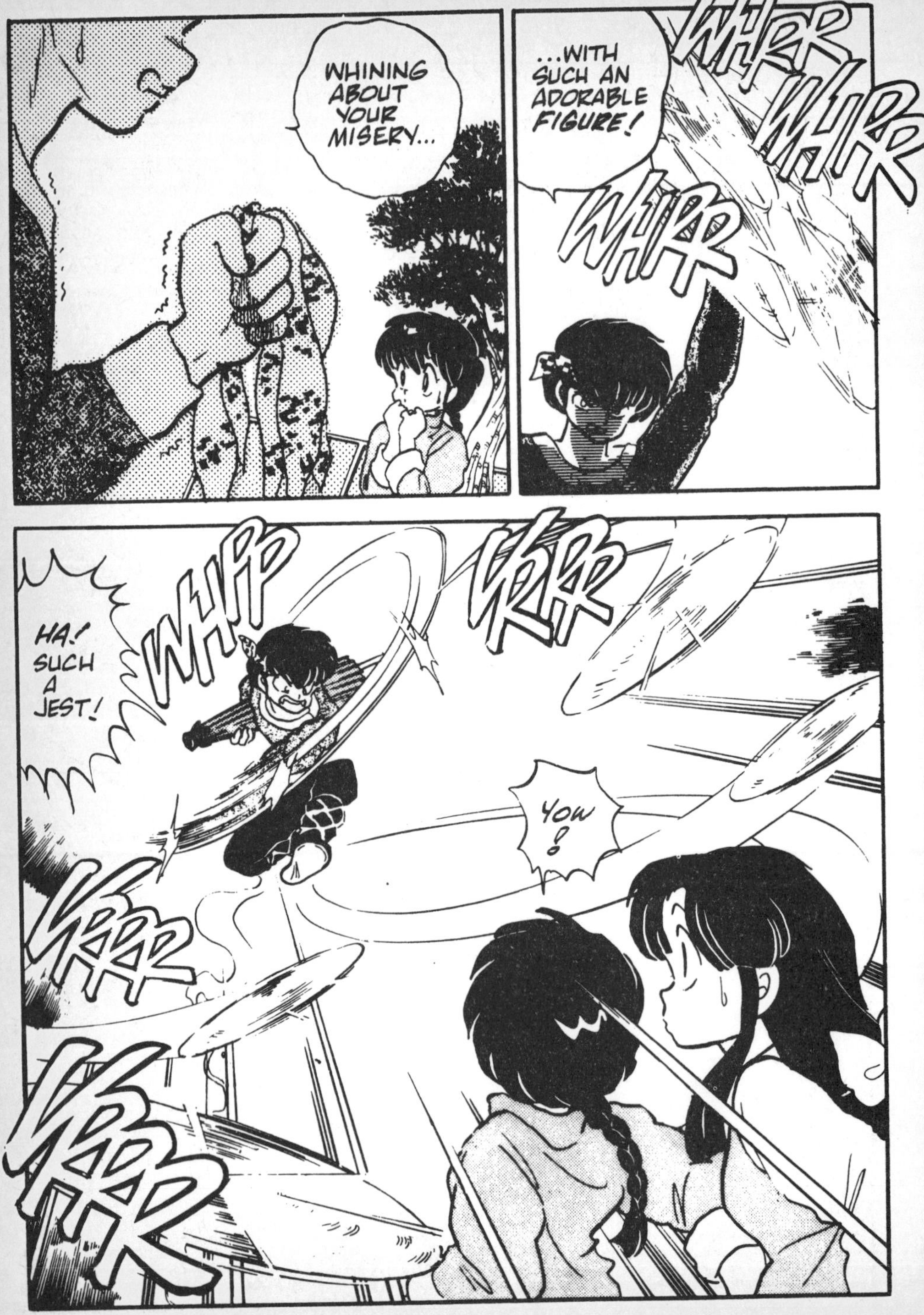
WHINING ABOUT YOUR MISERY...
...WITH SUCH AN ADORABLE FIGURE!
WHIRR WHIRR
WHIRR
HA! SUCH A JEST!
WHIRR
VRRR
YOW!
VRRR
VRRRR

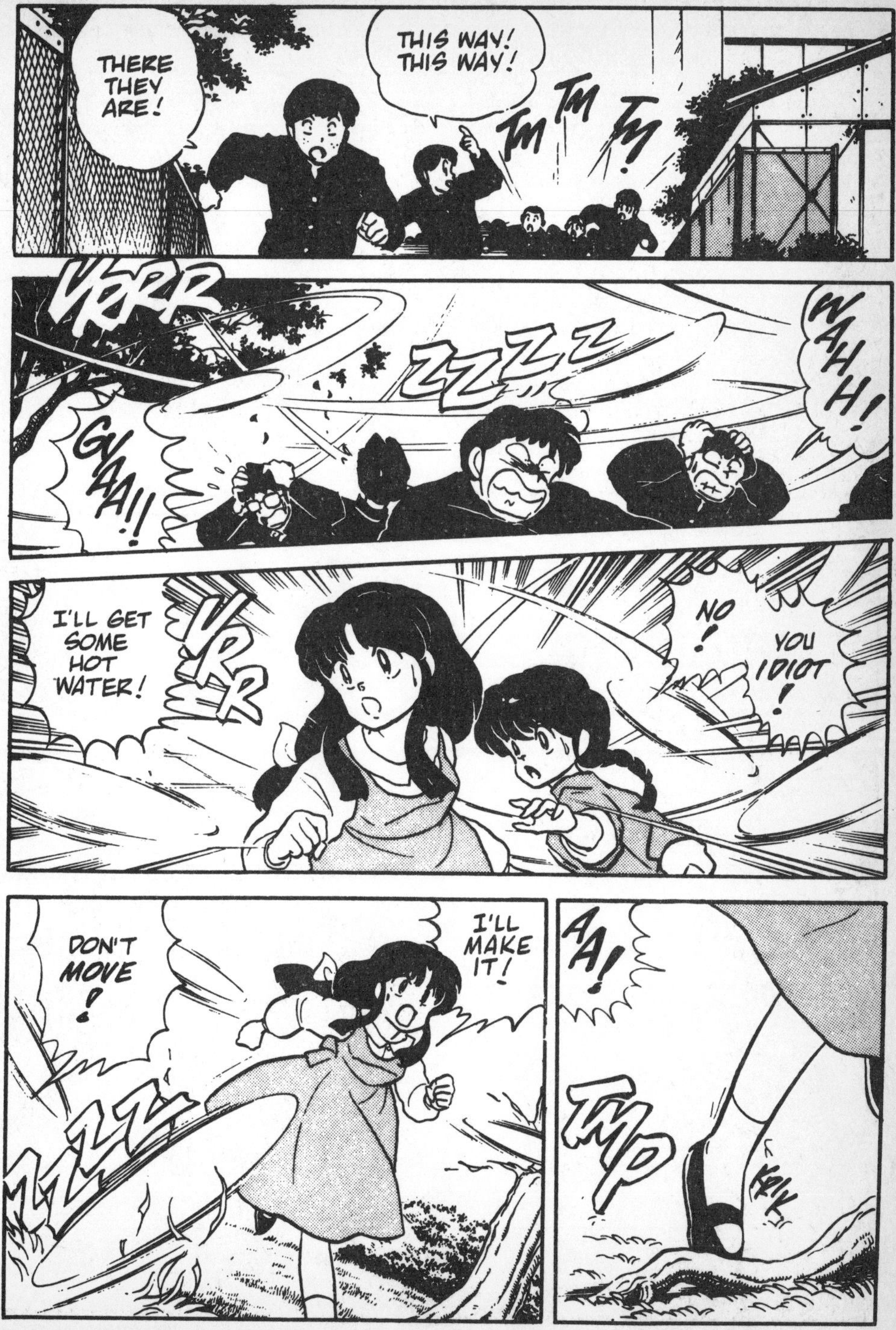
THIS WAY! THIS WAY!
THERE THEY ARE!
TM TM TM!
VRRR
WAHHH!
ZZZZZZ
GYAAA!!
NO! YOU IDIOT!
VRR
I'LL GET SOME HOT WATER!
I'LL MAKE IT!
DON'T MOVE!
ZZZZ
AAA!
TMP
KRIK

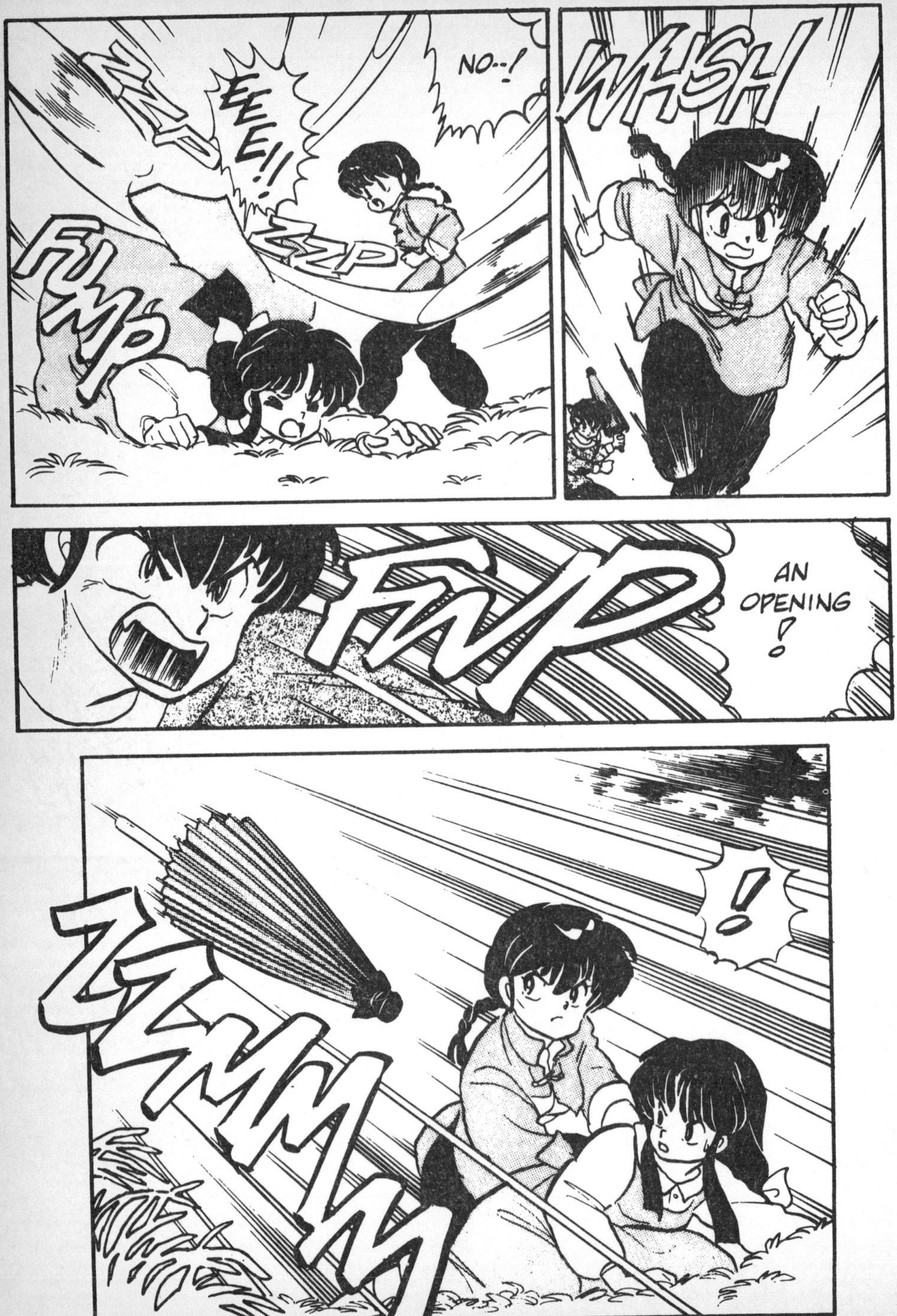
WHSH
NO--!
EEEE!!
ZZZP
ZZZP
FUMP
AN OPENING!
FWP
!
ZWMMM

PART THIRTEEN
A Bad Cut

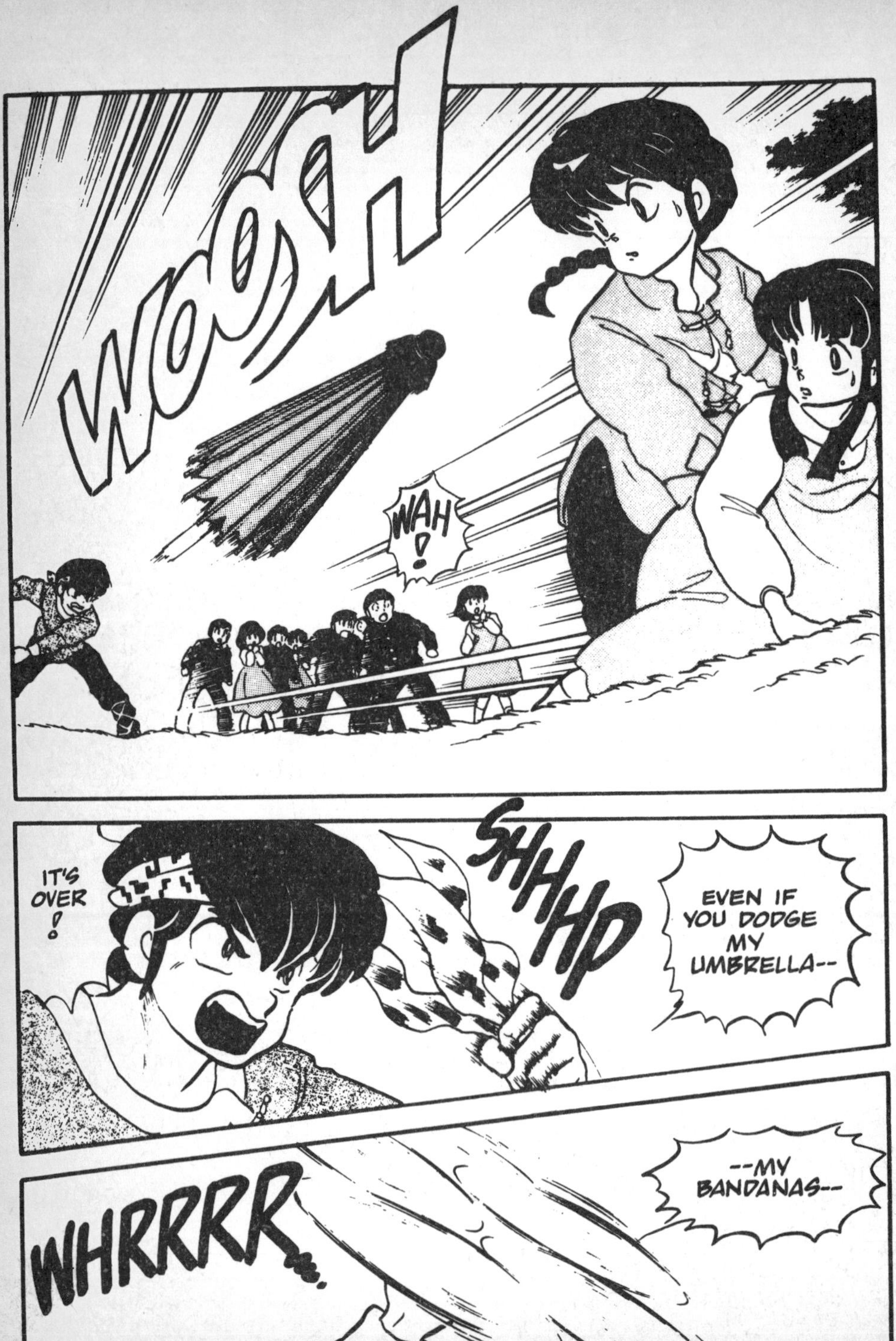
WOOSH
WAH!
SHHHP
EVEN IF YOU DODGE MY UMBRELLA--
IT'S OVER!
WHRRRR...
--MY BANDANAS--

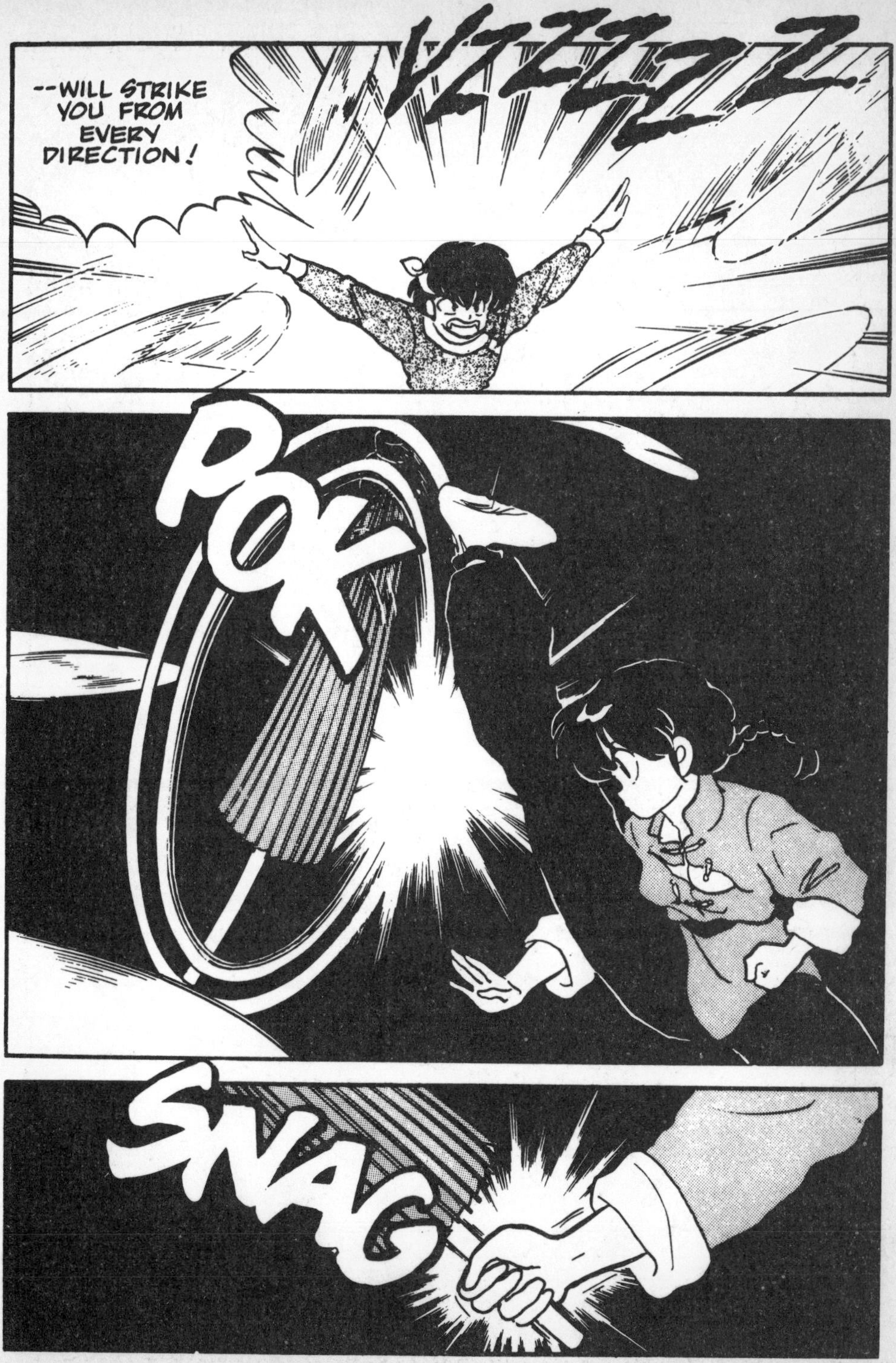
--WILL STRIKE YOU FROM EVERY DIRECTION!
VZZZZZ
POK
SNAG

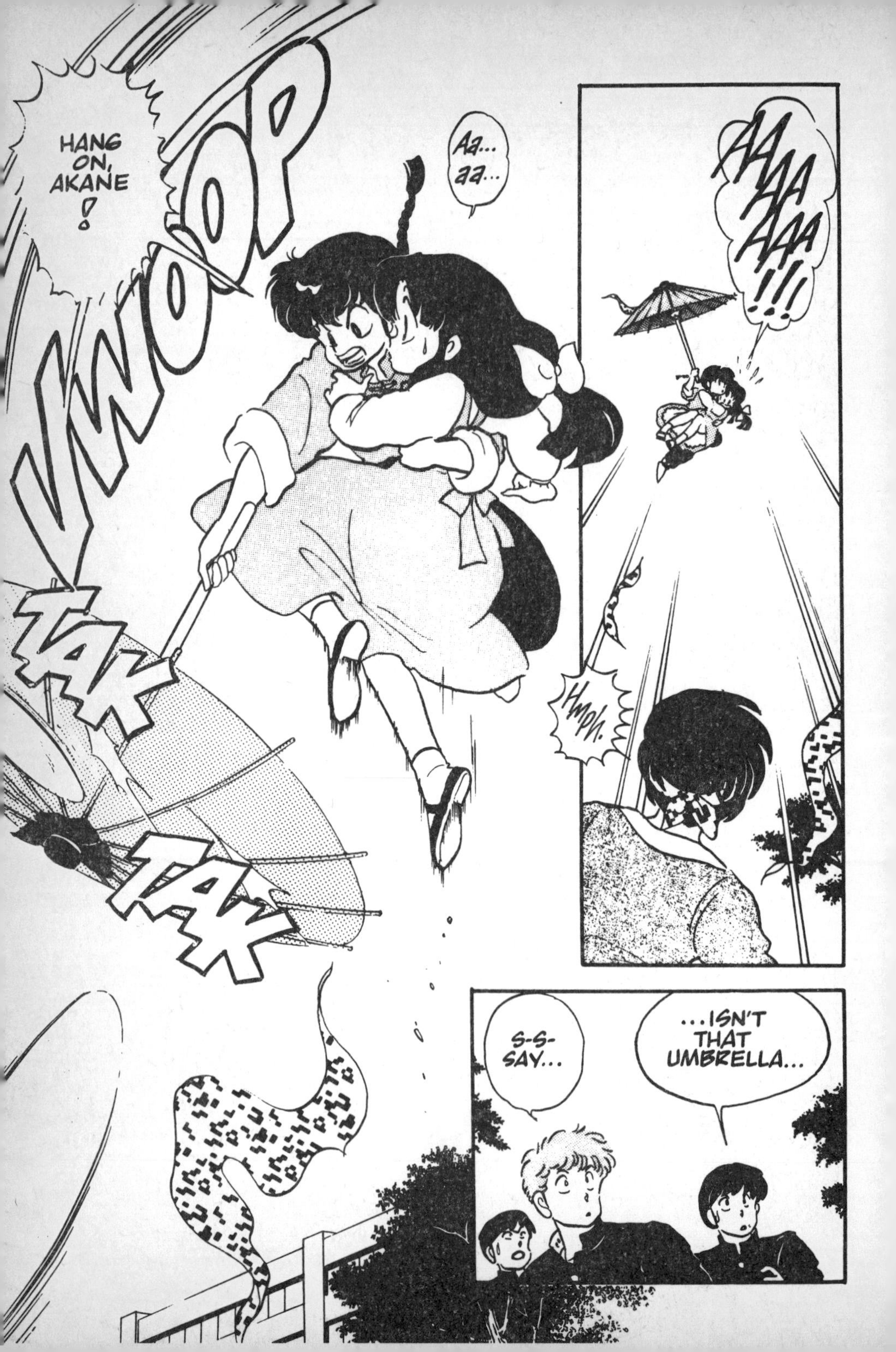

AAAAAAAA!!!
Aa... aa...
HANG ON, AKANE!
VWOOOP
TAK
TAK
Hmph.
...ISN'T THAT UMBRELLA...
S-S-SAY...

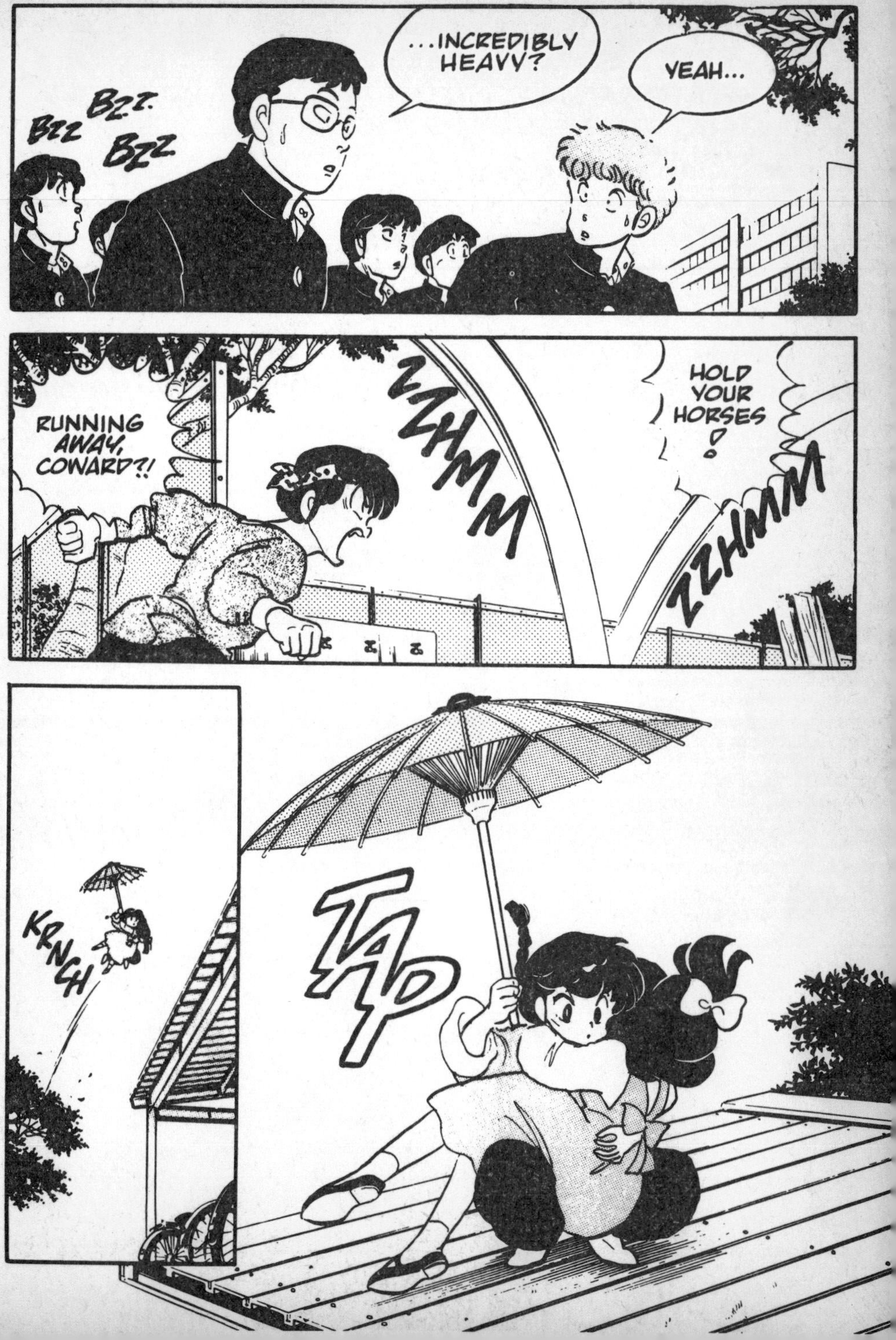
BZZ
BZZT.
BZZ
...INCREDIBLY HEAVY?
YEAH...
RUNNING AWAY, COWARD?!
VVHMMM
HOLD YOUR HORSES!
ZZHMMM
KRNCH
TAP

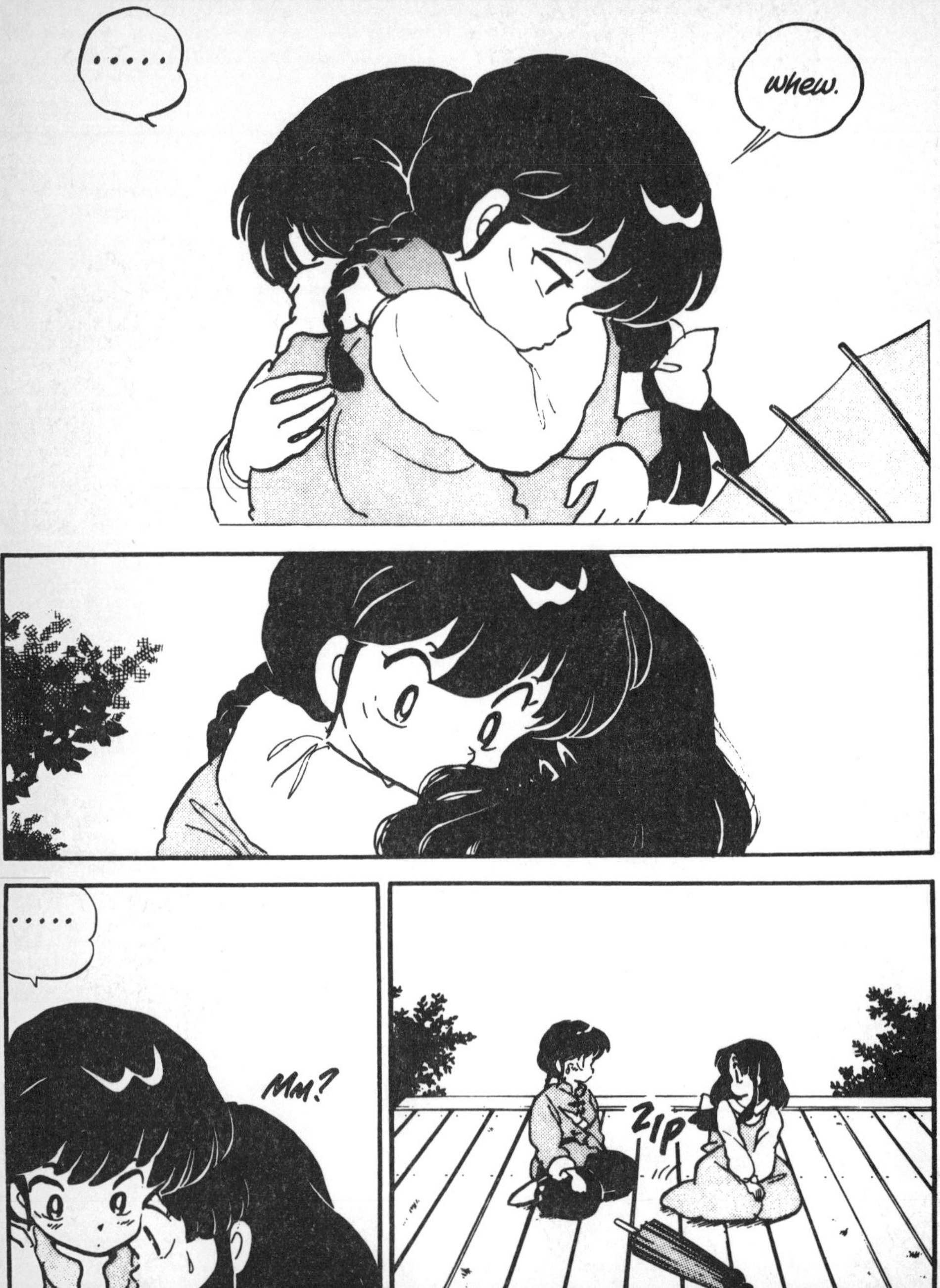

whew.
......
.....
Mm?
ZIP

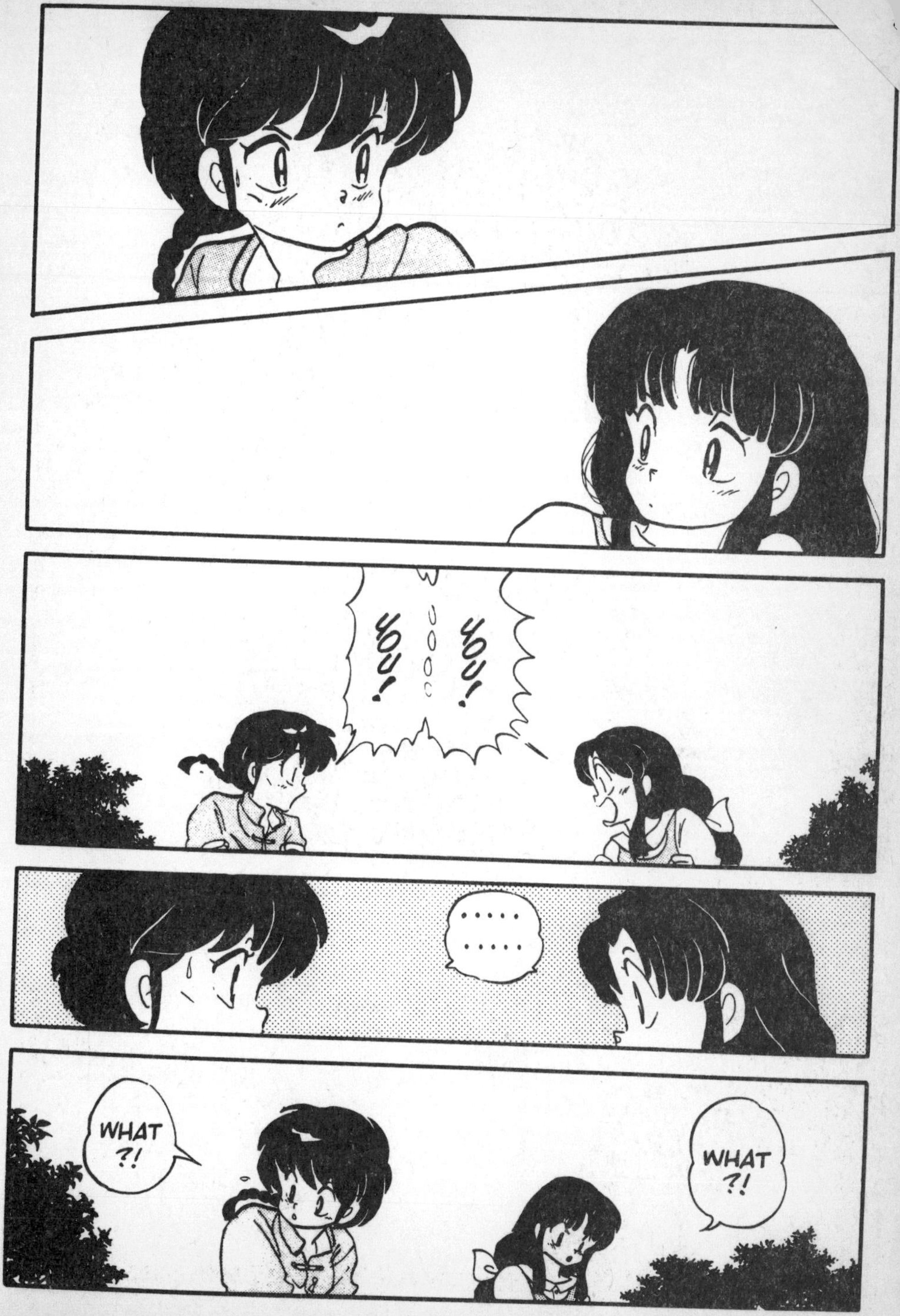
YOU!
YOU!
......
......
WHAT ?!
WHAT ?!

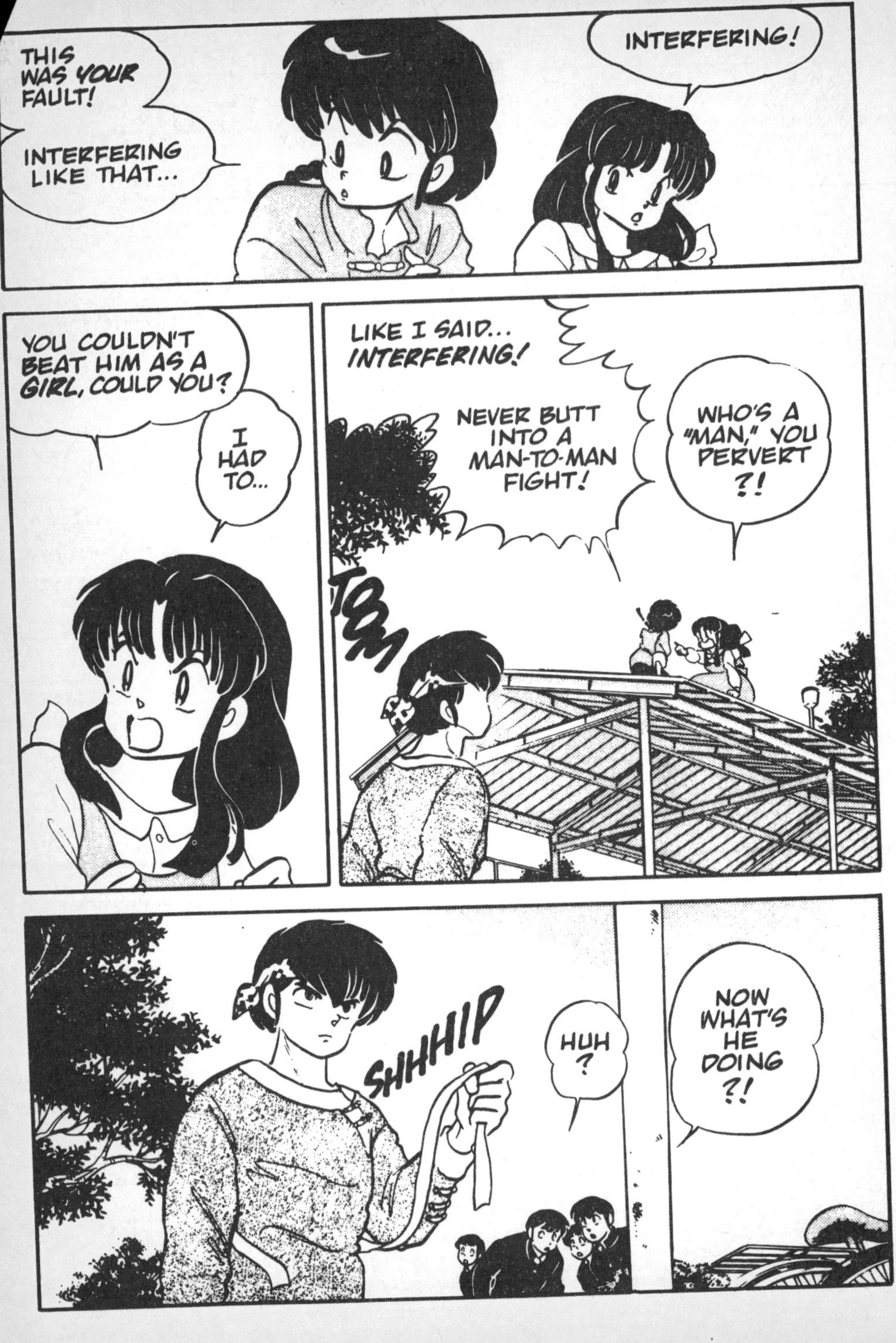
INTERFERING!
THIS WAS YOUR FAULT!
INTERFERING LIKE THAT...
LIKE I SAID... INTERFERING!
NEVER BUTT INTO A MAN-TO-MAN FIGHT!
WHO'S A "MAN," YOU PERVERT ?!
TOOM
YOU COULDN'T BEAT HIM AS A GIRL, COULD YOU?
I HAD TO...
NOW WHAT'S HE DOING ?!
HUH ?
SHHHIP

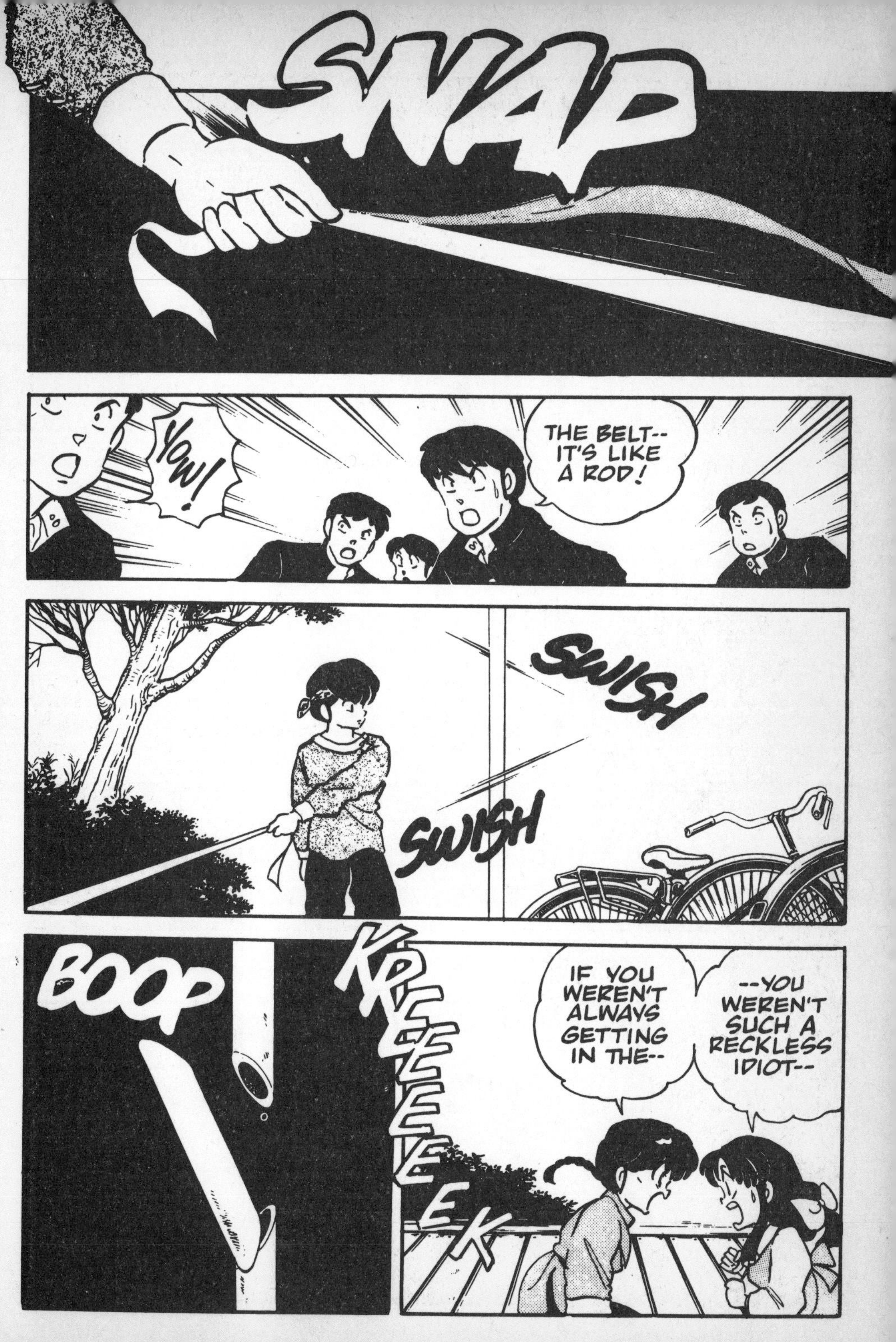
SNAP
YOW!
THE BELT-- IT'S LIKE A ROD!
SWISH
SWISH
BOOP
KREEEEEEEK
IF YOU WEREN'T ALWAYS GETTING IN THE--
--YOU WEREN'T SUCH A RECKLESS IDIOT--

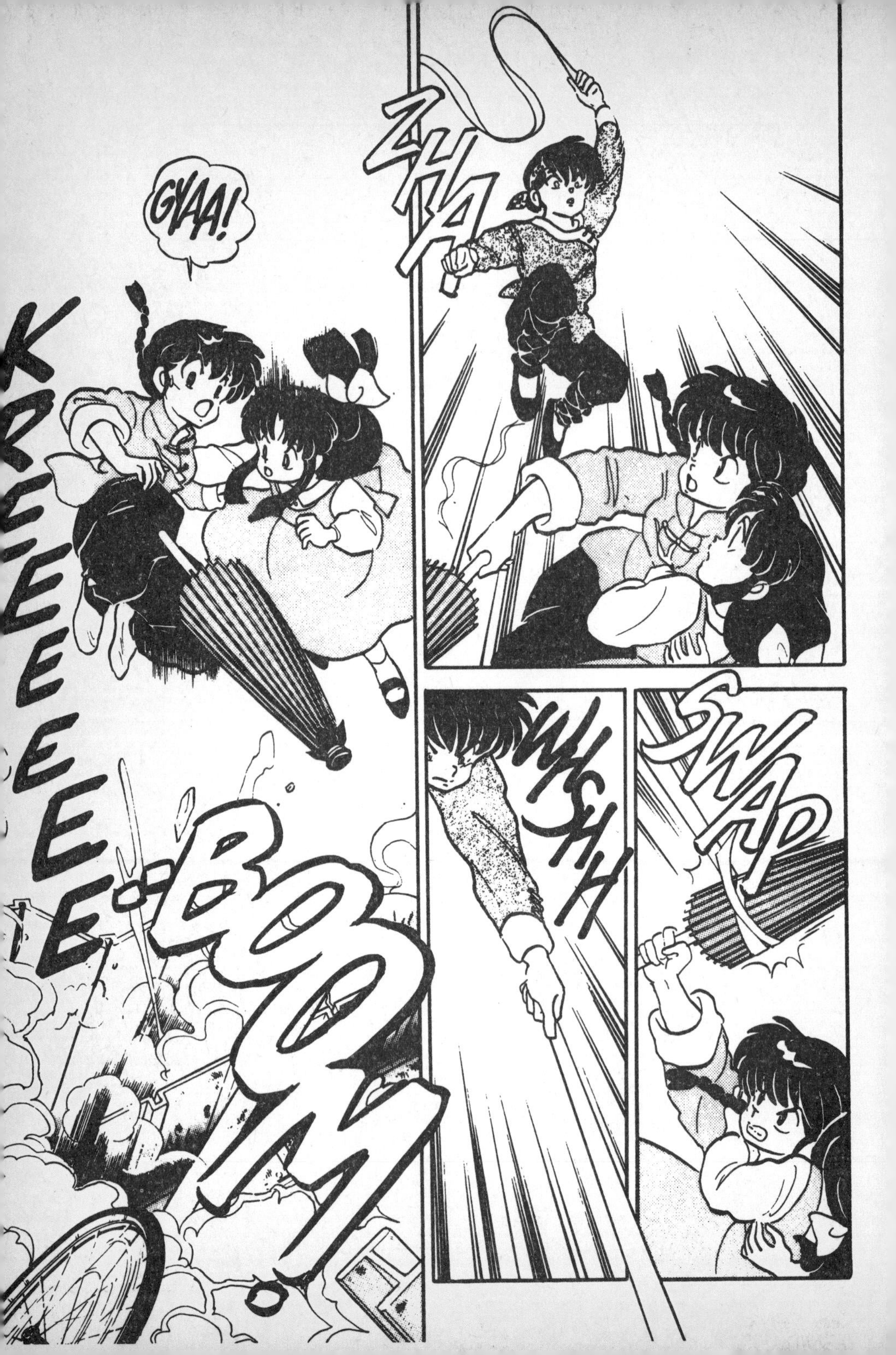
ZHA
SWAP
WHSHH
GYAA!
KREEEEEE-BOOM

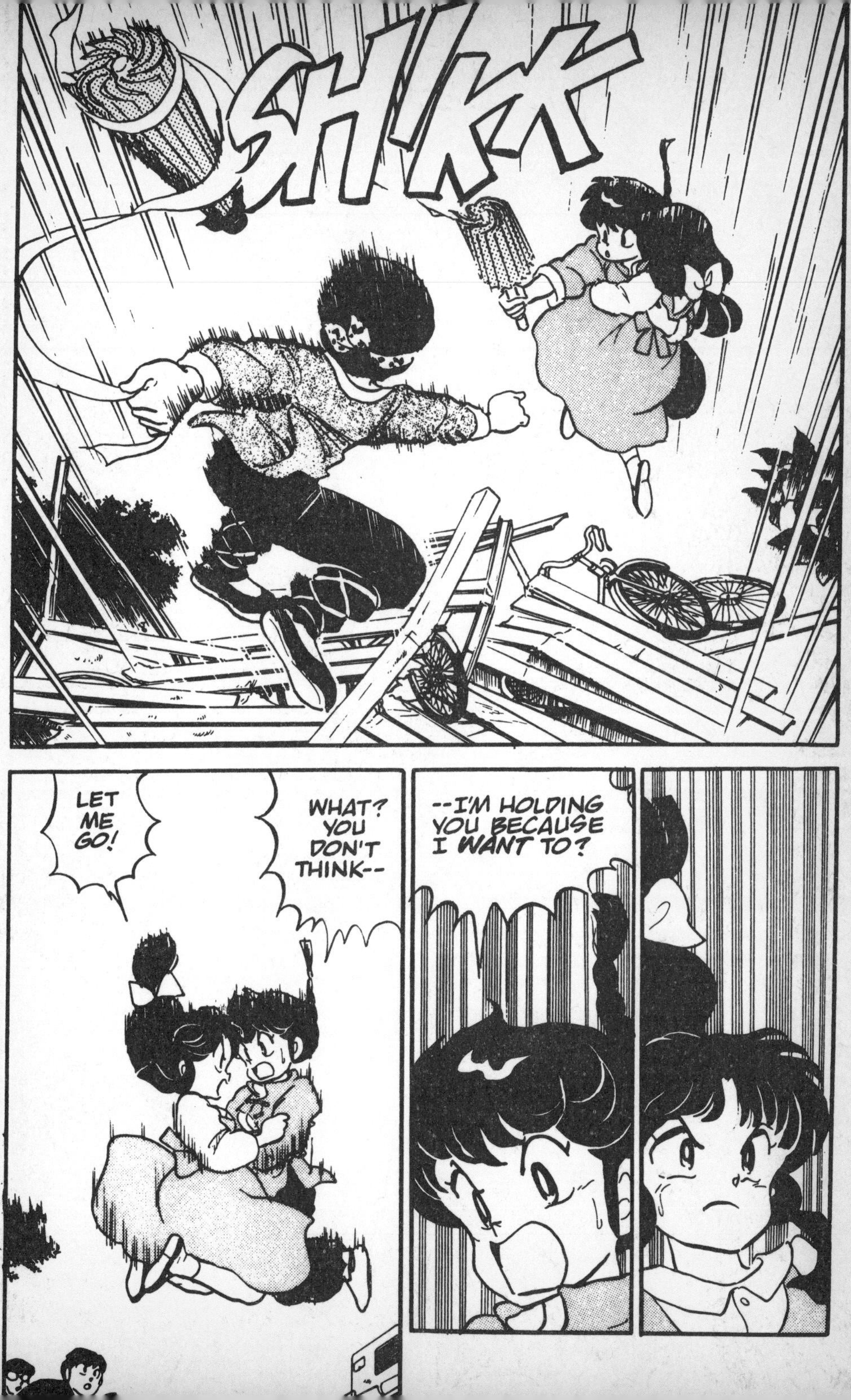
SHKK
LET ME GO!
WHAT? YOU DON'T THINK--
--I'M HOLDING YOU BECAUSE I WANT TO?

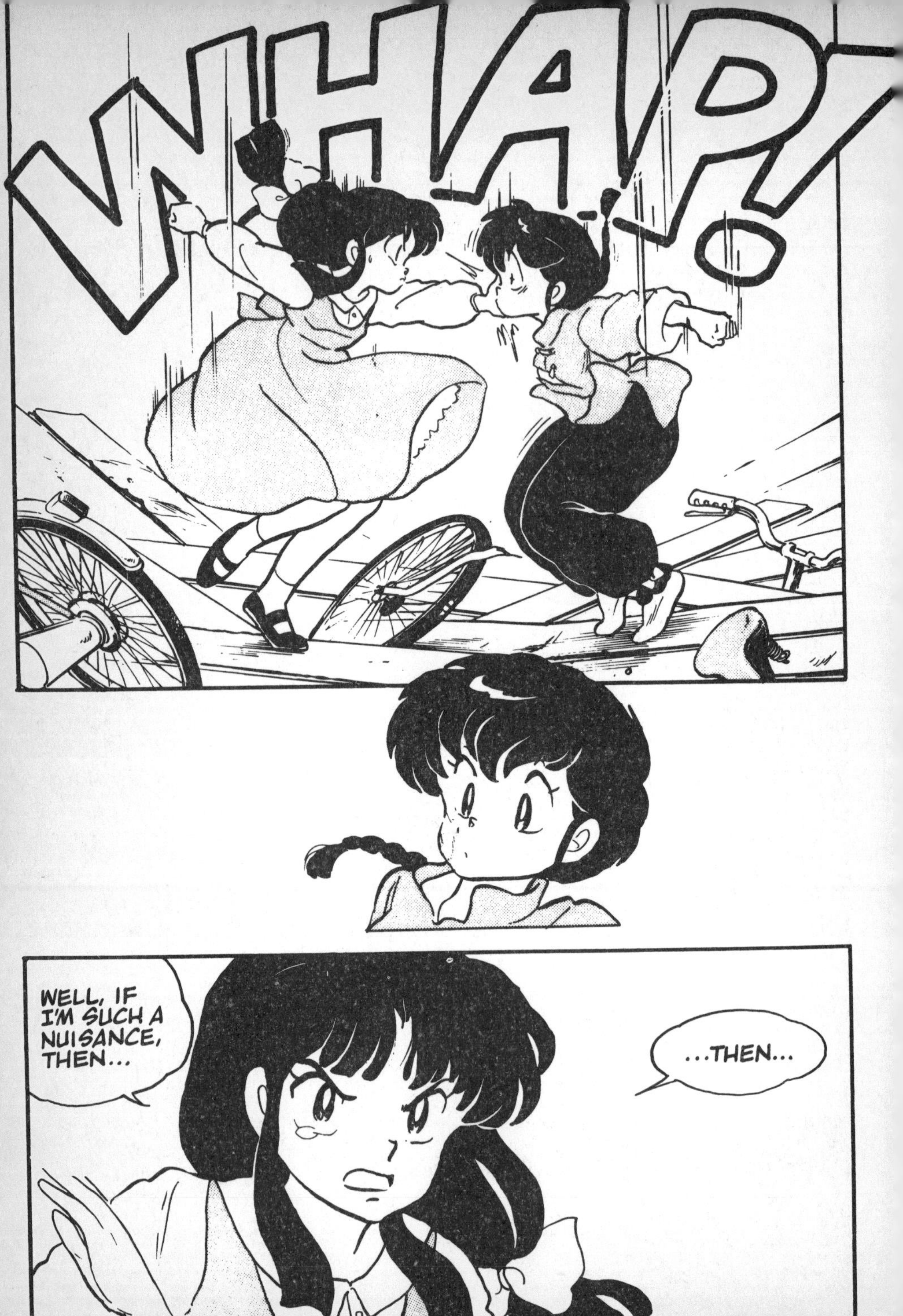
WHAP!
WELL, IF I'M SUCH A NUISANCE, THEN...
...THEN...

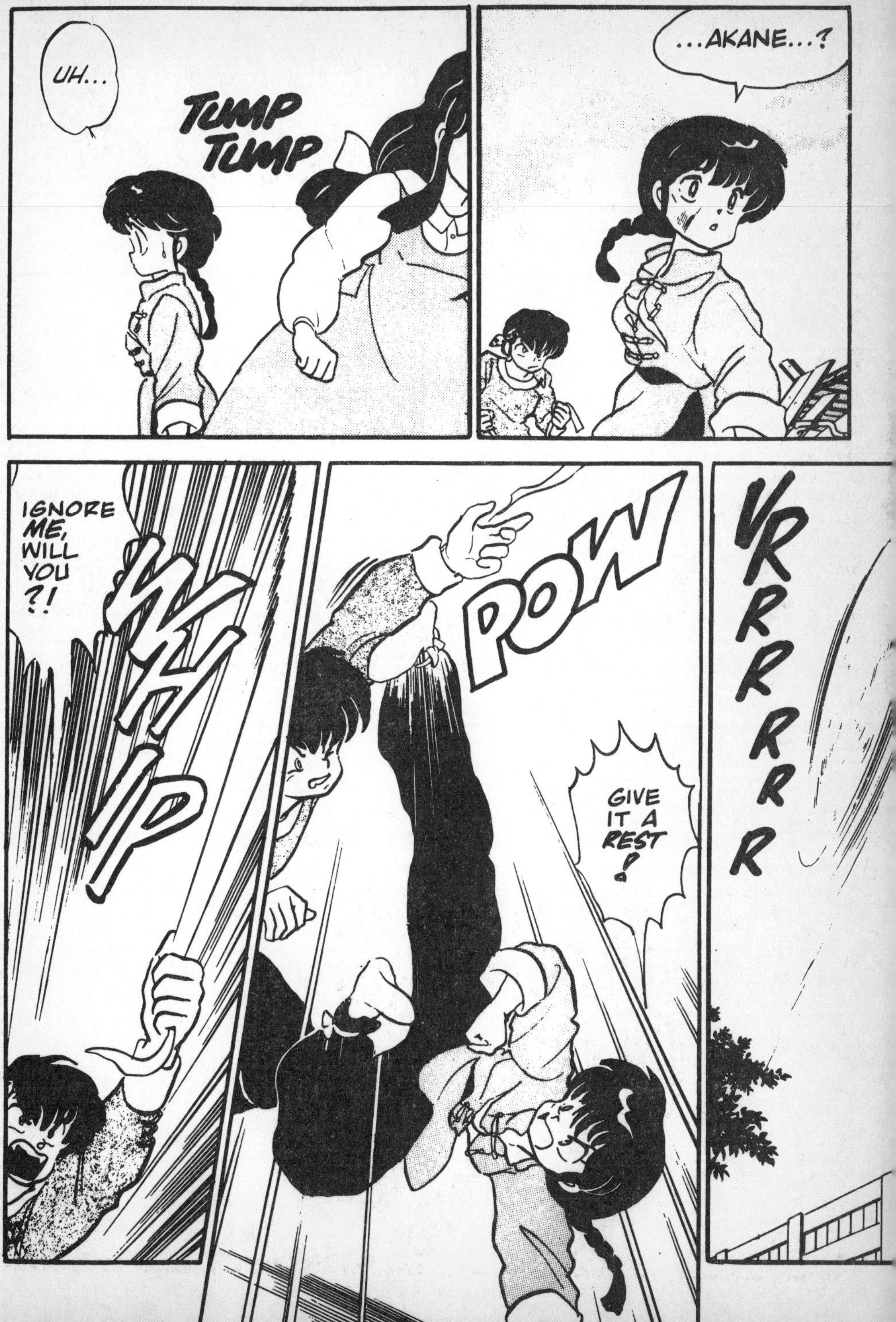
...AKANE...?
UH...
TUMP TUMP
VRRRRRR
POW
GIVE IT A REST!
IGNORE ME, WILL YOU?!
WHIP

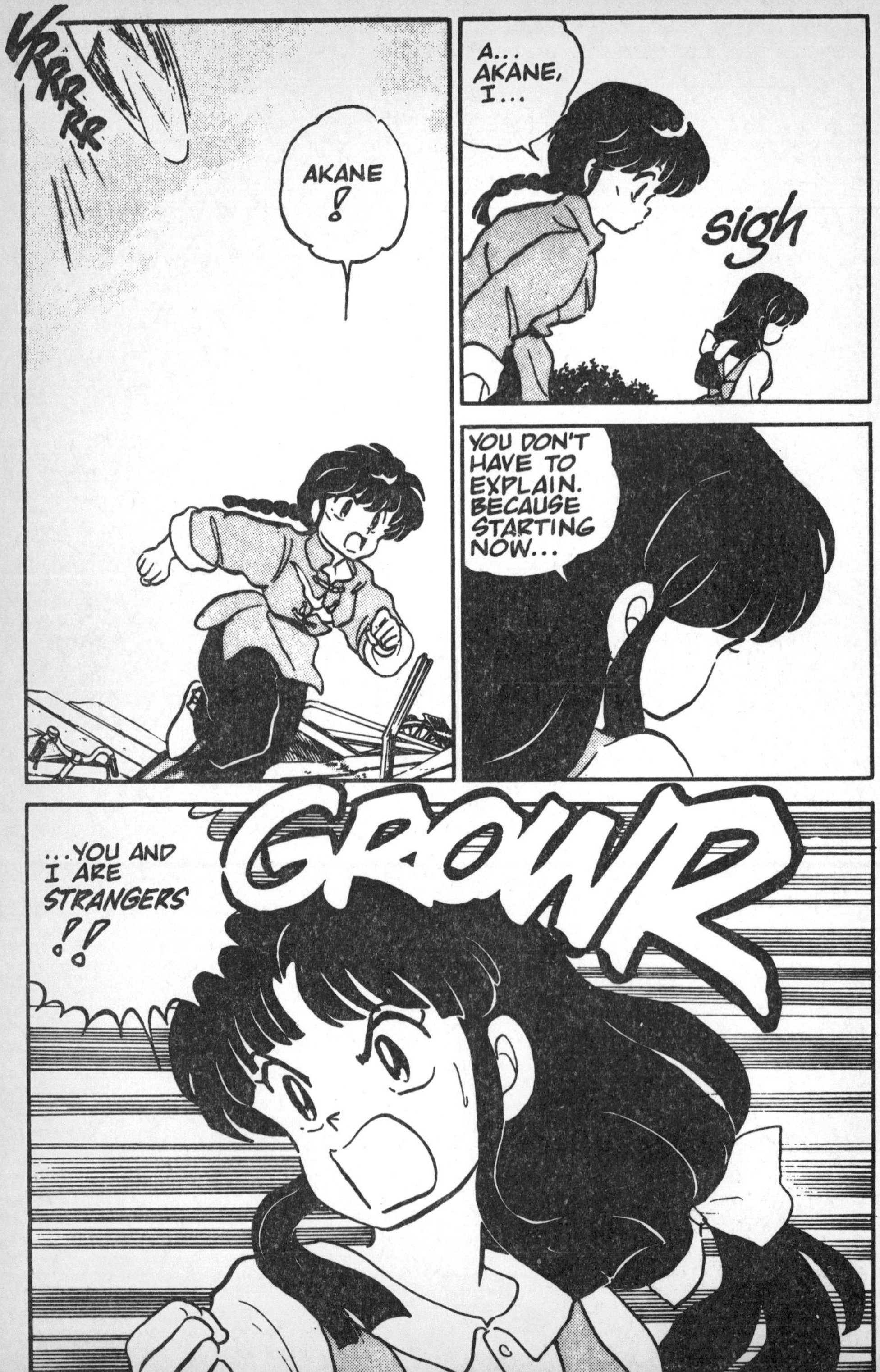

A... AKANE, I...
sigh
VRRRRR
AKANE!
YOU DON'T HAVE TO EXPLAIN. BECAUSE STARTING NOW...
GROWR
...YOU AND I ARE STRANGERS!!

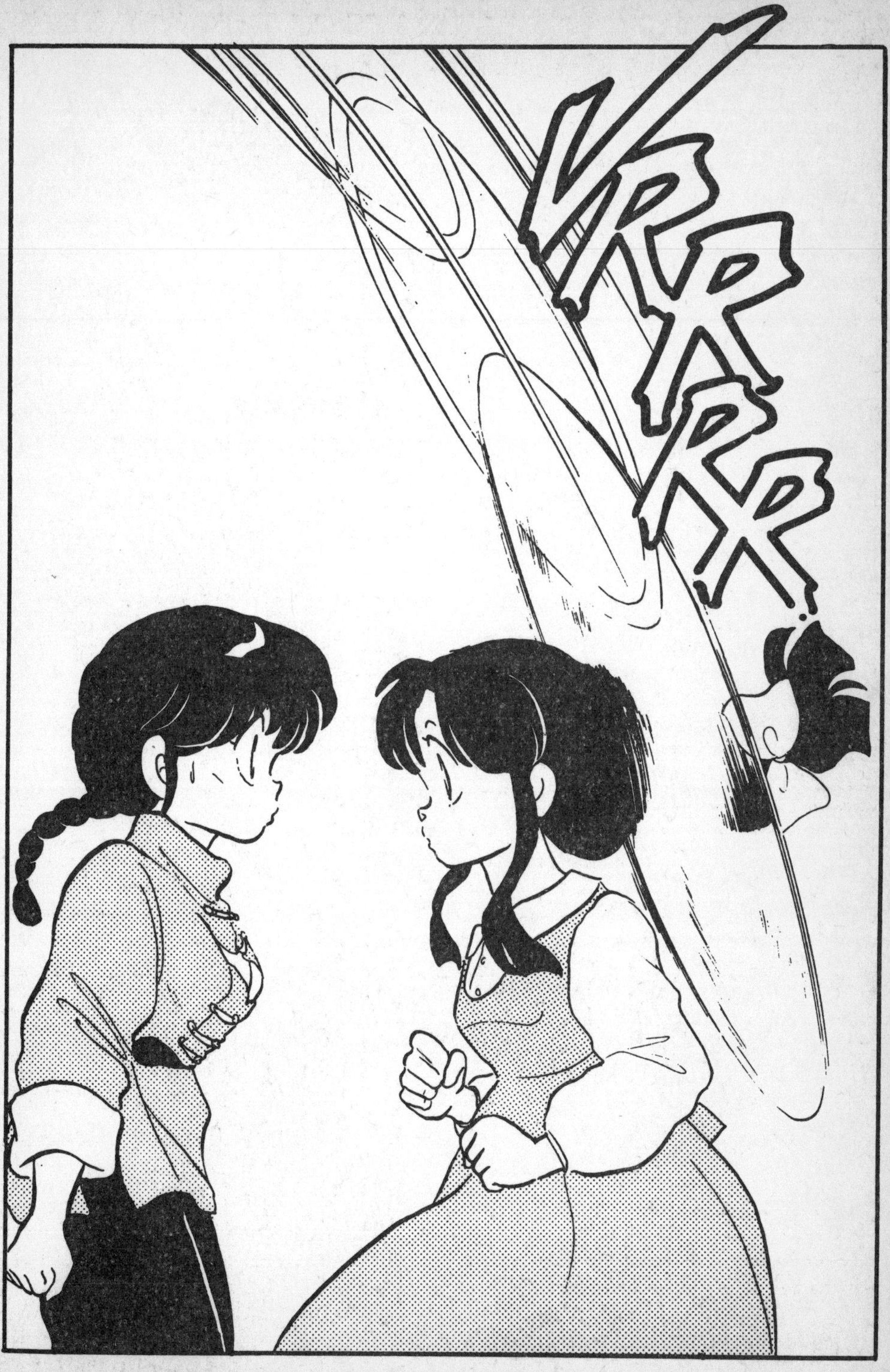
VRRRR

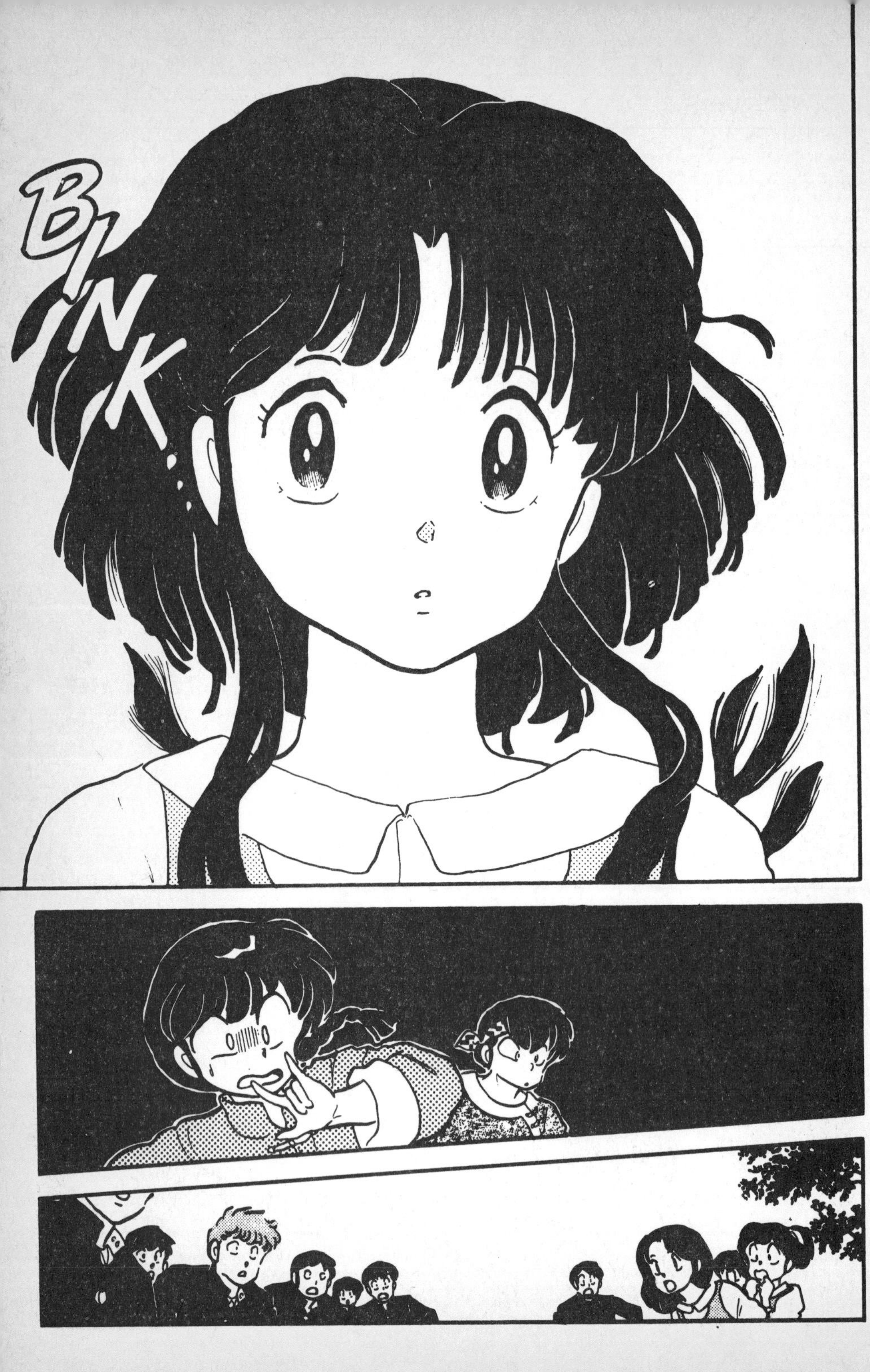
BLINK

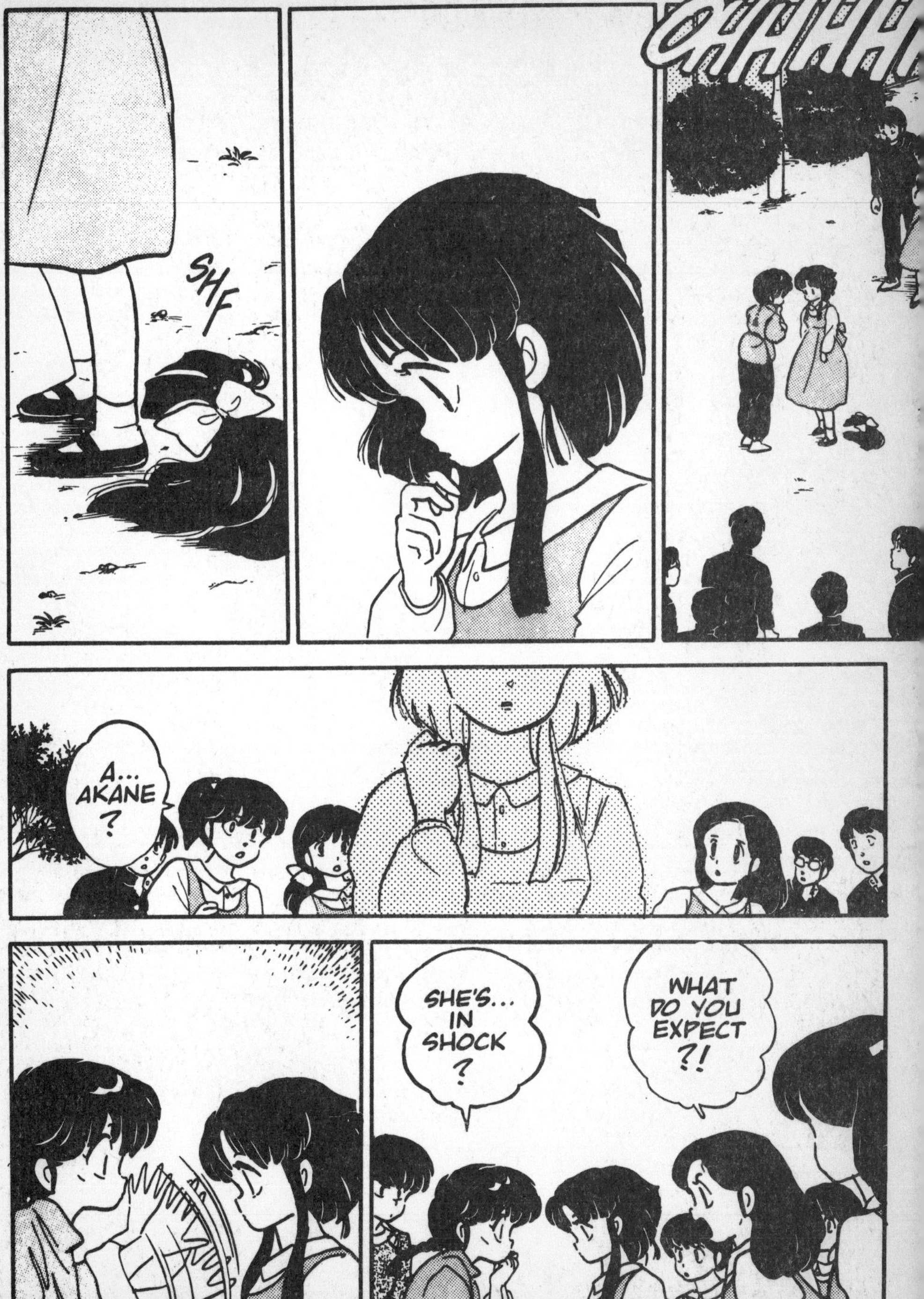
OHHHH
SHF
A... AKANE ?
WHAT DO YOU EXPECT ?!
SHE'S... IN SHOCK ?

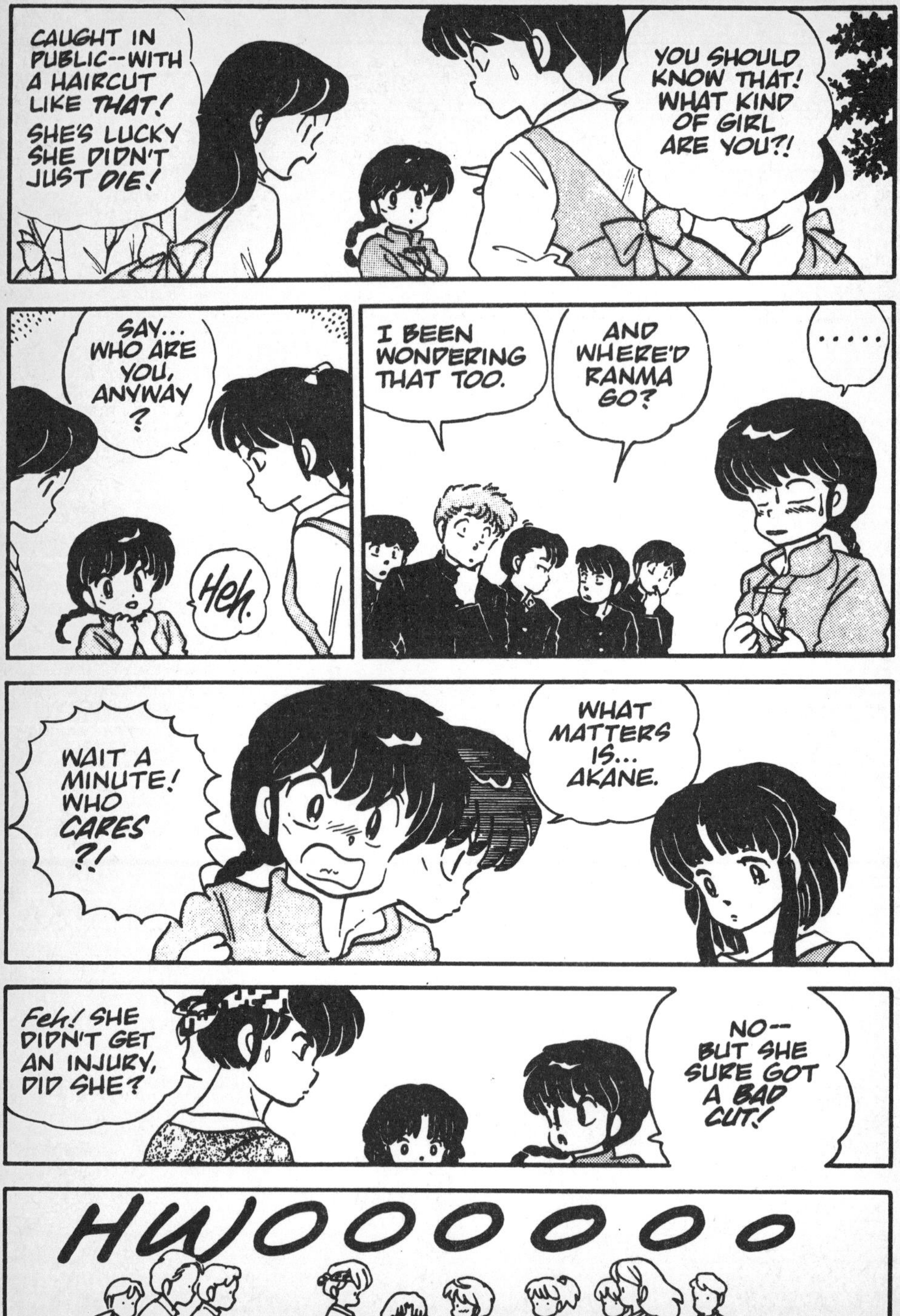

CAUGHT IN PUBLIC--WITH A HAIRCUT LIKE THAT! SHE'S LUCKY SHE DIDN'T JUST DIE!
YOU SHOULD KNOW THAT! WHAT KIND OF GIRL ARE YOU?!
SAY... WHO ARE YOU, ANYWAY ?
Heh.
I BEEN WONDERING THAT TOO.
AND WHERE'D RANMA GO?
.....
WAIT A MINUTE! WHO CARES ?!
WHAT MATTERS IS... AKANE.
Feh! SHE DIDN'T GET AN INJURY, DID SHE?
NO-- BUT SHE SURE GOT A BAD CUT!
HWOOOOOO

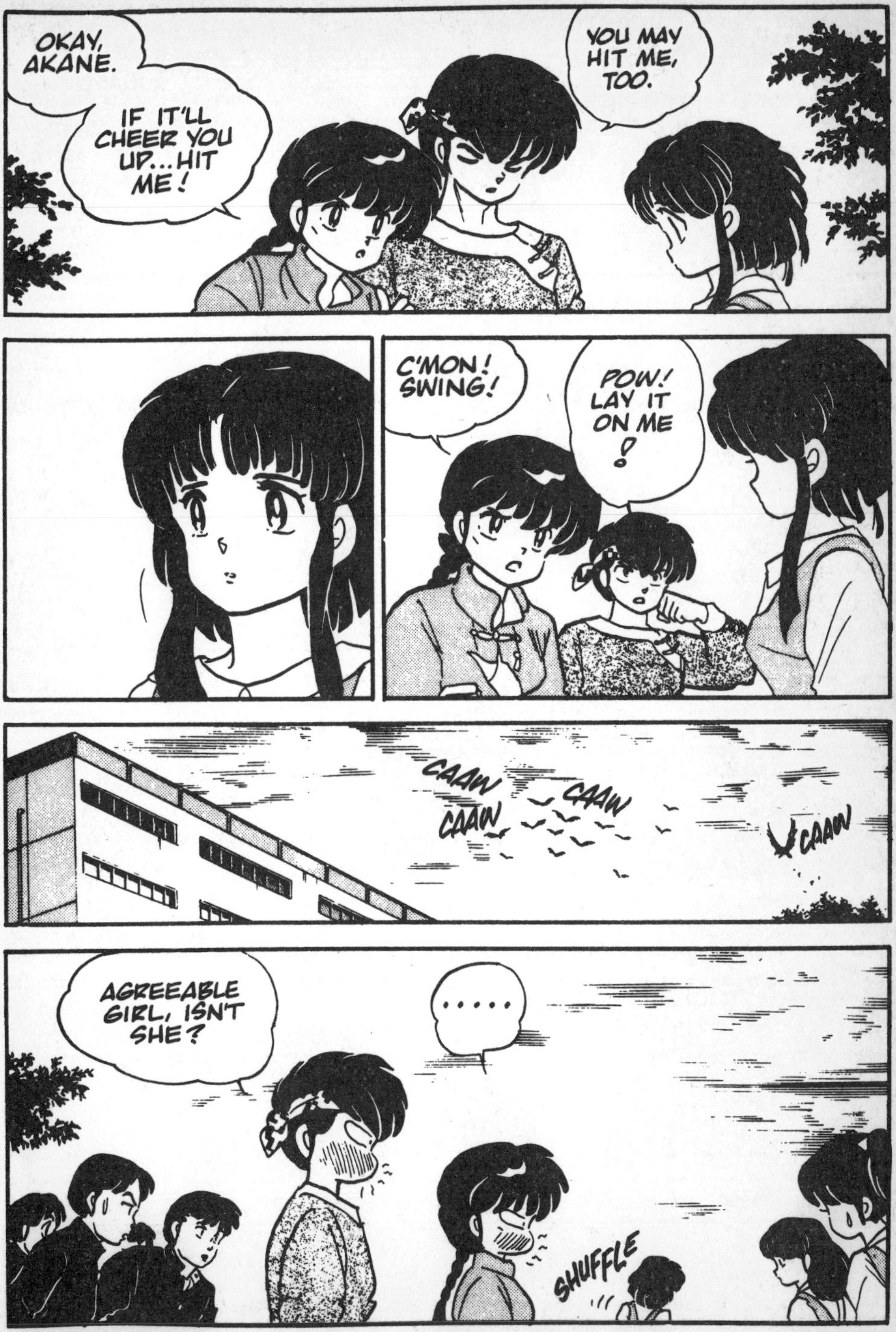
OKAY, AKANE.
IF IT'LL CHEER YOU UP...HIT ME!
YOU MAY HIT ME, TOO.
C'MON! SWING!
POW! LAY IT ON ME!
CAAW
CAAW
CAAW
CAAW
AGREEABLE GIRL, ISN'T SHE?
.....
SHUFFLE

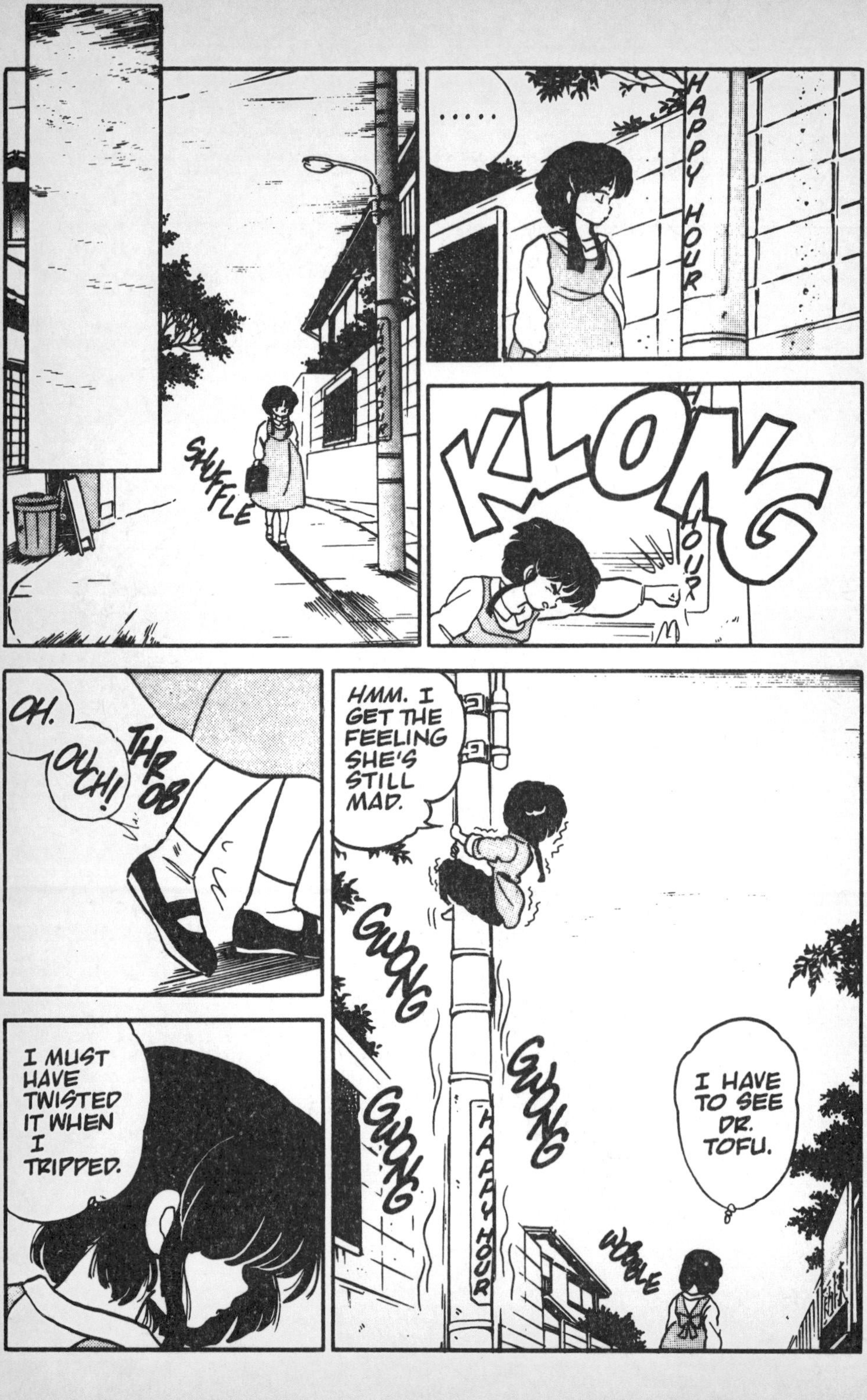
SHUFFLE
......
HAPPY HOUR
KLONG
HOUR
OH.
OUCH!
THROB
I MUST HAVE TWISTED IT WHEN I TRIPPED.
HMM. I GET THE FEELING SHE'S STILL MAD.
GWONG
GWONG
GWONG
HAPPY HOUR
I HAVE TO SEE DR. TOFU.
WOBBLE

PART FOURTEEN
Who Says You're Cute

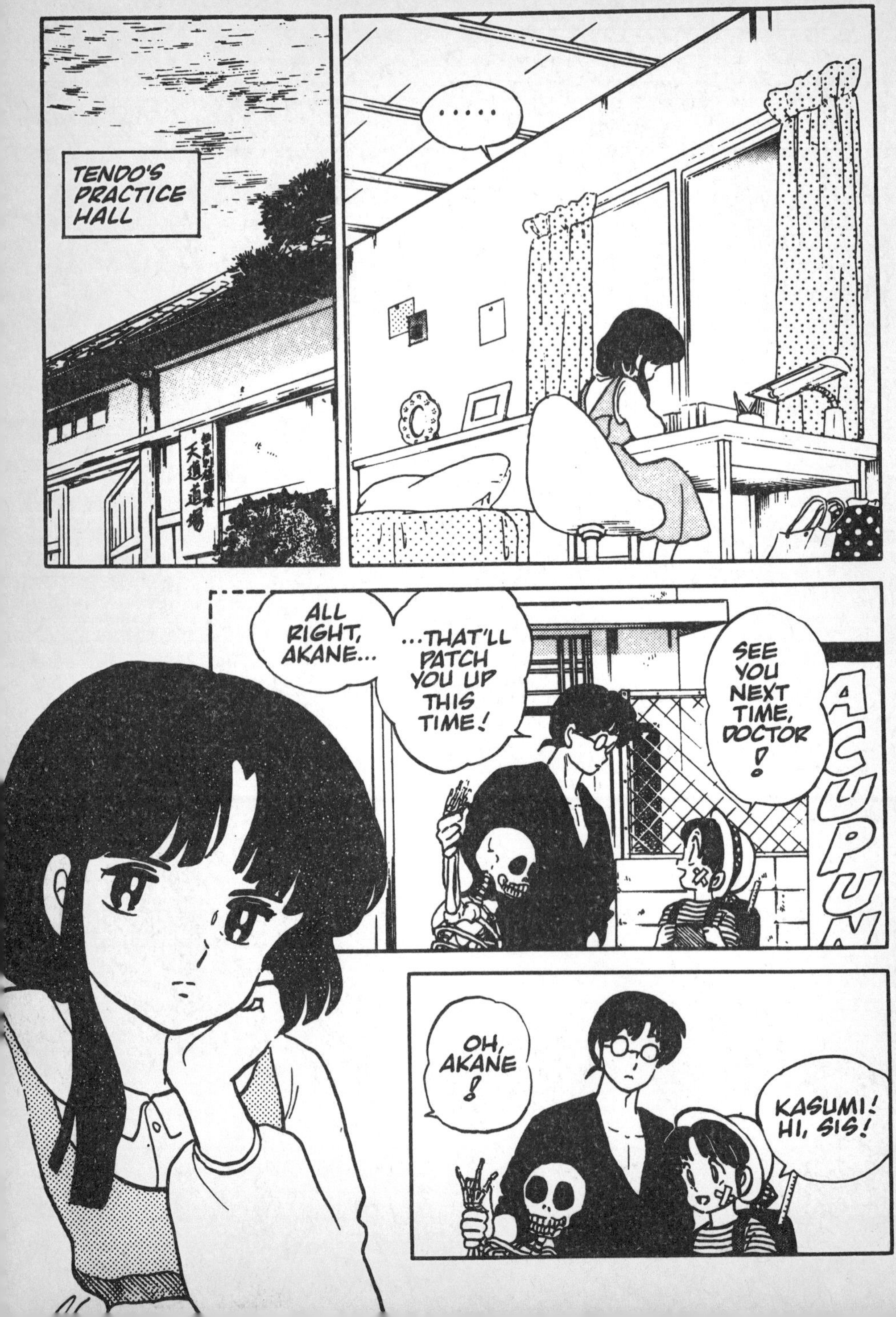
TENDO'S PRACTICE HALL
.....
ALL RIGHT, AKANE...
...THAT'LL PATCH YOU UP THIS TIME!
SEE YOU NEXT TIME, DOCTOR!
ACUPUN
OH, AKANE!
KASUMI! HI, SIS!

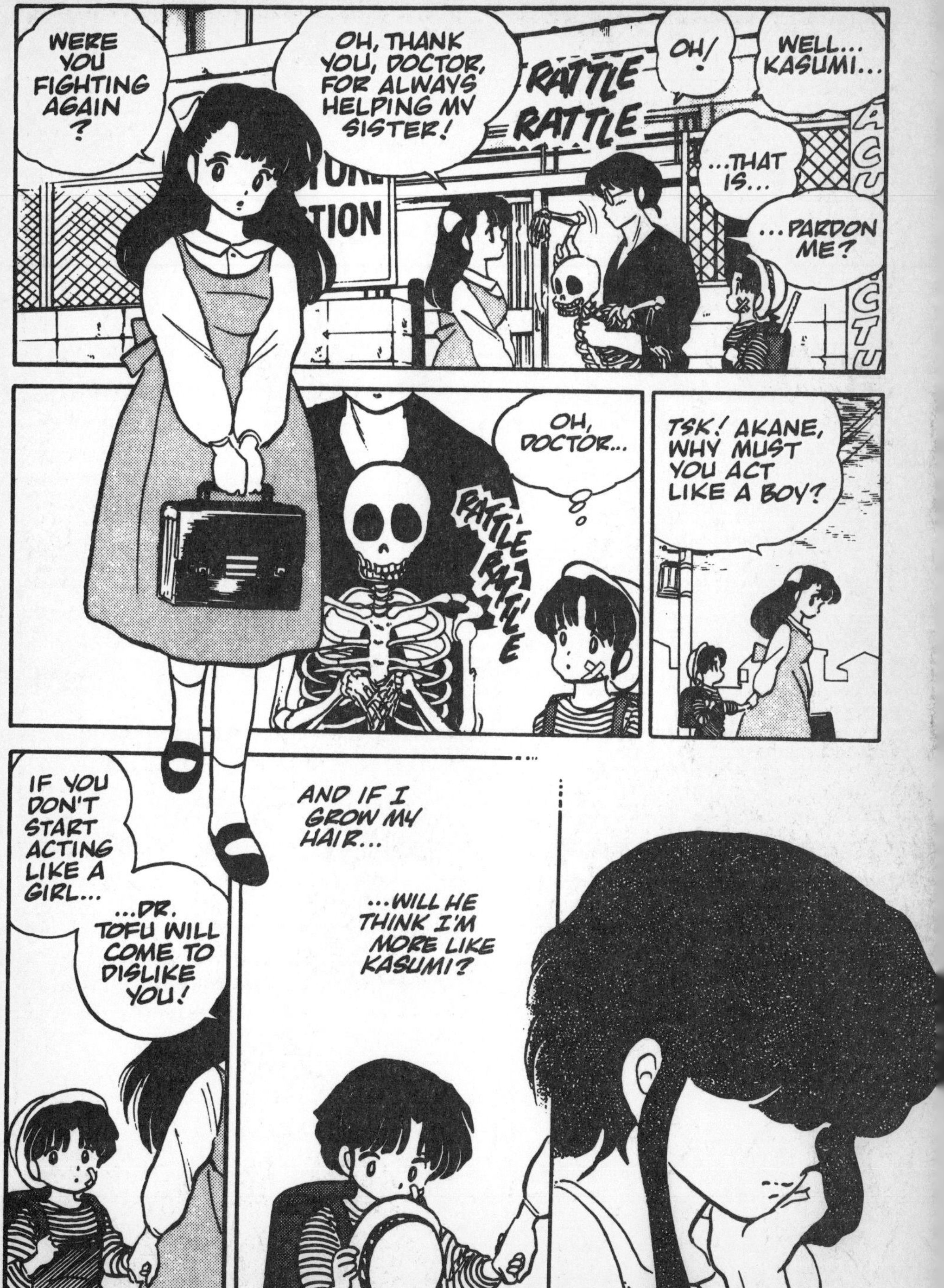
WERE YOU FIGHTING AGAIN?
OH, THANK YOU, DOCTOR, FOR ALWAYS HELPING MY SISTER!
RATTLE RATTLE
OH!
WELL... KASUMI...
...THAT IS...
...PARDON ME?
OH, DOCTOR...
RATTLE RATTLE
TSK! AKANE, WHY MUST YOU ACT LIKE A BOY?
IF YOU DON'T START ACTING LIKE A GIRL...
...DR. TOFU WILL COME TO DISLIKE YOU!
AND IF I GROW MY HAIR...
...WILL HE THINK I'M MORE LIKE KASUMI?

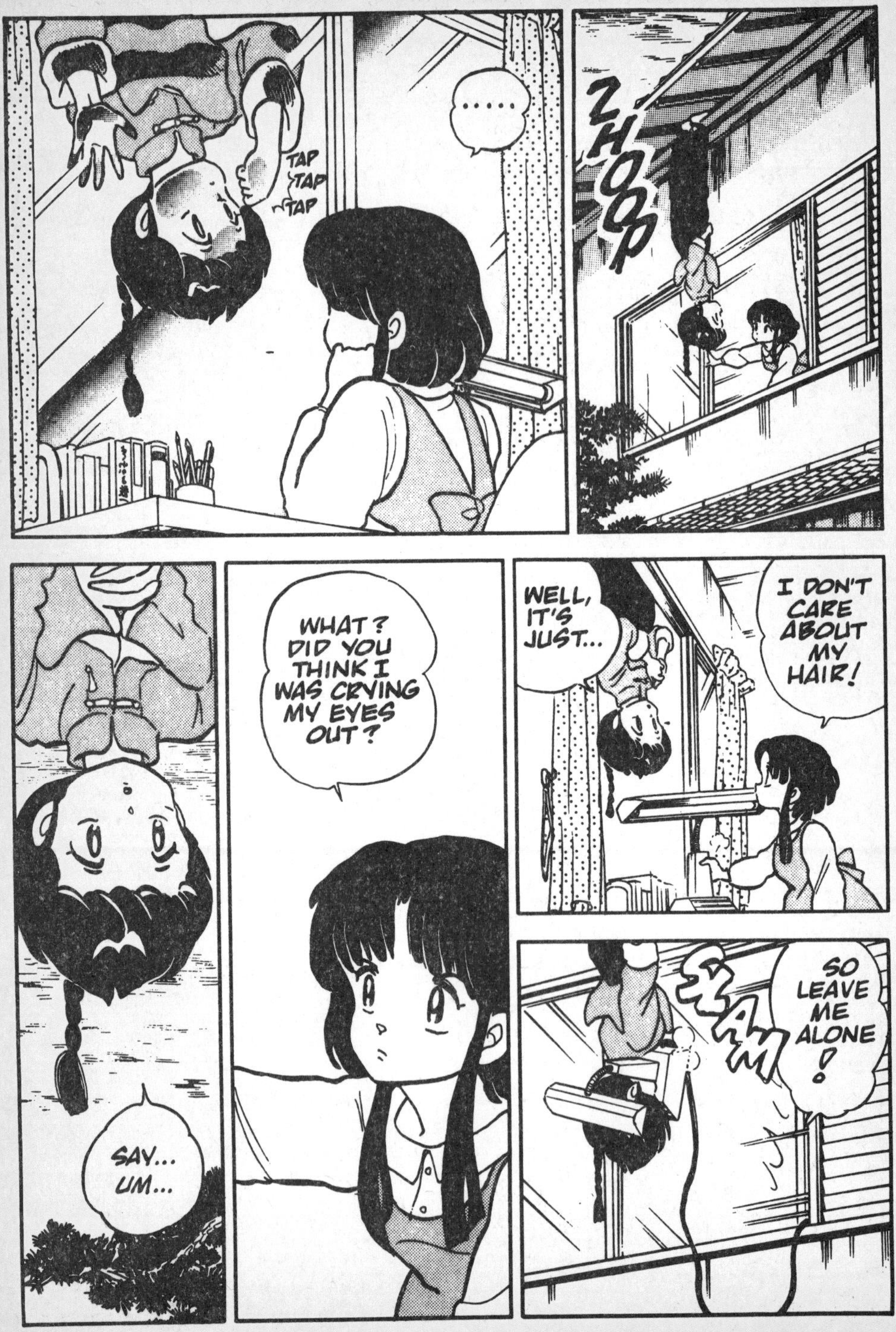

ZHOOP
TAP TAP TAP
......
I DON'T CARE ABOUT MY HAIR!
WELL, IT'S JUST...
WHAT? DID YOU THINK I WAS CRYING MY EYES OUT?
SAY... UM...
SO LEAVE ME ALONE!
SLAM

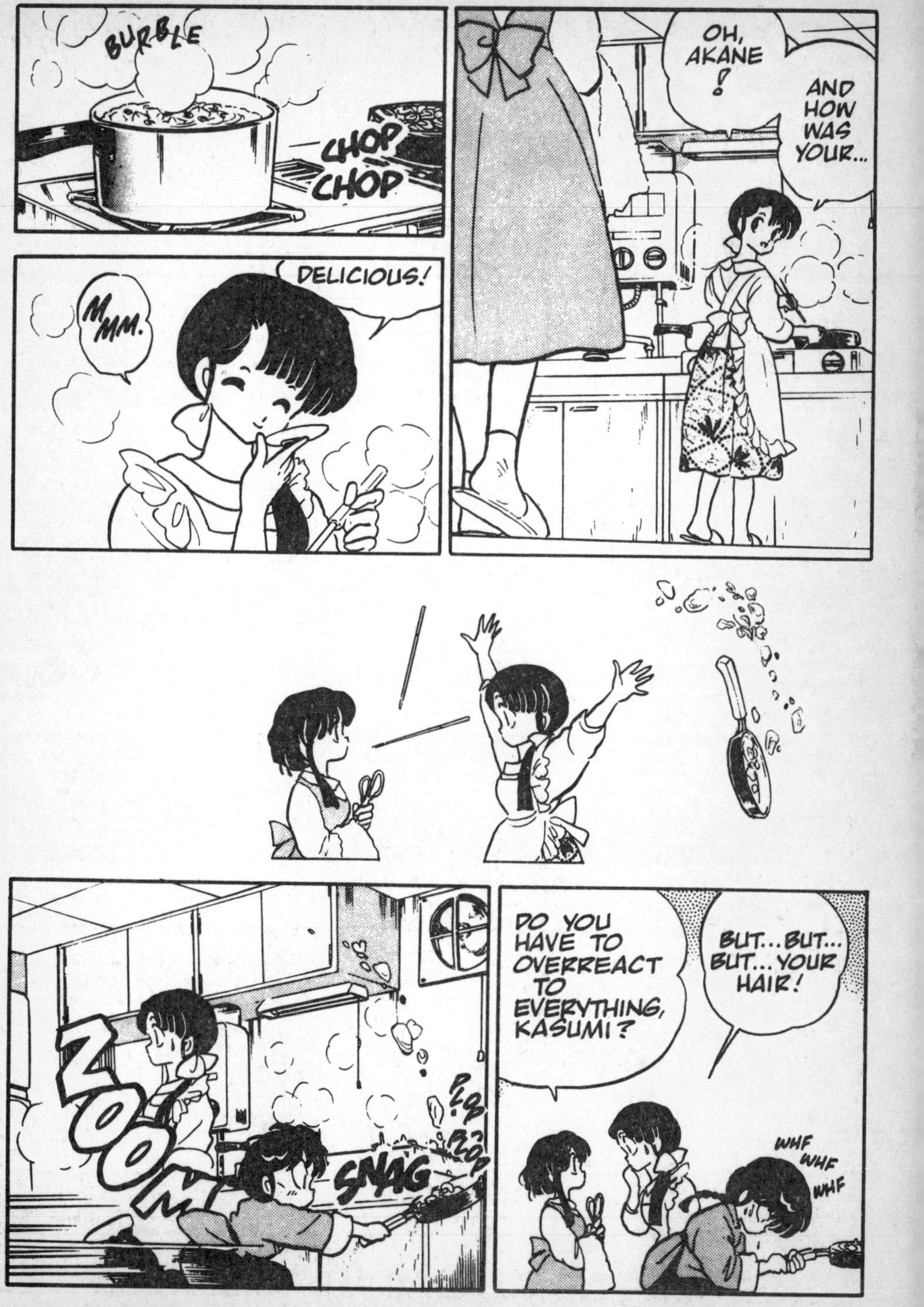

BURBLE
CHOP CHOP
OH, AKANE!
AND HOW WAS YOUR...
DELICIOUS!
M MM.
DO YOU HAVE TO OVERREACT TO EVERYTHING, KASUMI?
BUT...BUT... BUT...YOUR HAIR!
ZOOM
SNAG
PLOP PLOP
WHF WHF WHF

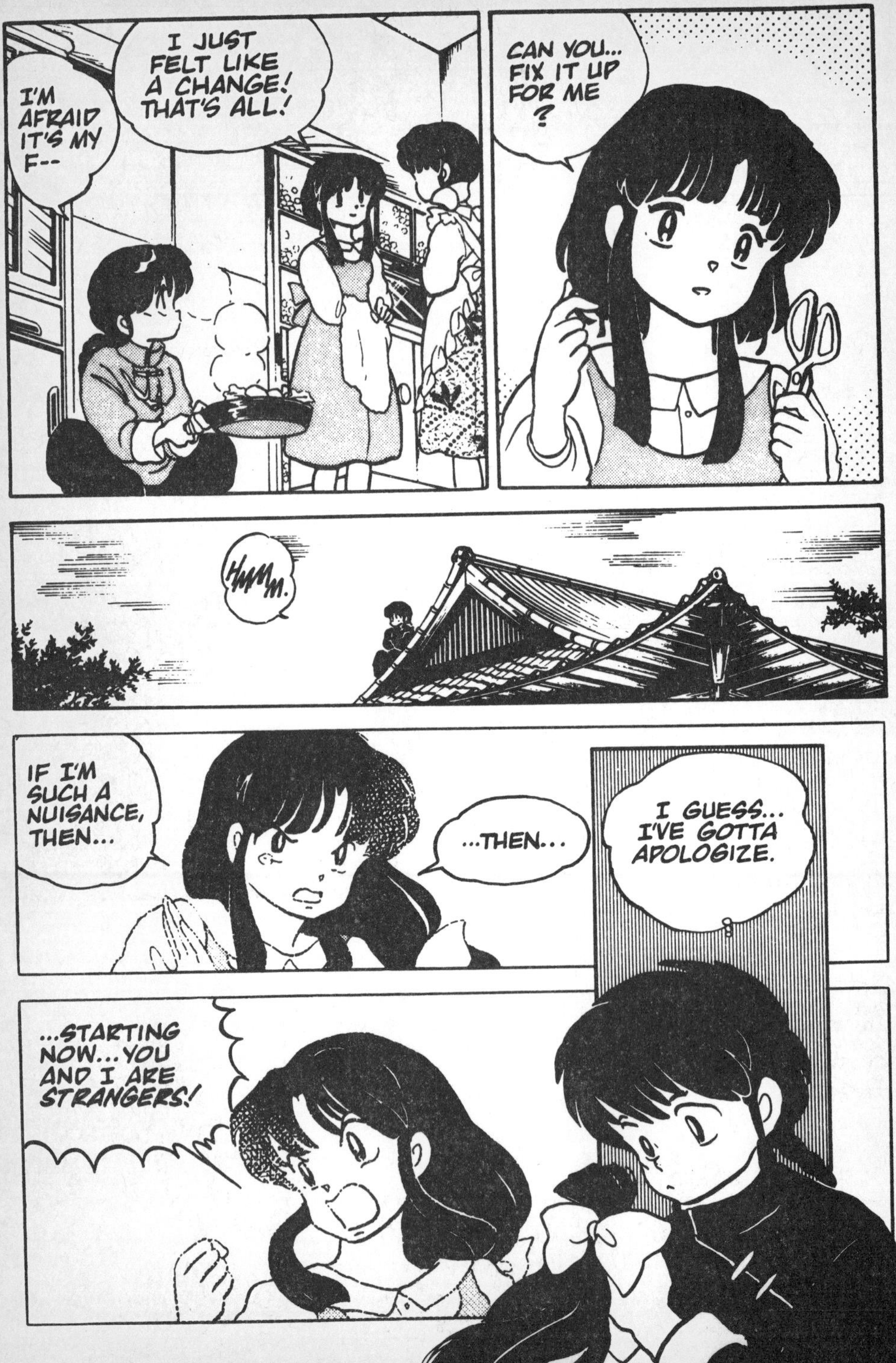
CAN YOU... FIX IT UP FOR ME ?
I JUST FELT LIKE A CHANGE! THAT'S ALL!
I'M AFRAID IT'S MY F--
HMMM.
IF I'M SUCH A NUISANCE, THEN...
...THEN...
I GUESS... I'VE GOTTA APOLOGIZE.
...STARTING NOW... YOU AND I ARE STRANGERS!

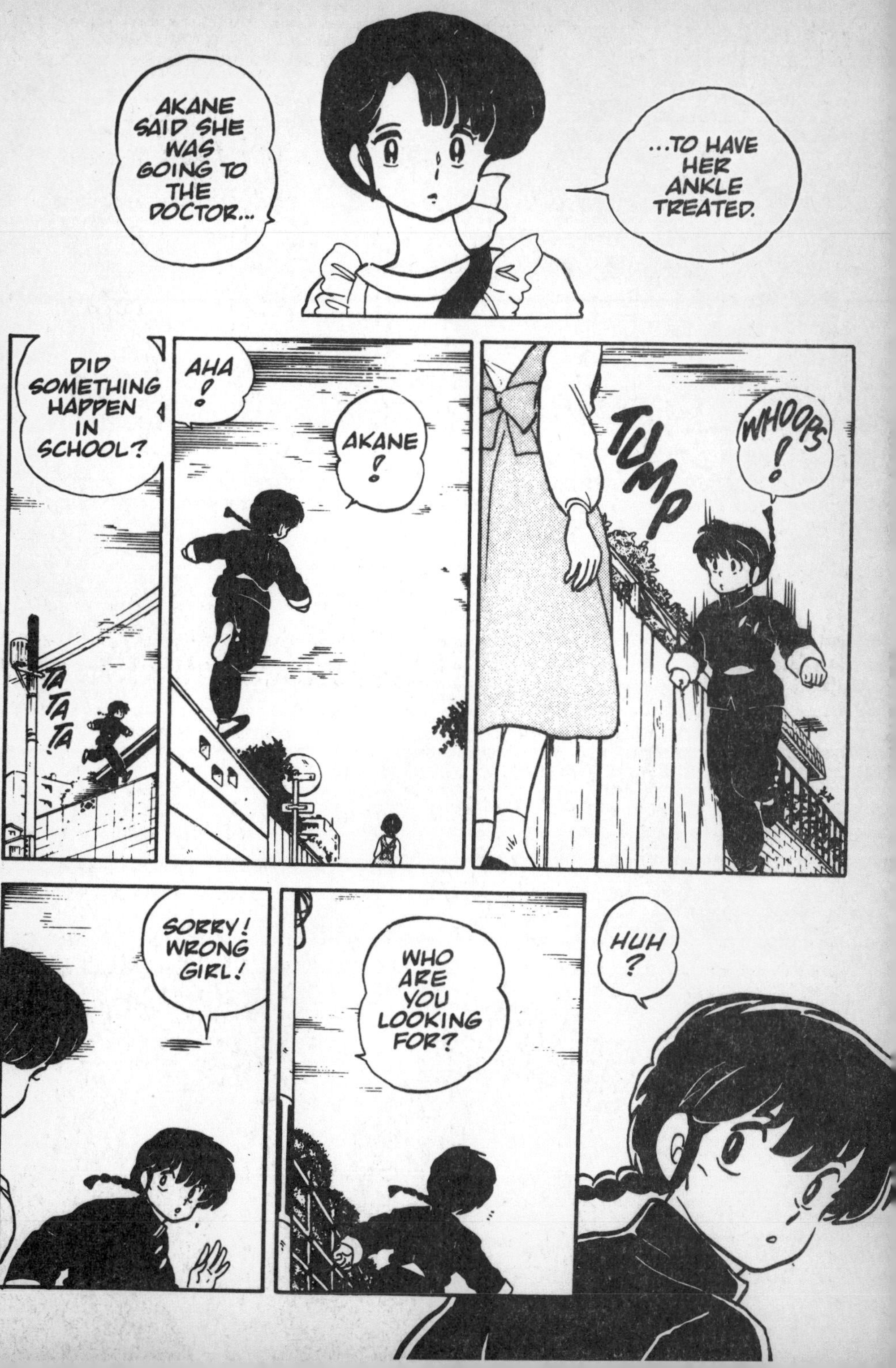
AKANE SAID SHE WAS GOING TO THE DOCTOR...
...TO HAVE HER ANKLE TREATED.
DID SOMETHING HAPPEN IN SCHOOL?
TATATA
AHA!
AKANE!
TUMP
WHOOPS!
SORRY! WRONG GIRL!
WHO ARE YOU LOOKING FOR?
HUH?

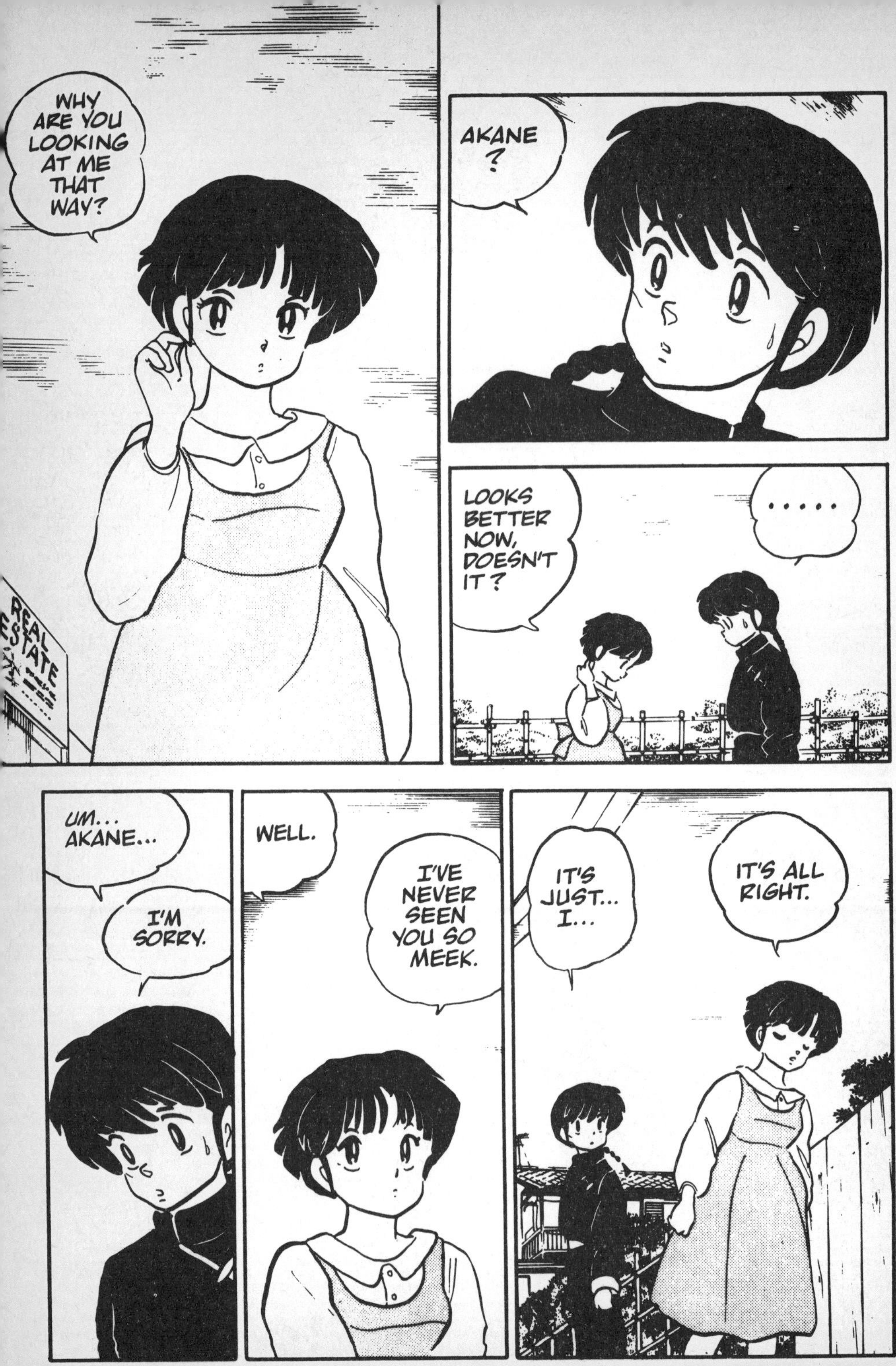
WHY ARE YOU LOOKING AT ME THAT WAY?
REAL ESTATE
AKANE ?
LOOKS BETTER NOW, DOESN'T IT ?
. . . . . .
UM... AKANE...
I'M SORRY.
WELL.
I'VE NEVER SEEN YOU SO MEEK.
IT'S JUST... I...
IT'S ALL RIGHT.

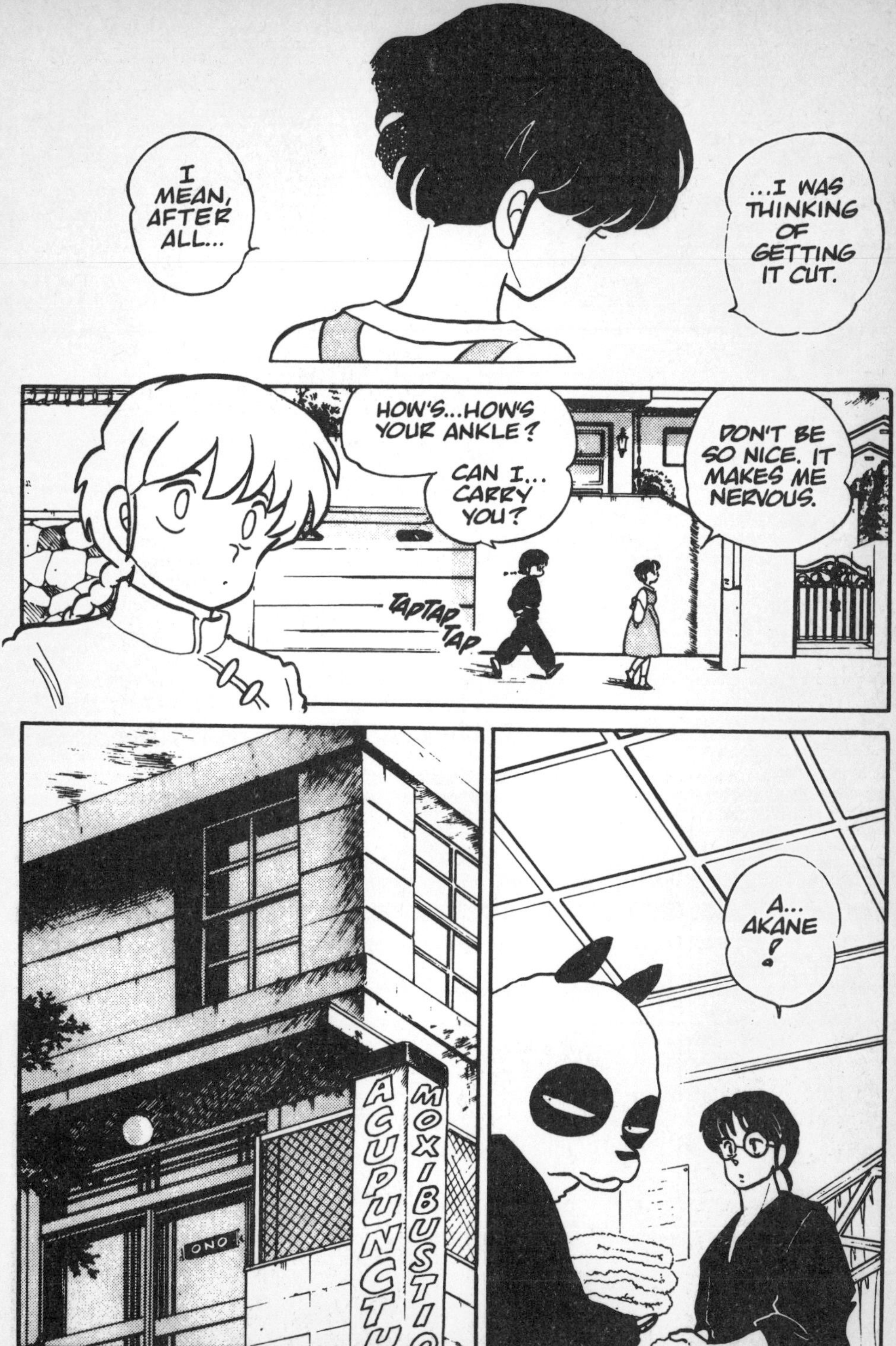
...I WAS THINKING OF GETTING IT CUT.
I MEAN, AFTER ALL...
DON'T BE SO NICE. IT MAKES ME NERVOUS.
HOW'S...HOW'S YOUR ANKLE?
CAN I... CARRY YOU?
TAPTAP TAP
A... AKANE?
MOXIBUSTIO
ACUPUNCTU
ONO

HELLO, DR. TOFU!

· · · · ·

WELL, WELL. CUT IT SHORT AGAIN, EH?

MM-HM.

"AGAIN"?

LOOKS LIKE JUST A LIGHT SPRAIN.

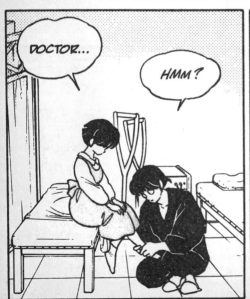

DOCTOR...

HMM?

DO YOU THINK IT... LOOKS GOOD?

OH, YES. IT'S VERY CUTE.

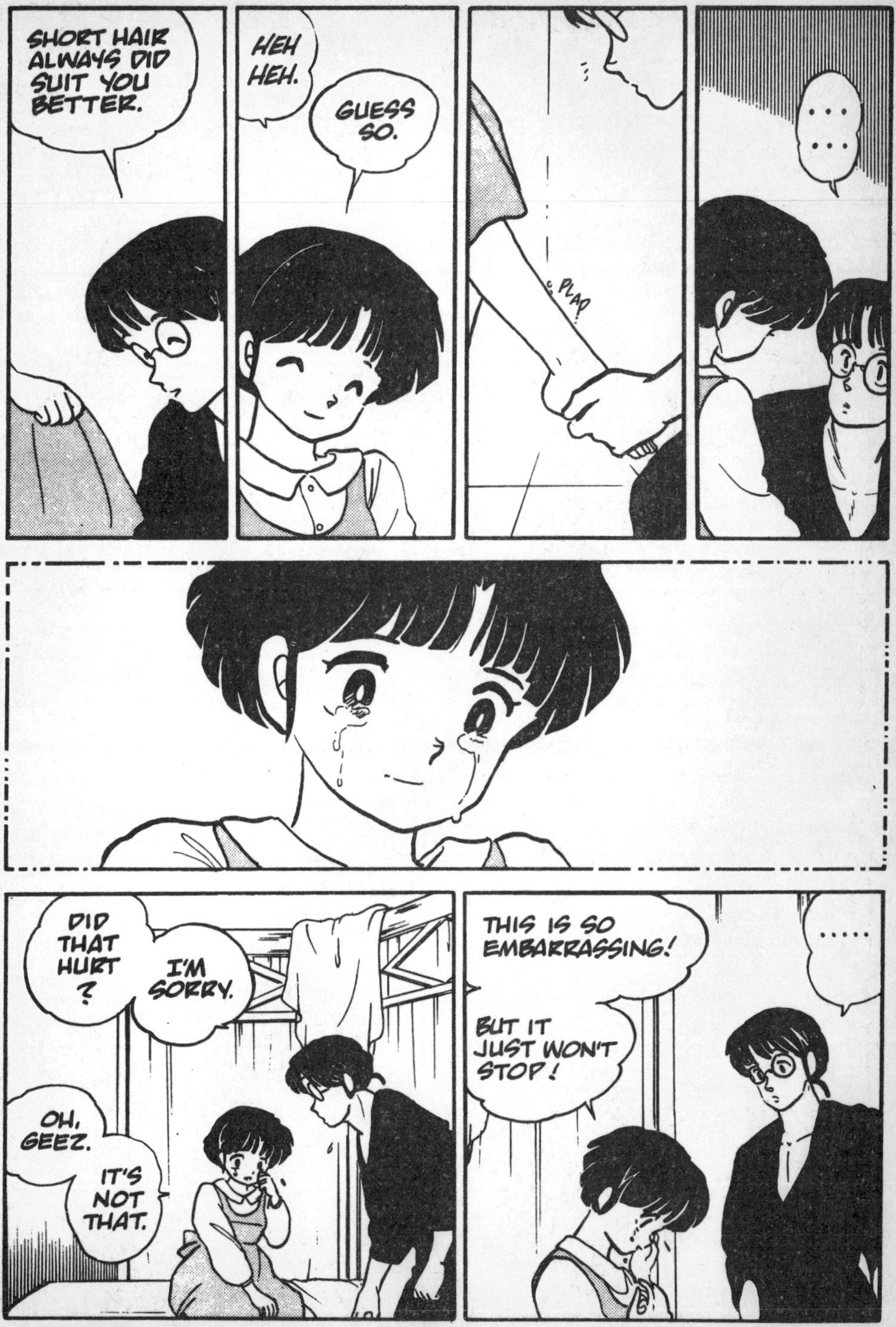
SHORT HAIR ALWAYS DID SUIT YOU BETTER.
HEH HEH.
GUESS SO.
PLAP
....
DID THAT HURT?
I'M SORRY.
OH, GEEZ.
IT'S NOT THAT.
THIS IS SO EMBARRASSING!
BUT IT JUST WON'T STOP!
.....

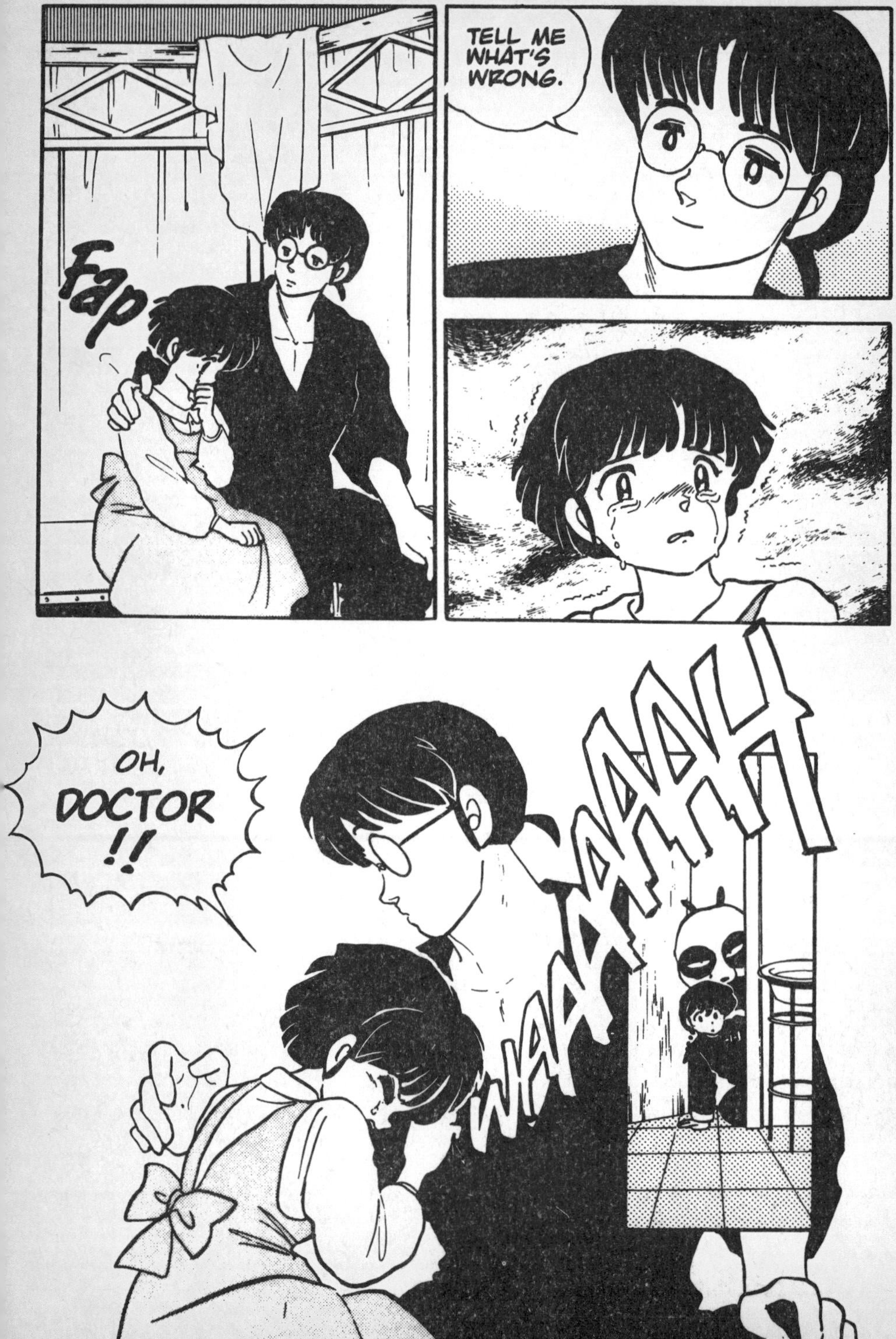
TELL ME WHAT'S WRONG.
Fap
OH, DOCTOR !!
WAAAAAAAAH

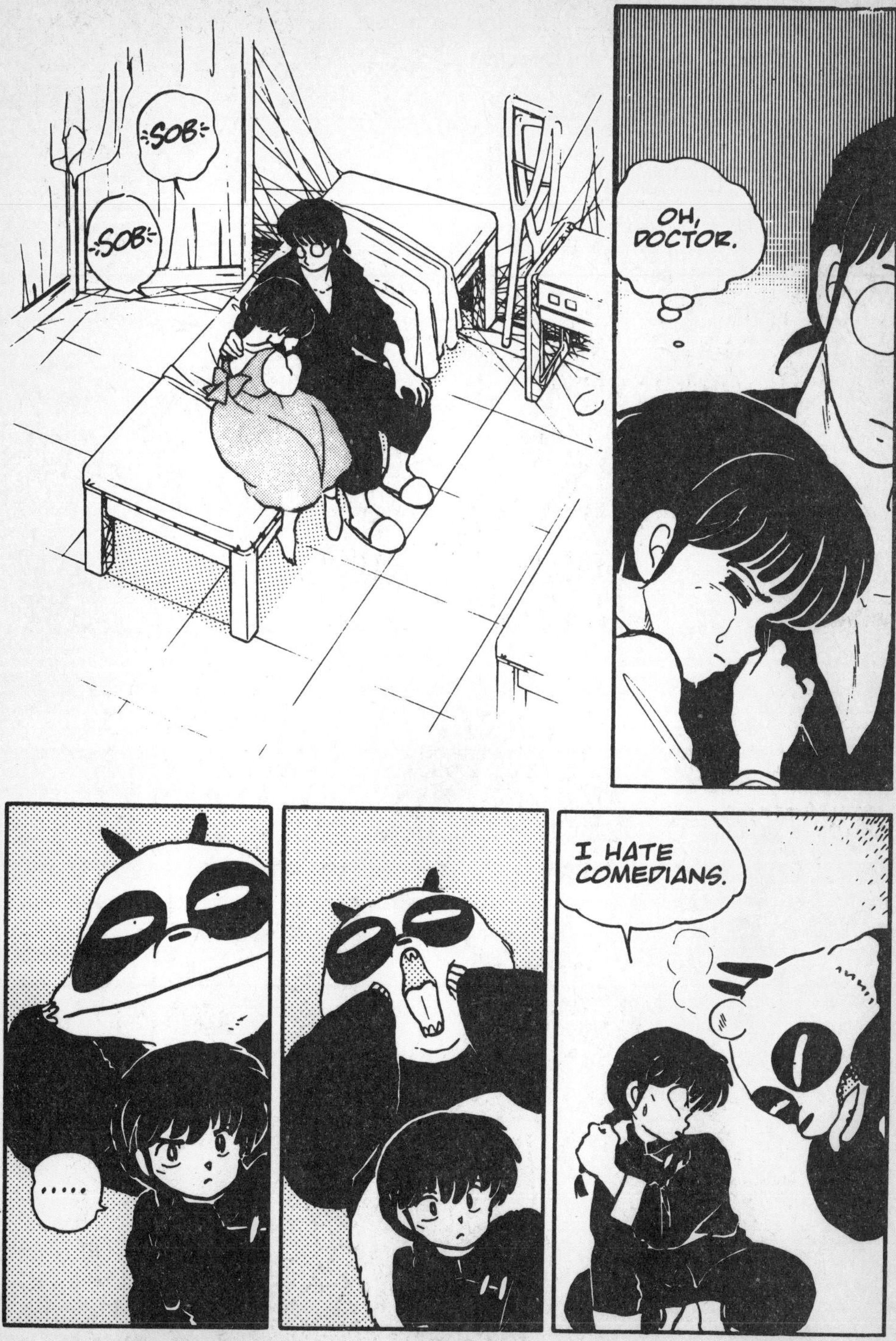
OH, DOCTOR.
SOB
SOB
I HATE COMEDIANS.
......

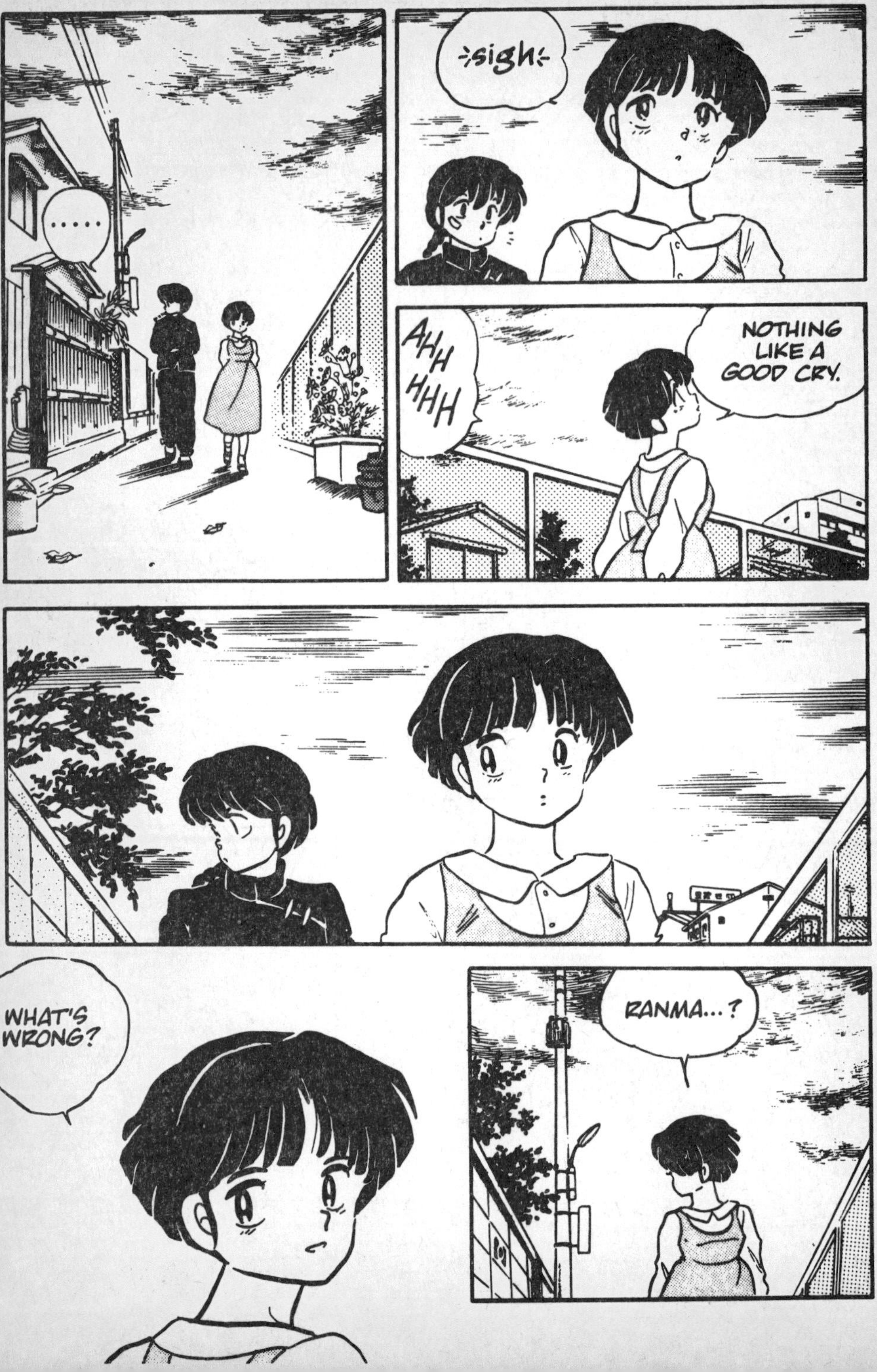

......
sigh
NOTHING LIKE A GOOD CRY.
AHHHHH
WHAT'S WRONG?
RANMA...?

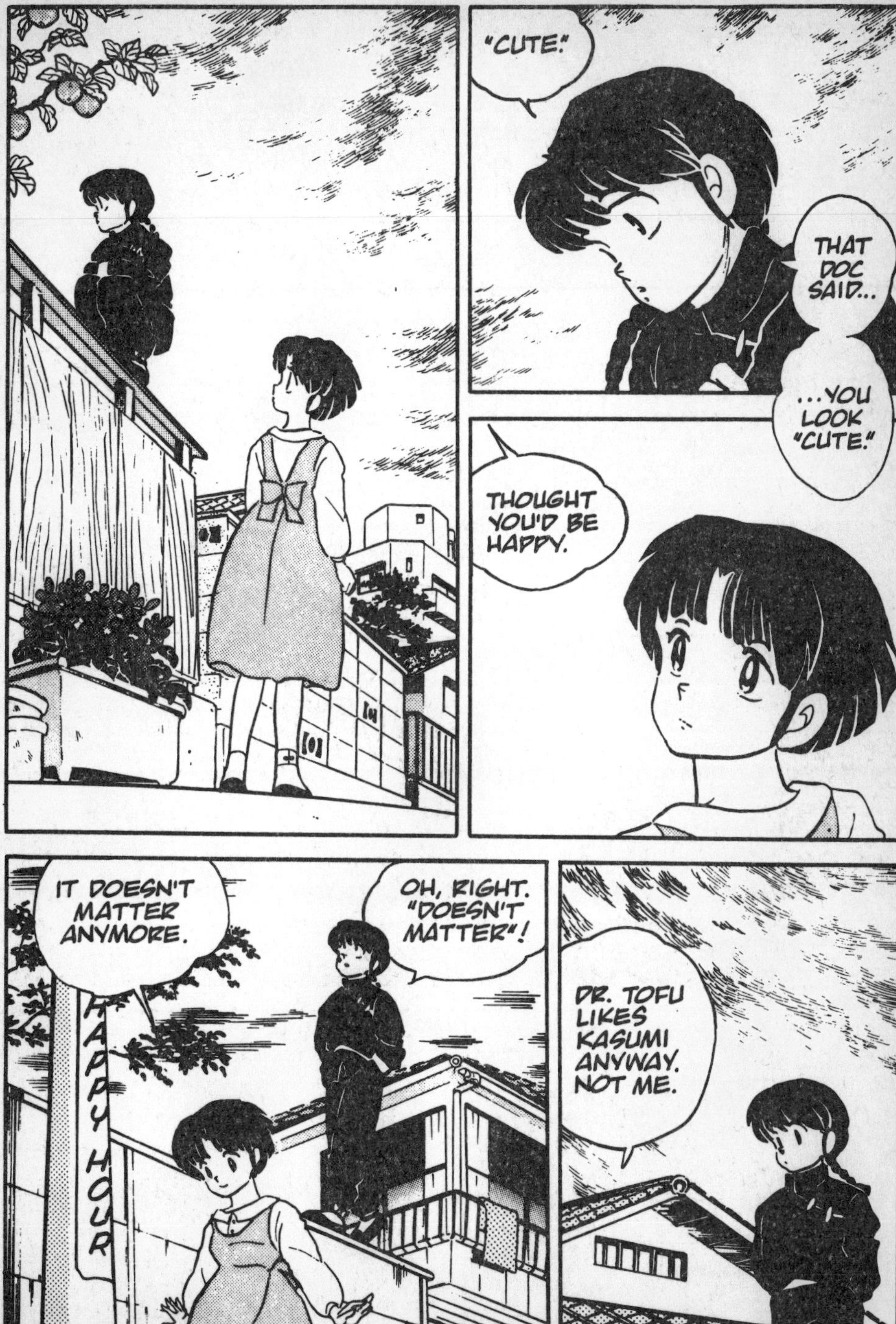
"CUTE."
THAT DOC SAID...
...YOU LOOK "CUTE."
THOUGHT YOU'D BE HAPPY.
IT DOESN'T MATTER ANYMORE.
OH, RIGHT. "DOESN'T MATTER"!
HAPPY HOUR
DR. TOFU LIKES KASUMI ANYWAY. NOT ME.

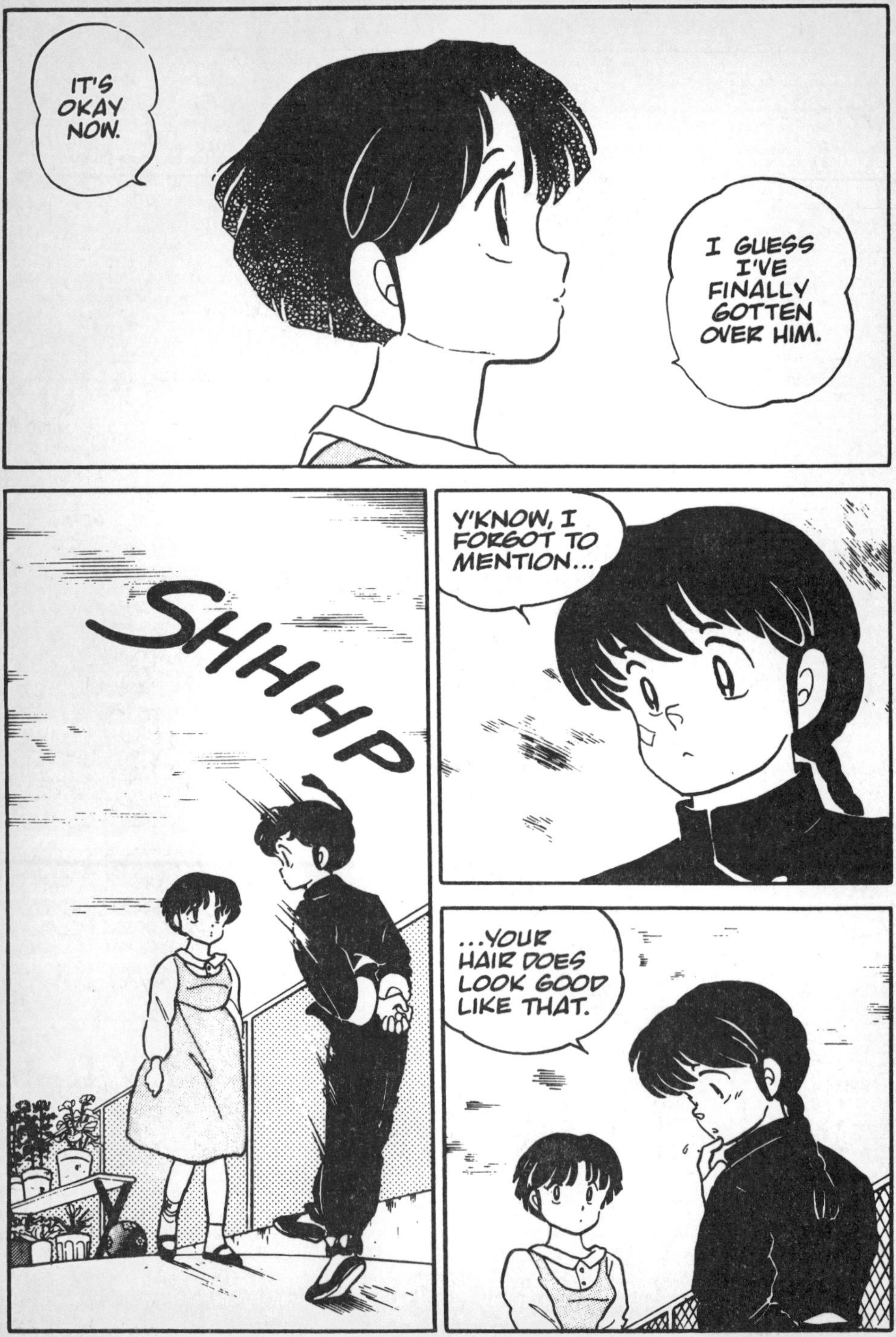
IT'S OKAY NOW.
I GUESS I'VE FINALLY GOTTEN OVER HIM.
Y'KNOW, I FORGOT TO MENTION...
SHHHP
...YOUR HAIR DOES LOOK GOOD LIKE THAT.

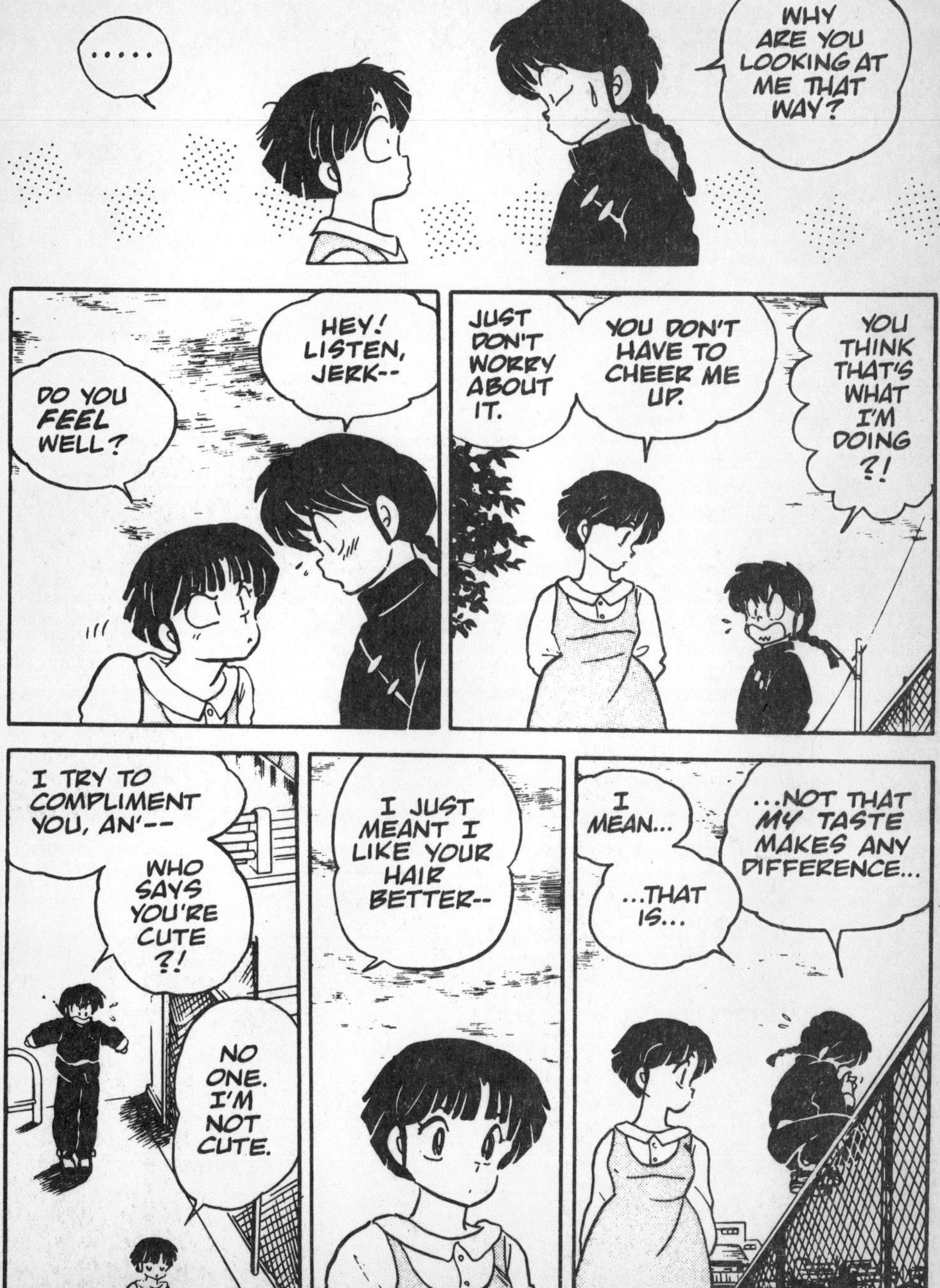
......
WHY ARE YOU LOOKING AT ME THAT WAY?
DO YOU FEEL WELL?
HEY! LISTEN, JERK--
JUST DON'T WORRY ABOUT IT.
YOU DON'T HAVE TO CHEER ME UP.
YOU THINK THAT'S WHAT I'M DOING?!
I TRY TO COMPLIMENT YOU, AN'--
WHO SAYS YOU'RE CUTE?!
NO ONE. I'M NOT CUTE.
I JUST MEANT I LIKE YOUR HAIR BETTER--
I MEAN...
...THAT IS...
...NOT THAT MY TASTE MAKES ANY DIFFERENCE...

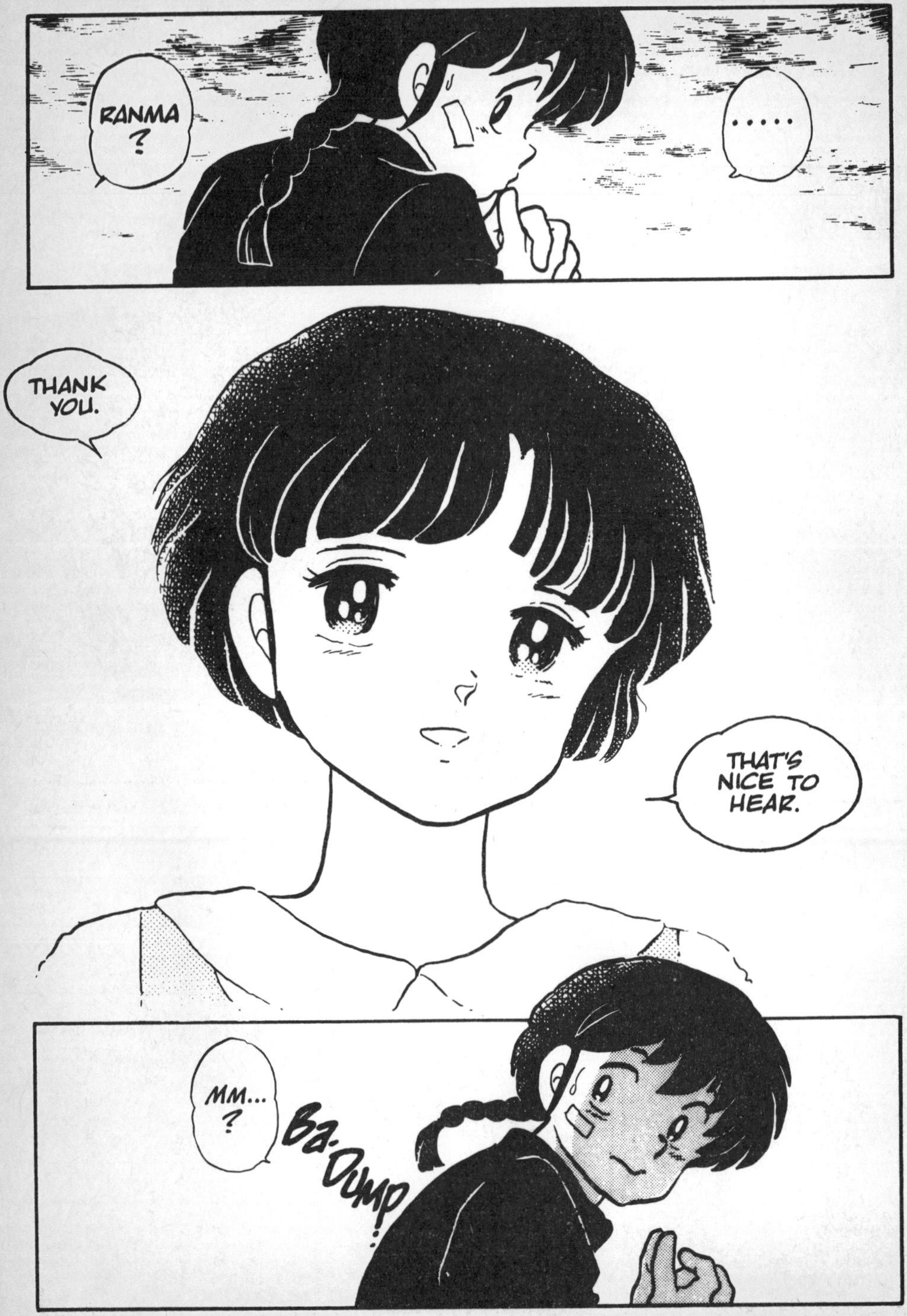
RANMA ?
.....
THANK YOU.
THAT'S NICE TO HEAR.
MM... ?
BA-DUMP

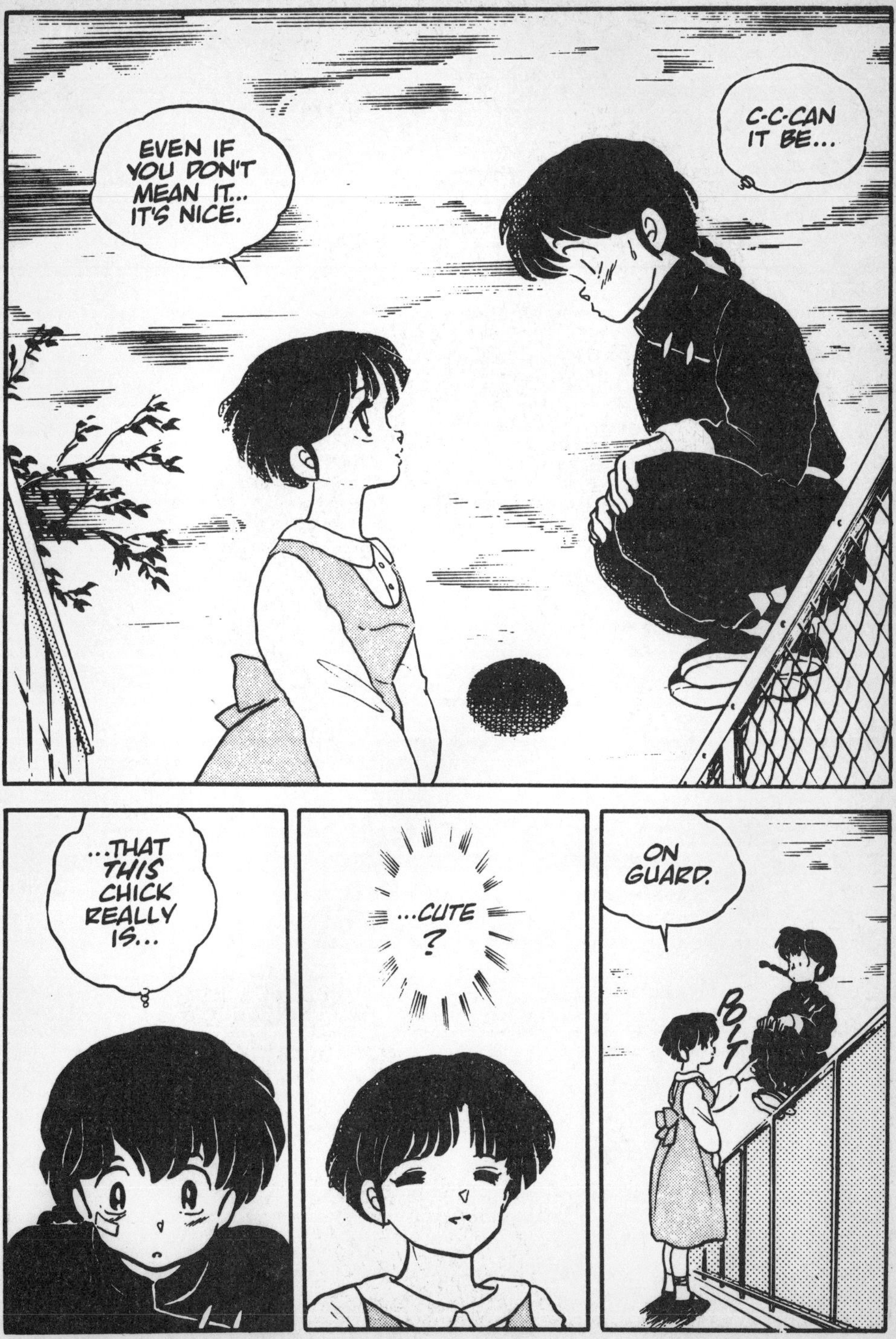
C-C-CAN IT BE...
EVEN IF YOU DON'T MEAN IT... IT'S NICE.
...THAT THIS CHICK REALLY IS...
...CUTE ?
ON GUARD.
POIT

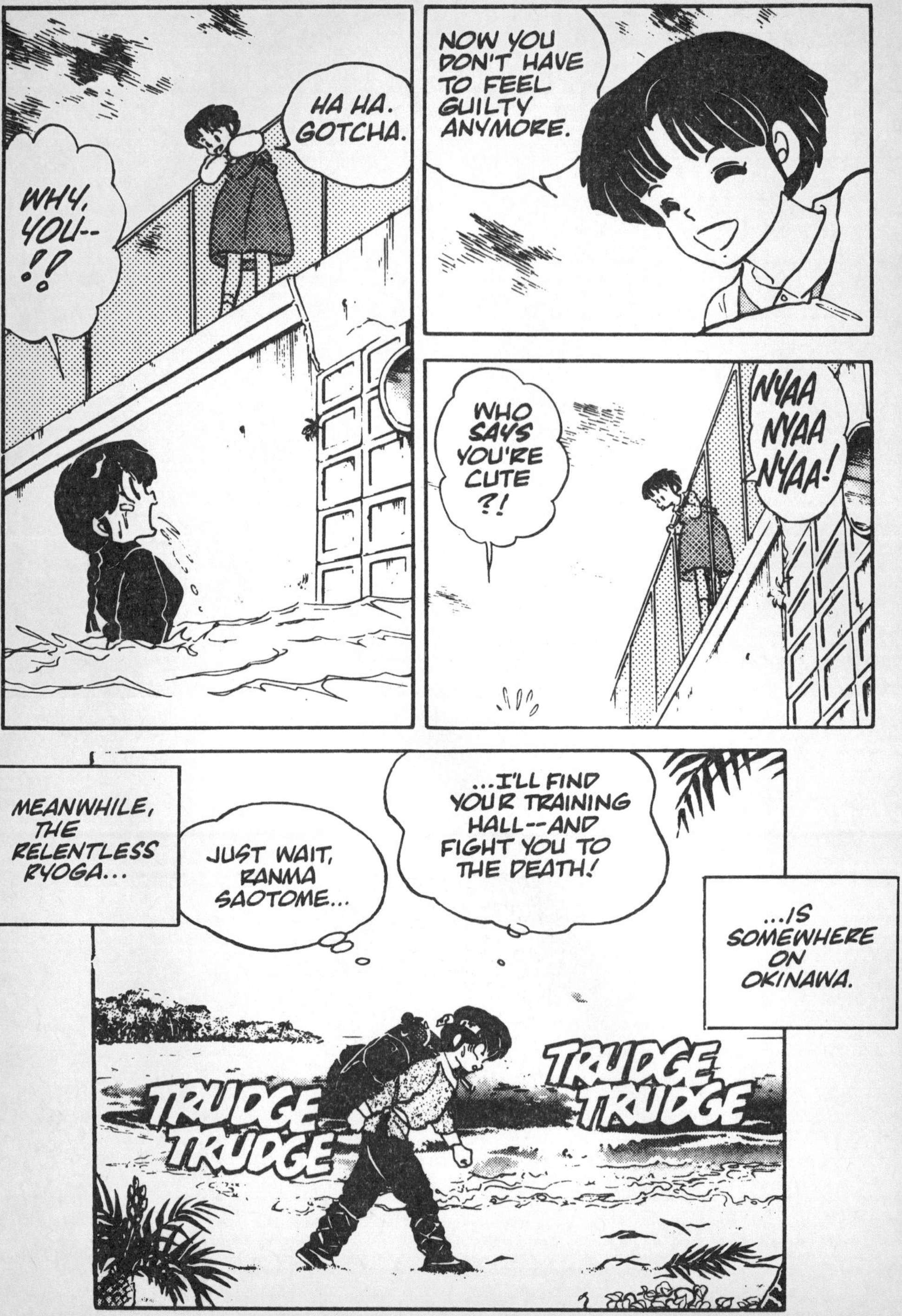
HA HA. GOTCHA.
WHY, YOU-- !!
NOW YOU DON'T HAVE TO FEEL GUILTY ANYMORE.
WHO SAYS YOU'RE CUTE ?!
NYAA NYAA NYAA!
MEANWHILE, THE RELENTLESS RYOGA...
JUST WAIT, RANMA SAOTOME...
...I'LL FIND YOUR TRAINING HALL--AND FIGHT YOU TO THE DEATH!
...IS SOMEWHERE ON OKINAWA.
TRUDGE TRUDGE
TRUDGE TRUDGE

THE END.

Rumiko Takahashi

Rumiko Takahashi was born in 1957 in Niigata, Japan. She attended a women's college in Tokyo, where she began studying comics with Kazuo Koike, author of *Crying Freeman*. In 1978, she won a prize in Shogakukan's annual "New Comic Artist Contest," and in that same year her series *Lum * Urusei Yatsura* began appearing in the weekly manga magazine *Shonen Sunday*. This phenomenally successful series ran for nine years and would go on to eventually sell 22 million copies. Takahashi is considered by many to be the most popular comic writer in Japan or America. Other titles include *Ranma 1/2*, *One-Pound Gospel* and *Maison Ikkoku*.

OTHER TITLES AVAILABLE FROM BOXTREE

OTHER GRAPHIC NOVELS:

☐ 0-7522-0861-6	Ranma 2	£5.99
☐ 0-7522-0881-0	The Mask	£6.99
☐ 0-7522-0977-9	Robocop: Prime Suspect	£6.99
☐ 0-7522-0856-X	The Shadow	£6.99
☐ 0-7522-0962-0	Necroscope	£6.99
☐ 0-7522-0876-4	Spiderman – Return of the Sinister Six	£9.99

Star Wars

☐ 0-7522-0987-6	Dark Empire	£9.99
☐ 0-7522-0962-0	Classic	£7.99
☐ 0-7522-0817-9	Tales of the Jedi	£8.99

Star Trek:

☐ 0-7522-0928-0	Deep Space Nine I	£7.99
☐ 0-7522-0933-7	Deep Space Nine II	£7.99

X-Men

☐ 1-85283-390-4	Ghost Rider	£5.25
☐ 1-85283-395-5	Wolverine	£6.99
☐ 0-7522-0892-6	X-Men Adventures 1 & 2	£9.99

All these books are available at your local bookshop or newsagent or can be ordered direct from the publisher. Just tick the titles you want and fill in the form below.

Prices and availability are subject to change without notice.

Boxtree Cash Sales, P.O. Box 11, Falmouth, Cornwall TR10 9EN

Please send a cheque or postal order for the value of the book and add the following for postage and packing:

U.K. including B.F.P.O. – £1.00 for one book plus 50p for the second book, and 30p for each additional book ordered up to a £3.00 maximum.

OVERSEAS INCLUDING EIRE – £2.00 for the first book plus £1.00 for the second book, and 50p for each additional book ordered.

OR please debit this amount from my Access/Visa Card (delete as appropriate).

Card Number ☐☐☐☐☐☐☐☐☐☐☐☐☐☐☐☐

Amount £ ....

Expiry Date ....

Signed ....

Name ....

Address ....

Kurt

694-8418